EAT LIKE THE HOGS

WIS CARPENTER SWITZER

JACKSON MORRIS TAYLOR

HELAN TURNER MORRISON

CUS GAMMILL HENRY FORTE

H-THOMAS ADAMS FALCON

WASHINGTON BULL CLARY

PITTMAN MONCRIEF NUTT

BROWN-CAMPBELL FOLIART

KJERSTAD BREWER TABOR

EAT LIKE THE HOGS

A Collection of Favorite Recipes from Razorback® Greats

EDITED BY

KAREN VAN HORN

AND

BECKY BULL

THE UNIVERSITY OF ARKANSAS PRESS

Fayetteville ▸ 2025

ISBN: 978-1-68226-281-8
eISBN: 978-1-61075-843-7

29 28 27 26 25 5 4 3 2

Manufactured in the United States of America

Designed by William Clift

∞ The paper used in this publication meets the minimum requirements of the American National Standard for Permanence of Paper for Printed Library Materials Z39.48–1984.

LIBRARY OF CONGRESS CATALOGING-IN-PUBLICATION DATA

Names: Van Horn, Karen, 1965– editor | Bull, Becky, 1952– editor
Title: Eat like the Hogs : a collection of favorite recipes from Razorback Greats / edited by Karen Van Horn and Becky Bull.
Description: Fayetteville : The University of Arkansas Press, 2025. | Includes index.
Identifiers: LCCN 2025010560 (print) | LCCN 2025010561 (ebook) | ISBN 9781682262818 cloth | ISBN 9781610758437 ebook
Subjects: LCSH: Cooking | University of Arkansas (System)—Sports—Miscellanea. | LCGFT: Cookbooks
Classification: LCC TX714 .E226 2025 (print) | LCC TX714 (ebook) | DDC 641.59767—dc23/eng/20250326
LC record available at https://lccn.loc.gov/2025010560
LC ebook record available at https://lccn.loc.gov/2025010561

Appetizers part opener photo: Natasha Bhogal
Brunch and Bread part opener photo: Rosa Sepanta
Soups, Salads, and Sandwiches part opener photo: Leanna Myers
Side Dishes part opener photo: Brent Hofacker
Main Dishes part opener photo: Jeswin Thomas
Desserts part opener photo: James Trenda

To order a copy of this book by phone, please call the Chicago Distribution Center at 1-800-621-2736.

This cookbook is dedicated to the student-athletes and coaches, past and present, who have worn a Razorback uniform. For your dedication, effort, loyalty, and time, we, along with Razorback Nation, recognize and appreciate all you have done.

Thank you, and Wooo Pig Sooie!

Taste and see that the Lord is good

—**PSALM 34:8**

CONTENTS

SOUPS, SALADS, AND SANDWICHES

SIDE DISHES

MAIN DISHES

DESSERTS

FOREWORD

WHEN I MARRIED MY wife, Caroline, and brought her to Arkansas in 1970, little did we know that we had found our forever home. How does a guy from Wisconsin and a gal from Hawaii end up in Fayetteville, Arkansas? It truly is an improbable story.

Yet from the beginning, Caroline and I knew we had found something special. There is nothing like the Razorback family and the devoted fan base that extends to every corner of Arkansas and well beyond. For more than fifty-three years, we have raised our family here and experienced the devotion this state has for family, friends, food, and, of course, the Razorbacks.

So what better way to celebrate the unique legacy of our state and our beloved home team than sharing time together while enjoying recipes from Razorback legends from various sports and generations?

I had the privilege of serving as the head baseball coach of the Arkansas Razorbacks for thirty-three seasons. It truly was an honor to coach so many tremendous players and watch the program grow in success and popularity. When I decided it was time to retire following the 2002 season, I went to our director of athletics, Frank Broyles. Shortly after I shared my desire to step down following the season, Coach Broyles had one pressing question: "Do you think [Dave] Van Horn would be interested?"

As it would play out, Dave Van Horn, my former player and graduate assistant coach, would come to Fayetteville after a successful career at numerous other programs, including the University of Nebraska. What has transpired since then is simply remarkable, and the Razorback baseball program has blossomed into what one outlet recently recognized as the best collegiate baseball program in the nation.

So, when Karen Van Horn, Dave's wife, and Becky Bull, wife of former Razorback football quarterback and baseball pitcher Scott Bull, asked me to participate in this cookbook, it was an easy call. The time and effort they have put into this cookbook reflects the love and passion they have for the Razorbacks and the state of Arkansas.

As you flip through the pages, you will not only find a wide variety of recipes, you'll also be taken on a trip down memory lane with some of the most beloved players, coaches, and administrators in Razorback history. Just as you have treasured special Razorback moments through the years, I hope you will savor those memories as you enjoy these wonderful tastes of home!

Go Hogs!

Norm DeBriyn
Head Baseball Coach, 1970–2002
University of Arkansas

ACKNOWLEDGMENTS

WE WOULD LIKE TO acknowledge those who helped make this cookbook a reality.

Those who provided exceptional assistance to the cookbook project: Kevin Trainor, Hunter Yurachek, Jeri Thorpe, Dean Weber, Lyndy Lindsey, Scott Bull, Dave Van Horn, Leigh Ann Sandlin, Kaylyn Sandlin, Tony Bua, and the Razorback Foundation.

Those who served on the recipe-testing committee with us: Susan Bakewell, Elisabeth Beasley, Marcia Bertram, Amy Bull, John Scott Bull, Teri Eklund, Mindy Iverson, Margie Myers, and Amy Woodard.

Our dear families, who helped us cook and taste these recipes. They encouraged us through the many long hours of meetings, phone calls, text messages, emails, and letters required to collect and test recipes and produce this cookbook. We are forever grateful!

INTRODUCTION

WE ARE EXCITED THAT you have chosen our cookbook, *Eat Like the Hogs*!

You may wonder where the idea to collect recipes from former players, coaches, and athletic staff came from. The inspiration was planted decades ago when the baseball cookbook *Recipes from Home Plate* was published, as well as the *Souper Bowl of Recipes*, a collection of NFL players' recipes written by the wives of four Miami Dolphins coaches.

While the idea remained only an idea for years, a mutual friend, Elisabeth Beasley, connected us over lunch, and *Eat Like the Hogs* was born!

This book is filled with delicious recipes and heartwarming stories from amazing people who happen to also be remarkable Razorback athletes, coaches, and staff.

When we collected these recipes, some handed down for generations, a common phrase was shared over and over: "Once a Razorback, always a Razorback." As we tested each recipe, we remembered each person and what they meant to their teams, the university, and the state of Arkansas.

We are thankful that the contributors took the time to share their favorite recipes and remind us of two of our favorite things … Razorbacks and good food!

GO HOGS!

APPETIZERS

BARBECUE SHRIMP

Pat Morrison
Football
Tight End, 1967–1970

1 cup (2 sticks) unsalted butter

6 tablespoons Worcestershire sauce

1 tablespoon black pepper

1 teaspoon salt

⅛ teaspoon Tabasco sauce (optional)

1 lemon, sliced

1 garlic clove, minced

2 pounds unpeeled raw shrimp

French bread, for serving

Preheat the oven to 400°F.

In a large skillet, melt the butter over medium heat. Add the Worcestershire, pepper, salt, Tabasco, lemon slices, and garlic and stir to combine. Pour the sauce into a large baking dish. Dump the shrimp into the sauce and mix well. Bake for 15 to 20 minutes, turning once, until the shrimp are pink and firm. Serve with French bread for dipping. *Makes 4 to 6 servings.*

The shrimp recipe is a close version from one of our favorite restaurants in New Orleans, Pascal's Manale Restaurant and Bar. My wife, Ann, and I attended Sugar Bowl games while in college and have visited many times.

BEST CHEESE BALL EVER

Scott Bull
Football and Baseball
Quarterback, 1971–1975
Pitcher, 1972, 1976

1 cup shredded cheddar cheese

1 cup chopped pecans

½ cup chopped green onions

½ cup cream cheese, at room temperature

¼ to ½ cup pepper jelly

Crackers, for serving

In a medium bowl, stir together the cheddar, pecans, green onions, and cream cheese. Pack into a small mold or form into a flattened ball and place on a plate. Cover and refrigerate for at least 1 hour or up to 2 days.

When ready to serve, unmold onto a plate (if necessary) and spoon the pepper jelly over the top. Serve with crackers. *Makes 12 to 14 servings.*

BROCCOLI DIP

Norm DeBriyn
Baseball
Head Coach, 1970–2002

½ cup (1 stick) unsalted butter

1 small onion, chopped

2 celery stalks, chopped

1 (8-ounce) can mushrooms, drained and chopped

1 (10.5-ounce) can condensed cream of mushroom soup

1 (10.8-ounce) package frozen broccoli (do not thaw)

16 ounces Velveeta or garlic cheese, cubed

Garlic powder or garlic salt

Bread, crackers, or veggie sticks, for serving

In a large skillet, melt the butter over medium heat. Add the onion, celery, and mushrooms and cook, stirring occasionally, until tender. Stir in the cream of mushroom soup. Add the broccoli and cook until softened. Add the Velveeta and stir until melted. Season with garlic powder or garlic salt to taste. Serve warm, with fresh bread, crackers, or veggie sticks. *Makes 12 to 16 servings.*

Norm DeBriyn

CHILI DIP

Norm DeBriyn
Baseball
Head Coach, 1970–2002

1 (15-ounce) can tamales

1 (15-ounce) can chili, with or without beans

½ onion, chopped

16 ounces Velveeta cheese, cubed

Tortilla chips, for serving

In a large saucepan, combine the tamales, chili, onion, and Velveeta. Cook over medium heat, breaking up the tamales as you stir, until the Velveeta has melted and the mixture is well combined. Serve with chips. *Makes 10 to 12 servings.*

So good, you'll want to eat it with a spoon.

CHIPOTLE HUMMUS WITH TAJÍN

Eddie Jackson
Football and Men's Track & Field
Defensive Back, 2000–2003
110m Hurdles, 2000–2003

2 (15-ounce) cans chickpeas, drained, liquid reserved

½ cup tahini

Juice of 1 large lemon

1 tablespoon adobo sauce (from a can of chipotle peppers in adobo)

1½ teaspoons ground cumin

1¼ teaspoons garlic salt with parsley

¼ teaspoon freshly ground black pepper

¼ cup olive oil, plus more for drizzling

Tajín seasoning

Pita and vegetable sticks, for serving

Place the chickpeas in a food processor and pulse 2 or 3 times just to begin breaking them down. Add the tahini, lemon juice, adobo sauce, cumin, garlic salt, and pepper. Pulse 2 or 3 times more to incorporate the ingredients. While pulsing, drizzle in the olive oil, then pulse until the mixture is smooth. While pulsing, drizzle in the reserved chickpea liquid until the desired consistency is achieved. The hummus should be smooth, with no visible signs of whole chickpeas. Transfer the hummus to a serving bowl. Drizzle with olive oil, then sprinkle with Tajín. Serve with pita and vegetable sticks. *Makes 8 to 10 servings.*

At my beer garden in Houston, Texas, my friend has a Mediterranean food truck called Pitas Bites. I swear, he makes the best hummus I've ever had! Imported olive oil helps him keep his menu as authentic as possible. He shares a few of his recipes, but his hummus stays under lock and key. I've tried at least a dozen times to crack the code, to no avail, so I decided to create my own sacred hummus recipe with a little Tex-Mex flair. This one's *not* under lock and key!

COACH'S PIGSKIN NACHOS

Jimmy Johnson
Football
Defensive Lineman, 1961–1964
Defensive Coordinator, 1973–1976

16 ounces tricolor tortilla chips

1 pound slow-roasted BBQ pulled pork, homemade or store-bought

½ cup sliced fresh bell peppers (a mix of colors)

¼ cup sliced banana peppers

¼ cup sliced fresh jalapeños

1 (2.25-ounce) can sliced pitted black olives

¼ cup chopped onion

½ cup shredded Monterey Jack cheese

½ cup shredded cheddar cheese

1 cup pico de gallo

¼ cup sour cream

¼ cup guacamole

Preheat the oven to 400°F.

Arrange half the tortilla chips in an overlapping layer in the bottom of a large cast-iron skillet. Spread half the pulled pork over the chips. Sprinkle half the bell peppers, banana peppers, jalapeños, olives, onion, and cheeses over the pork and chips. Repeat these layers with the remaining chips, meat, peppers, olives, onion, and cheese. Bake for 8 to 10 minutes, until the cheese is melted and bubbling. Remove from the oven and top with the pico de gallo, sour cream, and guacamole. Serve immediately. *Makes 1 or 2 servings.*

When Coach Johnson called to give us his recipe, he said, "We don't really cook that much, but we eat at Jimmy Johnson's Big Chill a lot, and my favorite menu item is Coach's Pigskin Nachos." Upon calling the restaurant and asking about the recipe, the manager, Amanda, said, "Oh yeah, he eats that a lot, and always with extra jalapeños!" The restaurant is in Key Largo, Florida, at Fisherman's Cove. If you're ever in the neighborhood, be sure to drop by, tell them that you are Razorbacks, and order some of the Coach's Pigskin Nachos with extra jalapeños.

CORN DIP

Jimmy Dykes
Men's Basketball
Point Guard, 1981–1984
Graduate Assistant Coach, 1984–1985

Women's Basketball
Head Coach, 2014–2017

1 (15.25-ounce) can whole kernel corn, drained

1 (11-ounce) can shoepeg corn, drained

1 (14.5-ounce) can Ro*Tel diced tomatoes and green chiles, with juices

1 (8-ounce) package cream cheese, cubed

1 teaspoon garlic salt

1 teaspoon chili powder

1 teaspoon ground cumin

Tortilla chips, for serving

In a microwave-safe medium bowl, combine the whole kernel corn, shoepeg corn, and tomatoes and green chiles. Add the cream cheese. Microwave for 4 minutes, then stir until creamy and well combined. Add the garlic salt, chili powder, and cumin and stir until fully combined. Serve with your favorite tortilla chips. *Makes 12 servings.*

DEER HORS D'OEUVRES

Reuben Reina Sr.
Men's Track & Field / Cross Country
1500m, 10,000m, 1986–1991

1 venison backstrap

Extra-virgin olive oil

Emeril's Original Essence

Cavender's All-Purpose Greek Seasoning

6 jalapeños, sliced into rings

12 bacon strips, sliced in half

Using a sharp knife, remove all the white fascia and fat from the venison. Slice the meat crosswise on an angle into twenty-four 3-inch-long strips, each about the width of a strip of bacon. Lightly coat the venison pieces with olive oil and generously dust them with Emeril's Original Essence and Greek seasoning. Place the meat in a large zip-top bag and marinate in the refrigerator for 24 hours.

The following day, heat an outdoor grill to about 325°F. (I prefer to cook over coal with a little hickory or mesquite thrown in, but they still taste great on an electric grill.) Soak 24 toothpicks in a bowl of water for 30 minutes before grilling to keep them from burning too much, then drain.

Pull the meat out of the refrigerator. Lay a venison strip flat on your work surface and top with a piece of jalapeño. Fold the venison around the jalapeño, then wrap with a strip of bacon and secure it with a toothpick. Repeat with the remaining venison.

Grill the bacon-wrapped venison for 2 to 3 minutes on each side, just enough that the bacon is ready. Do not overcook, or you'll dry out the meat too much. Enjoy! Great straight off the grill, with your beer of choice in hand, on game days or at tailgating parties! *Makes 24 pieces.*

This is a recipe that was introduced to me by some homegrown Arkansas friends of mine, and I have tweaked it to my liking and made it my own. Being an outdoorsman who loves to hunt and fish, this has been a great way for me to introduce venison to people who have never eaten venison before or who have tried it and been put off by the "wild taste" of the meat. This recipe uses the backstrap of a whitetail deer, the most coveted part of the animal due to its tenderness. I've made this several times, and everyone who's tried it has downright loved it (even some people who were skeptical about eating it). I process all my own meat from field to table, and I'm pretty meticulous on how I go about doing it to keep the meat fresh and free of the "wild taste" people may associate with venison. But that process is another story altogether that I'll save for another book. ;)

DEVILED EGGS

Casey Jo Magee MacPherson
Gymnastics
All-Around, 2007–2010

6 large eggs

¼ cup mayonnaise

1½ to 2½ teaspoons stone-ground Dijon mustard

1 to 2 teaspoons yellow mustard

3 dashes of balsamic vinegar

Paprika

Salt and black pepper

Bring a large pot of water to a boil over medium-high heat. Add the eggs and boil for 13 to 15 minutes. Meanwhile, fill a large bowl with ice and water and set it nearby. Using a slotted spoon, transfer the eggs to the ice water and let cool.

Peel the eggs, then cut them in half lengthwise. Carefully separate the whites and yolks, placing the yolks in a small bowl; set the whites aside. Mash the yolks with a fork to break them up, then add the mayonnaise and both mustards. I usually start with 2 heaping tablespoons of mayonnaise and 1 heaping tablespoon of mustard. Add the vinegar and mix. Taste and season with paprika, salt, and pepper. Taste again and add more mayonnaise, mustard, vinegar, paprika, salt, and/or pepper. Once the flavor is to your liking, scoop the yolk mixture into a zip-top bag, cut off one bottom corner, and pipe the mixture into egg whites. Sprinkle paprika over the deviled eggs. *Makes 12 pieces.*

NOTES *When making the filling, I start with less than the full quantity of mayo and mustard, because you can always add more. If you like, use any mustard you prefer instead of the Dijon and yellow mustard.*

For a finishing touch, you can slice some fresh chives and sprinkle them over the deviled eggs.

Deviled eggs were a staple at family and friend get-togethers, potlucks, and holiday gatherings growing up. My sister and I would help our mom make them, and of course we'd taste-test along the way. We had to keep our dad and brother from eating them all before anyone else could get some. At Arkansas, our coaches hosted a Thanksgiving potluck where everyone brought a favorite dish from holidays at home, so naturally I made deviled eggs. It was such a fun evening spent together learning about everyone's traditions, and a memory I will have forever.

DORITOS CHICKEN TENDERS

Mark Smith

Football

Linebacker, 1993–1996

1 (15-ounce) bag Doritos (any flavor, such as nacho cheese)

1 large egg

2 tablespoons milk

2 boneless, skinless chicken breasts, cut into roughly ¾-inch-wide strips

Nonstick cooking spray

Dipping sauces, such as ranch or sour cream, for serving

Preheat the oven to 400°F. Line a baking sheet with foil.

Place the Doritos in a zip-top bag and crush them with a rolling pin or the bottom of a heavy glass. You should have 1½ cups crushed Doritos. In a shallow bowl, whisk together the egg and milk. Dip each chicken strip into the egg mixture, ensuring it's fully coated, then into the bag of crushed Doritos, pressing the chips onto the chicken to ensure they adhere and that the chicken is evenly coated. Place the coated chicken strips on the prepared baking sheet. Lightly spray the tops of the chicken strips with cooking spray to help them crisp in the oven.

Bake for 15 to 17 minutes, until the chicken is cooked through and the Doritos coating is crispy and golden. Serve hot, with your favorite dipping sauces. Enjoy these delicious Doritos chicken tenders as an appetizer or a main dish! *Makes 4 to 6 servings.*

ENERGY BITES

Amy Yoder Begley

Women's Track & Field / Cross Country

3000m, 10,000m, 15,000m, 1996–2001

2 cups old-fashioned oats (see Notes)

2 cups unsweetened coconut flakes (see Notes)

1 cup seeds (use any variety, such as hulled sunflower seeds, hemp hearts, hulled pumpkin seeds, etc.; I prefer flaxseed and chia seeds)

4 ounces miniature chocolate chips

½ cup oat flour

1½ cups smooth peanut butter

½ cup honey

1 teaspoon pure vanilla extract or your favorite flavoring

½ teaspoon kosher salt

In a large bowl, combine the oats, coconut flakes, seeds, chocolate chips, oat flour, peanut butter, honey, vanilla, and salt. Stir until evenly combined. For easier rolling, cover and refrigerate the mixture for 1 hour.

Scoop heaping tablespoons of the mixture and roll them into balls, placing them on a baking sheet as you go. Refrigerate for 1 hour, then transfer to an airtight container or zip-top bag. Store them in the refrigerator for up to 2 weeks. *Makes 48 (1-inch) balls.*

NOTES *You can really mix up the variety with the mix-ins, but these are my staples.*

If gluten is a concern, make sure the rolled oats and oat flour are labeled "gluten-free."

If you can only find sweetened coconut flakes, just reduce the amount of honey.

For added flavor, toast the oats and coconut flakes before using.

I made these and traveled with them to a lot of meets while coaching. TSA does not always appreciate a bag of them in my carry-on!

GAME-DAY CHEESE DIP

Eric Musselman
Men's Basketball
Head Coach, 2019–2024

1 pound lean ground beef

16 ounces Velveeta cheese, cubed

1 (10-ounce) can Ro*Tel diced tomatoes and green chiles, with juices

2 tablespoons taco seasoning

Tortilla chips, for serving

In a large skillet, brown the ground beef over medium-high heat until it's cooked thoroughly. Drain the fat. Add the Velveeta, Ro*Tel, and taco seasoning and stir until the Velveeta has melted. Transfer to a slow cooker on the Warm setting and serve with tortilla chips. *Makes 12 to 16 servings.*

"Our family is always hosting the team and staff, and this is a dish that we like to serve as an appetizer no matter what the occasion. I don't think there's been a time that the entire Crock-Pot hasn't been empty at the end of the night. It's a quick, easy crowd-pleaser . . . and Mexican is Coach's favorite!" —Danyelle Musselman

GAME-DAY NUTS

Deena Drossin Kastor
Women's Track & Field / Cross Country
5000m, 10,000m, 1991–1996

Neutral oil, for greasing

1 large egg white

1½ cups raw almonds

1½ cups raw cashews

½ cup unsweetened coconut flakes

¼ cup sugar

½ teaspoon Maldon sea salt

½ teaspoon red pepper flakes

Preheat the oven to 300°F. Grease a baking sheet with oil or line it with parchment paper.

In a large bowl, whisk the egg white until foamy. Add the almonds and cashews and stir to coat. Add the coconut, sugar, salt, and red pepper flakes and mix. Spread the nut mixture evenly over the prepared baking sheet. Bake for 25 to 30 minutes, until golden brown. Let cool before serving.
Makes 8 to 10 servings.

Nuts are a great source of protein, calcium and other essential nutrients. Great for your own performance or sustained energy while watching game day.

GREEK DIP

Dave England
Assistant Athletic Trainer, 1984–1989
Head Athletic Trainer, 1989–2019
Director of Sports Medicine, 2019–2022

1 (8-ounce) container hummus

1 (8-ounce) container tzatziki dip

1 cucumber, seeded and diced

4 to 6 ounces cherry tomatoes, chopped or halved

1 small red onion, diced

Honey

Pita bread or naan bread, sliced vegetables, and/or chips, for serving

Spread the hummus over the bottom of an 8-inch square baking dish or 9-inch pie plate. Spread the tzatziki over the hummus and top with the cucumber, tomatoes, and onion. Drizzle honey over the top. Refrigerate for an hour or two before serving. Serve with veggies, flatbreads, chips, etc.
Makes 8 to 10 servings.

We take this appetizer to all potlucks, and everybody loves it. Go Hogs!

GREG LASKER'S FAVORITE MEATBALLS

Greg Lasker
Football
Safety, 1982–1985

1½ pounds ground pork

8 ounces ground turkey

4 to 8 ounces ground veal

6 large eggs, lightly beaten

8 ounces ricotta cheese

8 ounces Pecorino Romano or Parmesan cheese (or mix 4 ounces of each), grated

1½ pounds breadcrumbs

2 tablespoons all-purpose flour

½ bunch flat-leaf parsley, finely chopped, or 2 tablespoons dried parsley

3 garlic cloves, minced

1 tablespoon salt

1½ teaspoons black pepper

4 to 5 (24-ounce) jars marinara sauce

In a very large, deep container, use clean hands to combine the ground pork, turkey, and veal (see Note). (You may want to wear a clean pair of plastic gloves for mixing.) Add the eggs and ricotta. Set aside 2 tablespoons each of the pecorino and the breadcrumbs, then add the remainder to the bowl with the meat mixture along with the parsley and garlic, salt, and pepper to taste. Mix it all very well.

In a separate medium bowl or deep dish, stir together the flour and the reserved 2 tablespoons each pecorino and breadcrumbs. Place a small amount of the meatball mixture in one hand and place the palm of your other hand in the breadcrumb mixture. Then rub the hand with the mixture over the meatball to coat. As you are rubbing both hands together, the breadcrumb mixture will coat the meatball, smoothing it out and keeping it from crumbling as it cooks in the sauce. Place the coated meatballs in a separate large dish.

Pour 4 jars of the marinara into a large deep pot (make sure it's big enough that the meatballs will have room to expand a bit as they cook) and bring to a simmer over medium heat. Simmer for about 15 minutes, then place the meatballs in the sauce one at a time. Make sure there is enough sauce in the pot to cover the meatballs completely; pour in more marinara as needed. Cover and cook for at least 1 hour and until their internal temperature reaches 165°F on the meat thermometer, stirring every 10 minutes or so.
Makes 20 to 30 meatballs—6 to 10 servings.

NOTE *You can substitute other types of ground meat or use only one kind per your preference.*

This is my favorite recipe from my mother-in-law.

GRILLED SPICY KOREAN CHICKEN WINGS

Joe Adams
Football
Receiver, 2008–2011

SAUCE

3 garlic cloves, minced

2 teaspoons fresh ginger, minced

¼ cup mirin

¼ cup soy sauce

2 tablespoons untoasted sesame oil

2 tablespoons gochujang (Korean chile paste)

2 tablespoons honey

WINGS

3 pounds chicken wingettes

2 tablespoons olive oil

Salt and ground black pepper

Make the sauce: In a large bowl, stir together the garlic, ginger, mirin, soy sauce, sesame oil, gochujang, and honey until thoroughly combined; set aside.

Make the wings: Heat a grill to medium heat. Coat the chicken wings with the olive oil, then season with salt and pepper. Grill the wings for 20 to 30 minutes, flipping them every 5 minutes. Remove from the grill and add to the bowl with the sauce. Toss to coat. Return the wings to the grill and cook for 10 to 15 minutes, flipping them every 5 minutes, until the sauce is crisp. Take the wings off the grill and place them in a pan to cool slightly, then serve. *Makes 4 to 6 servings.*

GUACAMOLE

Houston Nutt
Football and Basketball
Quarterback and Guard, 1976–1977
Head Coach, 1998–2007

4 ripe avocados, pitted

1 tomato, diced

½ white onion, finely diced

½ jalapeño, seeded and finely diced

3 tablespoons chopped fresh cilantro

1 to 2 tablespoons fresh lime juice

½ teaspoon salt

Tortilla chips and sliced veggies, for serving (optional)

Scoop the flesh from the avocados into a medium bowl. Mash with a fork or potato masher to the desired consistency. (Some like their guacamole smooth, some like it chunky.) Add the tomato, onion, jalapeño, cilantro, lime juice, and salt and stir until combined. Serve with tortilla chips and sliced veggies, or pair it with your favorite Mexican dishes. *Makes 6 to 8 servings.*

HOT ARTICHOKE DIP

Scott Bull
Football and Baseball
Quarterback, 1971–1975
Pitcher, 1972, 1976

½ cup mayonnaise

½ cup sour cream

1 (14-ounce) can artichoke hearts, drained and chopped

½ cup grated Parmesan cheese

⅛ teaspoon hot pepper sauce

Crackers, for serving

In a 1-quart microwave-safe bowl, combine the mayonnaise, sour cream, artichoke hearts, Parmesan, and hot sauce. Zap in the microwave on high for 3½ minutes, until hot and bubbling, stopping once to stir halfway through. Serve with crackers of your choice. *Makes 4 to 6 servings.*

QG FRENCH BREAD SAUSAGE DIP

Quinn Grovey
Football
Quarterback, 1987–1990

1 pound bulk pork sausage (if you're a meat lover like me, make it 2 pounds)

1 bunch green onions, thinly sliced

1 (8-ounce) container sour cream

1 (8-ounce) package cream cheese, at room temperature

1½ cups shredded cheddar cheese

1 loaf French bread

Fritos scoops or tortilla chips, for serving (optional)

Preheat the oven to 350°F.

In a large skillet, brown the sausage over medium-high heat, then drain the fat, leaving the sausage in the skillet. Add the green onions, sour cream, cream cheese, and 1 cup of the cheddar to the skillet with the sausage and stir well until the cream cheese has melted and all ingredients are fully incorporated.

Cut a roughly 1-inch-thick, slice off the top of the French bread and set the top aside. Remove half of the soft bread from inside the loaf to create a sturdy hollowed-out cavity. Spoon the sausage dip into the cavity. Sprinkle the remaining ½ cup cheddar on top of the dip and place on a baking sheet. Bake for 20 to 30 minutes, until the cheese topping has melted. Serve with Fritos scoops, tortilla chips, or the reserved bread top. *Makes 6 to 8 servings.*

Quinn Grovey

SALSA

Wendi Willits Wells
Women's Basketball
Guard, 1997–2001

5 or 6 garlic cloves, peeled

⅓ bell pepper

2 jalapeños: 1 seeded, 1 with seeds, or to taste

Small handful of cilantro

2 tablespoons distilled white vinegar

1 tablespoon kosher salt

½ teaspoon onion powder

6 to 8 regular or 8 to 10 Roma (plum) tomatoes

In a food processor, combine the garlic, bell pepper, jalapeños, cilantro, vinegar, salt, and onion powder and process to the desired consistency (process less to keep it chunky or more to make it smooth). Pour into a bowl. Place all but 2 of the tomatoes in the food processor and pulse to the desired consistency. Pour into the bowl and stir to combine. Taste and add more tomatoes if it's too spicy. *Makes 8 to 10 servings.*

SEVEN-LAYER DIP

Norm DeBriyn
Baseball
Head Coach, 1970–2002

2 cups sour cream

1 (1-ounce) packet taco seasoning mix (I use the hot variety)

2 (9-ounce) cans bean dip

2 (1-ounce) packets guacamole dip mix

1 (8-ounce) package shredded Mexican-style cheese blend

1 (2.25-ounce) can sliced black olives, drained

4 Roma (plum) tomatoes, diced

1 bunch green onions, thinly sliced

¼ cup chopped jalapeños

Fritos and/or tortilla chips, for serving

In a small bowl, stir together the sour cream and taco seasoning.

In a 9 by 12-inch serving dish, layer the bean dip, guacamole mix, seasoned sour cream, cheese, olives, and tomatoes. Top with the green onions and jalapeños. Serve with Fritos, tortilla chips, or both. *Makes 12 servings.*

SOOIE GUACAMOLE

Mary Haff
Softball
Pitcher, 2017–2022

3 ripe Hass avocados

1½ teaspoons garlic salt, plus more as needed

1 tablespoon mayonnaise

¼ cup packed fresh cilantro leaves, plus more as needed

¼ teaspoon lime juice

Tortilla chips or raw veggies, for serving

Pit and peel the avocados, then scoop the flesh into a medium bowl and mash it. This takes about 1 minute, depending on your Razorback-level mastery of avocado mashing. Stir in the garlic salt, mayonnaise, cilantro, and lime juice. Taste and adjust the seasoning with additional garlic salt or cilantro to your desired flavor. Serve your guacamole with tortilla chips, raw veggies, or anything else crispy or crunchy. *Makes 6 to 8 servings.*

NOTES *The most important factor in all guacamole is the avocado ripeness. You want each one to be perfectly ripe, which means basically black on the outside; it should give just a bit when you grasp it. If the avocado is too hard, you won't get the same buttery, creamy flavor and texture. And if it's not ripe yet, there's not much you can do about it except wait.*

You can play with the classic guacamole recipe by adding all sorts of extra ingredients, such as jalapeños, onions, fresh garlic, tomatoes, green onions, and serrano chiles. Guacamole is a great spread or topping too, and not just for toast; it adds a deliciously fatty, silky texture to rice cakes, bagels, burgers, sandwiches and all sorts of tacos, burritos, and other Mexican favorites.

Reflecting on my time as a softball pitcher at the University of Arkansas, I'm filled with gratitude. The experience was transformative both on and off the field. The support from the team, coaches, and fans was incredible, and it helped me grow not just as a player but as a person. I'll always cherish those memories and the lessons I learned during those years.

SPICY KOREAN WINGS

Eddie Jackson
Football and Men's Track & Field
Defensive Back, 2000–2003
110m Hurdles, 2000–2003

Canola oil, for frying

SAUCE

1 tablespoon canola oil

1 tablespoon finely chopped shallot

¼ cup gochujang (Korean chile paste)

¼ cup light molasses

¼ cup low-sodium soy sauce

1 heaping tablespoon light brown sugar

1 tablespoon finely chopped fresh ginger

1 tablespoon finely chopped garlic

½ teaspoon kosher salt

⅛ teaspoon coarsely ground black pepper

¼ cup water

WINGS

2 pounds chicken wings

1½ cups rice flour

Alabama White Sauce (page 66), for serving

1 bunch thinly sliced green onions, for garnish

Fill a large Dutch oven halfway with canola oil and attach a deep-fry thermometer to the side of the pot. Heat the canola oil over medium heat to 375°F.

Meanwhile, make the sauce: In a small saucepan, heat the canola oil over medium heat until it begins to shimmer, 1 to 2 minutes. Add the shallot and cook, stirring, until softened, about 1 minute. Add the gochujang, molasses, soy sauce, sugar, ginger, garlic, salt, black pepper, and ¼ cup water and bring to a simmer. Cook until the sauce has reduced by one-third, 5 to 8 minutes. Reduce the heat to low and keep warm.

Make the wings: Use a sharp chef's knife to break down each wing into three separate pieces. Using your finger, locate the joint connecting the flat of the wing to the drumette, then use the tip of your knife to cut the skin so the joint is visible. Firmly press your knife between the pieces to separate them. Next, use your finger to locate the joint connecting the wingtip to the flat. You don't need to cut the skin this time; just press your knife through the joint, remove the wingtip, and discard. Repeat with the remaining wings.

Place the rice flour in a large bowl. Working in batches as needed, toss the wings in the rice flour until completely coated, then slowly lower them into the hot oil—they should be fully submerged. Fry, turning occasionally, until an instant-read thermometer inserted into the thickest part of a wing registers 165°F (see Note), 10 to 12 minutes. Transfer the cooked wings to a large bowl and toss with enough of the reserved sauce to coat them. Repeat with the remaining wings and sauce. Serve hot, drizzled with Alabama White Sauce and sprinkled with green onions. *Makes 2 or 3 servings.*

NOTE *For safety, don't try to test the temperature of the wings while they're still in the hot oil. Using tongs, transfer a wing to a cutting board and insert your thermometer to test the internal temperature.*

Gochujang, which is a Korean fermented chile paste, is what gives these wings a sweet heat you won't soon forget. I first discovered it in Koreatown in New York City, and immediately took to its sweet, savory, and spicy notes. Gochujang is a perfect condiment on its own, but the addition of soy sauce, ginger, green onions, and a little brown sugar takes it to a whole new dimension. Rice flour ensures a crust that remains crispy and soaks up all that addictive sauce. Pairing these wings with my Alabama White Sauce makes for a Southern fling with an Eastern swing—far, far Eastern, that is.

SPICY SAUSAGE MEATBALLS

Chuck Barrett

Voice of the Razorbacks

Baseball, 1992–2014

Football, 2007–present

Men's Basketball, 2010–present

Nonstick cooking spray

3 cups Bisquick all-purpose baking mix

1 (16-ounce) package Jimmy Dean hot premium pork sausage

1 (8-ounce) block medium cheddar cheese, shredded

1 (8-ounce) block pepper Jack cheese, shredded

6 tablespoons whole milk

2 tablespoons grated yellow onion

2 tablespoons chopped fresh cilantro

Jessica Field Phelan

Preheat the oven to 350°F. Coat two baking sheets with cooking spray.

In a large bowl, combine the Bisquick, sausage, cheddar, pepper Jack, milk, onion, and cilantro and press the ingredients together with clean hands until the mixture is well combined. Shape the mixture into 1-inch balls and place them 2 inches apart on the prepared baking sheets. Bake for 20 to 25 minutes, until lightly browned. Serve warm. *Makes 12 to 15 servings.*

SWEET-AND-SPICY PECANS

Lance Harter
Women's Track & Field / Cross Country
Head Coach, 1990–2023

¼ cup powdered sugar

½ teaspoon kosher salt

¼ teaspoon cayenne pepper

1 cup pecans

Preheat the oven to 350°F. Line a baking sheet with parchment paper.

In a medium bowl, stir together the powdered sugar, salt, cayenne, and 2 teaspoons water. Add the pecans and stir to coat. Spread the pecans in a single layer on the prepared baking sheet. Bake for 9 minutes, or until golden brown. Remove from the oven and let cool, then store in an airtight container at room temperature. *Makes 1 cup.*

Makes a nice holiday gift for friends and neighbors. Also a good addition to a charcuterie board.

VEGETABLE PIZZA

Jessica Field Phelan
Women's Volleyball
Middle Blocker, 1995–1998

3 (8-ounce) cans crescent rolls

1 cup mayonnaise

1 (1-ounce) packet dry Hidden Valley ranch seasoning mix

1 (8-ounce) package cream cheese, at room temperature

1 (8-ounce) package shredded cheese of choice

Toppings: chopped lettuce, tomatoes, broccoli, cauliflower, onion, or other vegetables of your choice

Spread the crescent rolls on a baking sheet and bake as directed on the package. Let cool.

In a medium bowl, stir together the mayonnaise, ranch mix, and cream cheese. Spread the mixture over the cooled crescent rolls. Sprinkle with the shredded cheese and the vegetables of your choice. Slice and enjoy immediately or cover and refrigerate for 1 hour, then serve cold. Leftovers will keep for up to 3 days. *Makes 6 to 8 servings.*

BRUNCH AND BREAD

Barry Foster

BANANAS FOSTER FRENCH TOAST

Dave Van Horn
Baseball
Second Base, 1981–1982
Graduate Assistant Coach, 1985–1988
Head Coach, 2002–present

1 large egg

¾ cup whole milk

1 tablespoon granulated sugar

1 teaspoon vanilla extract

½ teaspoon ground cinnamon

8 slices bread, preferably brioche

½ cup (1 stick) salted butter

½ cup packed light brown sugar

3 to 4 bananas, cut into ¼-inch-thick slices

Neutral oil, for greasing

Powdered sugar or whipped topping, for serving (optional)

Preheat the oven or a warming drawer to 170°F.

Heat a lightly oiled large griddle or skillet over medium heat. In a shallow dish, whisk together the egg, milk, granulated sugar, vanilla, and cinnamon. Quickly dip both sides of the bread into the milk mixture, then place the bread on the heated griddle (work in batches, if needed). Cook until browned on the bottom, then flip and cook until browned on the second side. Transfer to an oven-safe dish and keep warm in the oven or warming drawer while you prepare the sauce.

In a separate large skillet, melt the butter and brown sugar over medium heat. Stir well, then add the bananas, reduce the heat to medium-low, and cook until the sauce begins to thicken slightly. Remove from the heat.

Slice each piece of French toast diagonally, overlap 4 triangle shaped pieces across each plate, and spoon the sauce and bananas over the top. Sprinkle with powdered sugar or add a dollop of whipped topping, if desired, and serve. *Makes 4 servings.*

NOTE *This recipe also works well if you want to substitute fresh ripe peaches, peeled and sliced, for the bananas.*

BARRY FOSTER'S BANANA PANCAKES

Barry Foster
Football
Fullback, 1987–1989

1⅓ cups whole wheat flour

2 teaspoons baking powder

1 teaspoon ground cinnamon

¼ teaspoon salt

1 large egg

I cup whole milk

1 large ripe banana, mashed

¼ cup plain Greek yogurt

2 tablespoons light brown sugar

1 teaspoon vanilla extract

Butter, for greasing and serving

Warm maple syrup, for serving

In a large bowl, combine the flour, baking powder, cinnamon, and salt.

In a separate medium bowl, stir together the egg, milk, banana, yogurt, brown sugar, and vanilla until well combined. Add the wet ingredients to the dry and whisk until combined.

Heat a griddle over medium-high heat, then add a pat of butter and let it melt. Working in batches, scoop ¼ cup of batter onto the griddle for each pancake. Cook until bubbles form on the surface, the edges are slightly brown, and the bottom is light brown, 2 to 3 minutes. Flip and cook until light brown on the second side, 2 to 3 minutes more. Transfer the pancakes to a plate and repeat with the remaining batter.

Serve with more butter and warm syrup. *Makes 8 servings.*

This is my favorite breakfast recipe!

BRADY TOOPS'S BANANA BREAD

Brady Toops
Baseball
Catcher, 2000–2004

Neutral oil, for greasing

1½ cups all-purpose flour, plus more for dusting

1 teaspoon baking soda

4 tablespoons (½ stick) unsalted butter

1 cup sugar

1 large egg

3 overripe bananas, mashed

1 teaspoon vanilla extract

Preheat the oven to 350°F. Grease a 9 by 5-inch loaf pan with oil, then dust it with flour, tapping out any excess.

In a small bowl, dissolve the baking soda in 1 to 2 tablespoons water.

In a large bowl, cream the butter and sugar with a handheld mixer. Add the egg and bananas. One at a time, mix in the flour, vanilla, and baking soda. Pour the batter into the prepared loaf pan. Bake for 50 minutes, or until a toothpick inserted into the center comes out clean. *Makes one 9 by 5-inch loaf.*

NOTE *If you like, stir nuts and/or chocolate chips into the batter before pouring it into baking pan.*

BREAKFAST CASSEROLE

Ike Forte
Football
Running Back, 1974–1976

Butter or nonstick cooking spray, for greasing

12 large eggs, beaten

1 cup whole milk

1 (16-ounce) package frozen hash browns, thawed

1 cup shredded cheddar cheese

8 ounces sliced bacon, cooked and crumbled

1 teaspoon salt

¼ teaspoon black pepper

Picante sauce, for serving

Preheat the oven to 350°F. Grease a 9 by 13-inch baking dish with butter or cooking spray.

In a large bowl, whisk together the eggs and milk. Stir in the hash browns, cheese, bacon, salt, and pepper. Transfer to the prepared baking dish. Bake, uncovered, for 35 minutes, or until the eggs are set. Cut into squares and serve with picante sauce. *Makes 12 servings.*

NOTE *This is also very good spooned into flour tortillas. Serve with picante sauce and extra cheese.*

BUTTERMILK PANCAKES

Ralph Kraus
Baseball
Outfield and First Base, 1983–1986

1 cup all-purpose flour

1 cup buttermilk

½ cup sugar

2 large eggs

1 teaspoon salt

1 teaspoon baking powder

1 teaspoon baking soda

¼ cup shortening, melted

Neutral oil, for greasing

In a large bowl, stir together the flour, buttermilk, sugar, eggs, salt, baking powder, and baking soda until smooth. Add the melted shortening and mix until well combined.

Heat a lightly oiled griddle or large skillet over medium heat. Working in batches, ladle the batter into the pan, using about ¼ cup per pancake, and cook until bubbles form on the surface and begin to pop, 2 to 3 minutes. Flip and cook until golden on the second side, 2 to 3 minutes. Transfer to a plate and repeat with the remaining batter. *Makes 6 to 8 servings.*

This simple recipe has always been a staple in our home. Having a home full of very busy kids, we knew the one meal we could plan for and have as a family was breakfast. Add some syrup and it's a great start to the day.

CHOCOLATE GRAVY AND BISCUITS

Mark Smith
Football
Linebacker, 1993–1996

1 cup sugar

¼ cup Hershey's unsweetened cocoa powder

3 tablespoons all-purpose flour

2 cups whole milk

1 tablespoon unsalted butter, at room temperature

2 teaspoons vanilla extract

Biscuits, for serving

In a small saucepan, whisk together the sugar, cocoa powder, flour, and milk. Make sure there are no lumps. Bring to a boil over medium-high heat, stirring

frequently. Reduce the heat to medium and cook, stirring frequently, until the gravy's thickness is to your liking, about 5 minutes. Remove from the heat and stir in the butter and vanilla. Chocolate gravy should be a little runnier than normal gravy—it will thicken up as it sits. Serve with biscuits and enjoy!
Makes 6 to 8 servings.

COCONUT AND COTTAGE CHEESE PROTEIN PANCAKES

Jessica Koch Dailey
Women's Track & Field / Cross Country
1500m, 3000m, 5000m, 5K, 1997–2002

3½ large eggs

1 cup cottage cheese

½ cup pancake mix

1 cup blueberries

2 tablespoons unsweetened shredded coconut

Coconut oil or coconut oil spray, for greasing

In a large bowl, combine the eggs, cottage cheese, pancake mix, blueberries, and shredded coconut and mix until well combined.

Lightly grease a large skillet or griddle with coconut oil or spray and heat over medium-high heat. Working in batches as needed, pour the batter onto the hot griddle, using about ¼ cup per pancake, and cook until bubbles begin to form on the surface, 3 to 5 minutes. Flip and cook until golden brown on the bottom and cooked through, 3 to 5 minutes more. (It's necessary to cook these pancakes longer than regular pancakes because of the cottage cheese.) Transfer to a plate and repeat with the remaining batter.
Makes 2 to 4 servings.

This is a favorite recipe I love to cook for my family on the weekends when I have more time. They all love these! We usually double (7 eggs) or triple (10½ eggs) the recipe for our family of seven. We have a very sporty family, as my husband and I were both all-American cross country and track and field athletes at the U of A. Our kids are in sports from cross country, track and field, and water polo to lacrosse, baseball, and soccer! So it's important to get a high-protein meal served in the morning to start our busy Saturdays!

CORNBREAD

Kirk Botkin
Football
Tight End, 1989–1993
Assistant Coach, 2008–2009

½ cup (1 stick) salted butter

2 (8.5-ounce) boxes Jiffy cornbread mix

¼ cup sugar

1 (15-ounce) can creamed corn

1 (8-ounce) container sour cream

2 large eggs

Preheat the oven to 400°F.

Place the butter in a large cast-iron skillet or a 9 by 13-inch pan and place it in the oven to melt.

In a large bowl, combine the cornbread mix, sugar, creamed corn, sour cream, and eggs. Mix until well combined. Carefully remove the skillet or pan from the oven and pour the batter over the melted butter. Bake for 35 to 45 minutes, until lightly browned and a toothpick inserted into the center comes out clean.
Makes 12 servings.

As a kid growing up in Baytown, Texas, I did not know much about the University of Arkansas. Coming out of high school, I was recruited by many colleges and it finally came down to the University of Oklahoma and the University of Arkansas for me. I chose Arkansas! There were many reasons, but mostly because I wanted to win and be successful. Out of all my recruiting trips, Fayetteville and the people of Arkansas made me feel more at home than anyplace else I visited. I loved the people at the U of A, the campus, the town of Fayetteville, and the passion of the Razorback fans! Despite numerous coaching changes, I had a wonderful college athletic experience. My recruiting class had four head coaches—Ken Hatfield, Jack Crowe, Joe Kines, and Danny Ford. I became a four-year letterman, never missing a game or a practice. I achieved much in the game of football. I scored the last TD in the Southwest Conference for the Hogs, led the team in receptions my junior season, winning multiple All-SEC honors and being selected the first 1st Team All-SEC player in the history of the University of Arkansas. One of my greatest honors was being voted captain of the team my senior year, but nothing compared to the comradery of being part of the university and the Razorback Football team. I met the love of my life and married an Arkansas girl, who was on the Pom Squad at the U of A. I even had the opportunity to further my career and coach for my beloved Hogs football program. I have so many amazing memories and friends from my time on "The Hill." I still vacation in and make annual duck hunting trips to Arkansas with an outstanding group of men from my time spent at the university. Hog Nation and the University of Arkansas will always be a place I can call home, and you are ALL family. GO HOGS!

EASY CHEESE GRITS

Mike Kirkland
Football and Baseball
Quarterback, Kicker, and Punter, 1972–1975
Third Base, 1973–1974

Butter or cooking spray, for greasing

3 cups chicken broth

½ teaspoon salt

1 cup quick grits (not instant)

1½ cups sharp cheddar cheese

¼ cup grated Parmesan cheese

½ cup (1 stick) salted butter

⅓ cup whole milk or half-and-half

3 large eggs

1 teaspoon Worcestershire sauce

½ teaspoon garlic powder

¼ teaspoon cayenne pepper

Preheat the oven to 350°F. Grease an 8-inch square baking dish with butter or cooking spray.

In a small saucepan, bring the broth and salt to a boil over high heat. Slowly stir in the grits. Reduce the heat to low, cover, and cook until thickened, 5 to 7 minutes. Remove from the heat, add the cheddar, Parmesan, and butter, and stir until melted. Add the milk, eggs, Worcestershire, garlic powder, and cayenne. Pour the grits into the prepared baking dish and bake for about 45 minutes, until light golden brown. *Makes 6 to 8 servings.*

What's a game weekend without cheese grits!

EGG AND SAUSAGE MUFFINS

Bo Busby
Football
Safety, 1973–1976

Nonstick cooking spray

1 (10-count) can flaky biscuits, or
2 uncooked flour tortillas

1 pound bulk hot or mild pork sausage

6 large eggs, beaten

1½ cups shredded cheddar and
Monterey Jack cheese blend

¾ cup grated Parmesan cheese

Salt and black pepper

Chopped green onion (optional)

Preheat the oven to 350°F. Spray two or three 12-cup muffin tins with cooking spray (if using biscuits) or just one tin (if using tortillas).

Divide each biscuit in half or into thirds based on your preference for a thick or thin crust. Press one biscuit piece into each well of the prepared muffin tins. (Or cut each tortilla into 6 pieces and press them into the prepared tin.)

In a large skillet, brown the sausage over medium-high heat, then drain the fat. Transfer the sausage to a large bowl and let cool slightly. Add the eggs, shredded cheese blend, Parmesan, and salt and pepper to taste. Divide the mixture evenly among the muffin tins. Bake for 18 to 20 minutes, until browned on top. *Makes 12 servings.*

NOTE *If you want to make these bite size, use a mini muffin tin and omit the biscuits or tortillas. Bake until browned on top; they will not take as long to cook as full-size muffins.*

Great for early morning tailgating and breakfast on the go.

EGGS OLÉ!

Barry Switzer
Football
Center and Linebacker, 1955–1959
Assistant Coach, 1961–1965

Nonstick cooking spray

12 large eggs, beaten

1 cup sour cream

4 tablespoons (½ stick) salted butter or margarine

1 (15-ounce) can diced tomatoes, drained and mashed with fork

1 green bell pepper, diced

16 ounces Velveeta cheese, diced

1 pound ham steak, diced

Preheat the oven to 325°F. Coat a 9 by 13-inch baking dish with cooking spray.

In a very large bowl, stir together the eggs, sour cream, butter, tomatoes, bell pepper, Velveeta, and ham steak. Pour the mixture into the prepared baking dish. (You can assemble the dish to this point, cover, and refrigerate overnight to bake the next day. Uncover and let stand at room temperature for 30 minutes before baking.) Bake for about 1 hour, until brown and set on top but still a little shaky in the center. *Makes 12 servings.*

GRANDMOM ELLIS'S BISCUITS

Taylor Ellis-Watson Washington
Women's Track & Field / Cross Country
200m, 400m, 2013–2016

Butter, for greasing and serving

2 cups all-purpose flour

4 teaspoons baking powder

1 teaspoon salt

1 cup buttermilk

3 tablespoons corn oil

Preheat the oven to 400°F. Grease a 9 by 11-inch baking pan with butter.

In a large bowl, stir together the flour, baking powder, salt, and buttermilk. Begin kneading the dough with your hands, gradually incorporating the corn oil as you knead. Separate the dough into biscuit-size pieces and roll each into a ball. Place the biscuits in the prepared baking pan, press your knuckles down into each one to flatten them slightly, and bake for 12 to 14 minutes, until golden brown on top. Serve with butter. *Makes 8 to 10 biscuits.*

This is my grandfather's mom's recipe. She grew up in Wilson, North Carolina. They moved to Philadelphia for more opportunities for them and their children and to get away from the racism they faced in the South. My grandfather was the baby of seven kids. He said his mom made these biscuits every single day. Right before she put them in the oven, she pushed her knuckles gently down on top so you could see the imprint. When you take them out of the oven, you cut them in half and put butter in between—yum! My great-grandmother taught my grandmom how to make these for my grandfather after they were married. Then my grandmom taught me how to make them.

JOSH FOLIART'S BANANA BREAD

Josh Foliart

Football

Outside Linebacker, 1998–2001

½ cup (1 stick) unsalted butter, at room temperature, plus more for greasing

3 cups all-purpose flour

½ teaspoon kosher salt

1½ teaspoons baking powder

1½ teaspoons baking soda

1½ cups chopped pecans (optional)

2 cups sugar

2 large eggs, at room temperature

1 cup buttermilk

2¼ cups very ripe mashed bananas

Preheat the oven to 350°F. Grease two 9 by 5-inch loaf pans with butter and line them with parchment paper.

Sift the flour, salt, baking powder, and baking soda into a medium bowl. Add the pecans (if using), then set aside.

In a large bowl, cream the butter and sugar with a handheld mixer. Mix in the eggs one at a time, then add the bananas. Alternate adding the dry ingredients and the buttermilk, beginning and ending with the dry ingredients, and mix just until incorporated—do not overmix. Divide the batter between the prepared pans.

Bake for 1 hour, or until the loaves are golden and firm to the touch, and a toothpick inserted into the center comes out clean. Let cool completely before removing from the pans and slicing or storing. The banana bread will keep well wrapped at room temperature for 2 to 3 days. *Makes two 9 by 5-inch loaves.*

PEPPER JACK CHEESE AND HAM QUICHE

Troy Eklund

Baseball

Outfield, 1986–1989

Butter, for greasing

1 (24-ounce) package frozen shredded hash brown potatoes, thawed and drained

½ cup (1 stick) salted butter

1 cup whole milk

2 large eggs

¼ teaspoon salt

2 cups shredded ham

2 cups shredded pepper Jack cheese

2 cups shredded Swiss cheese

Preheat the oven to 400°F. Grease a 9 by 13-inch casserole dish with butter.

Spread the hash browns over the bottom of the prepared casserole dish. Pour the melted butter over the hash browns. Bake for 25 minutes.

Meanwhile, in a medium bowl, beat the milk, eggs, and salt.

Remove the hash browns from the oven and reduce the oven temperature to 325°F. Layer the ham and cheeses on top of the hash browns, then pour over the egg mixture and bake for 40 minutes, or until golden brown on top and a toothpick inserted into the center comes out clean. *Makes 10 to 12 servings.*

In 1985, as a senior in high school, I was playing in an America Legion Tournament in Omaha, Nebraska, and Arkansas was playing in the College World Series. Coach Norm DeBriyn and Coach Doug Clark came to watch me play and invited me to visit the U of A campus. I was immediately sold on the program and on Fayetteville. My four years of playing for Arkansas and wearing a Razorback jersey were truly an honor. Not only did I have the pleasure of playing baseball for Arkansas, I also had the honor of meeting my beautiful wife, Teri, at the end of my sophomore year. This recipe was what my mom made the first time I brought Teri to Kansas City to meet my family. It quickly became one of our family favorites.

REFRIGERATOR ROLLS

Kevin Trainor
Razorback Athletics Staff, 1995–2025
Sports Information Director, 2000–2010
Senior Associate Athletic Director for Public Relations, 2010–2025

½ cup (1 stick) margarine, melted

1 (¼-ounce) packet active dry yeast

1 cup warm water

¼ cup sugar

1 large egg

1 teaspoon salt

3 cups all-purpose flour, plus more for dusting

Butter, for greasing and serving

Place the yeast in a medium bowl and pour in the warm water. Add the sugar and stir. Add the melted butter, egg, and salt and stir.

Place the flour in the bowl of a stand mixer fitted with the dough hook. With the mixer running on medium speed, slowly add the yeast mixture and mix until thoroughly combined. (Alternatively, place the flour in a large bowl, pour in the yeast mixture, and mix by hand until thoroughly combined.) Cover the bowl with plastic wrap and refrigerate overnight to allow the dough to rise slowly.

The next day, grease two baking sheets with butter. If you have the time, remove the dough from the fridge and let it come to room temperature (this makes it easier to handle, but you can also roll and cut it while it's still cold.)

Dust the countertop with flour and rub some flour on your rolling pin and your hands. Deflate the dough by pushing it down in the bowl, then turn it out onto the counter and knead it until you can form it into a ball. Add a little flour if the dough seems sticky. Press the dough flat with the rolling pin, then roll it out to about ¼ inch thick (or leave it thicker for bigger rolls). Cut the dough into rounds with your preferred cutter (see Notes). Place the dough rounds on the prepared baking sheets right next to each other. Form the dough scraps into a ball, then roll out and cut more rounds of dough until all the dough has been used. Let rise for 2 to 3 hours, or until doubled in size (see Notes).

Preheat the oven to 375°F.

Bake the rolls for 15 minutes, or until golden brown. Serve with butter, or melt 2 tablespoons of butter and brush the melted butter over the tops of the rolls before serving.

NOTES *You can easily make a homemade dough cutter from a clean empty tomato paste can with both ends removed. The size of the can makes for a nice size roll. Keep this cutter in your flour container for repeated use. If you use a tomato paste can to cut the dough, you'll end up with 30 or more rolls from this recipe.*

If you're in a hurry, you can place the rolls in the oven at 170°F for about 10 minutes, or until they have doubled in size. Remove the rolls from the oven, then raise the oven temperature to 375°F before baking.

This recipe has been passed down through the generations of women in my wife's family. My wife and I married in 1998, three years after I was hired for a full-time position in the athletic department. For almost twenty-two years, my mother-in-law would prepare Sunday dinner for six of her seven children (her eldest son lives in Virginia) and their children. Every Sunday, she would make these rolls. During those twenty-two years, fourteen grandchildren came along, so she had to double the recipe in order to have enough rolls. There was nothing better than walking into "Mimi's" house to the smell of fresh-baked rolls.

SAUSAGE AND GREEN CHILE BREAKFAST QUICHE

Dave Van Horn
Baseball
Second Base, 1981–1982
Graduate Assistant Coach, 1985–1988
Head Coach, 2002–present

1 homemade or store-bought refrigerated piecrust

12 ounces Jimmy Dean hot premium pork sausage

1 (4-ounce) can diced green chiles, undrained

1 cup mild shredded cheddar cheese

1 cup whole milk or half-and-half

4 large eggs, beaten

¼ teaspoon dry mustard

Tony Chachere's seasoning

Red and green salsas, for serving

Preheat the oven to 350°F.

Place the piecrust in a 9-inch deep-dish pie plate and use a fork to prick holes over the bottom of the crust. Bake the crust for 8 minutes. Remove from the oven and set aside; keep the oven on.

In a large skillet, cook the sausage over medium heat until browned and cooked through, then drain the fat. Crumble the sausage well, then place it in the piecrust, add the green chiles, and top with the cheese.

In a medium bowl, whisk together the milk, eggs, dry mustard, and Tony Chachere's to taste. Pour the egg mixture over the sausage mixture. Place the pie pan on a baking sheet and bake for 45 minutes to 1 hour, until the center is set and the top is golden brown. Remove from the oven and let stand for 10 minutes before serving. Serve with red and green salsas. *Makes 6 to 8 servings.*

This is a family favorite when we have friends and relatives in town for baseball weekends.

SOUR CREAM COFFEE CAKE

Larry Brown
Football
Quarterback and Holder, 1972–1976

COFFEE CAKE

1 teaspoon unsalted butter, plus more for greasing

All-purpose flour, for dusting

1 (15.25-ounce) box Duncan Hines butter golden cake mix

½ cup granulated sugar

⅔ cup Wesson oil

4 large eggs

1 small (8-ounce) container sour cream

ICING

3 ounces cream cheese, at room temperature

1 tablespoon whole milk, plus more if needed

1 teaspoon vanilla extract

1½ cups powdered sugar, plus more if needed

Pecans, for topping (optional)

Make the coffee cake: Preheat the oven to 325°F. Grease a 10-inch Bundt pan with butter, then dust it with flour, tapping out the excess.

In the bowl of a stand mixer fitted with the paddle attachment, combine the cake mix, granulated sugar, oil, eggs, sour cream, and butter. Mix on low speed until combined, then beat on high speed for 7 minutes, stopping often to scrape down the sides. Pour the batter into the prepared pan and bake for about 50 minutes, until a toothpick inserted into the center comes out clean. Let cool slightly before icing.

Make the icing: In a medium bowl, cream together the cream cheese, milk, and vanilla, then add the powdered sugar and mix until combined. If the icing seems too thick, add more milk until it's thin enough for drizzling; if it seems too thin, stir in more powdered sugar.

Drizzle the icing over the warm cake. Top with pecans, if desired. *Makes 12 to 16 servings.*

SOURDOUGH LOAF

Sebastian Cappelen
Men's Golf
Golfer, 2010–2014

POOLISH

175g water

175g high-protein flour (>12% protein bread flour is preferred)

Pinch of instant yeast (15 to 20 grains)

BREAD

6g instant yeast

13g kosher salt

50g whole wheat flour (see Notes)

350g high-protein bread flour (about 13%)

280g lukewarm water

Semolina flour, for dusting

SPECIAL EQUIPMENT

Plastic wrap and large metal bowl, or large bowl with airtight lid

Dough whisk

Dutch oven (about 8 quarts)

Bread lame

11- to 12-inch linen-lined proofing basket

Parchment paper

Wire rack

Kitchen scale

Pizza stone (optional)

Make the poolish: In a large metal bowl or airtight container, stir together the water, flour, and yeast. Cover tightly with plastic wrap or a lid and let stand at room temperature for 24 hours.

Start the bread: In a large metal bowl, mix the poolish with the water and add the yeast—use a tablespoon for mixing. This helps dissolve and mix the dough in its entirety. Add the whole wheat flour and the bread flour, then add the salt, placing it on top of the flour (direct contact between the salt and yeast can kill the yeast). Mix with a dough whisk or a spoon until the ingredients are just combined. Use a wet hand to really mix the dough, making sure it is completely combined. (Keep wetting your hand to keep the dough from sticking.) Cover the bowl with a lid or plastic wrap and let rest for 30 minutes.

Now it is time for the first "stretch and fold." Picture the dough in the bowl as a clock. Grab the dough at 12 o'clock, lift, and stretch (be careful not to tear it—you will feel how much the dough has to give), then fold the stretched dough down toward 6 o'clock. Repeat, starting at 3 o'clock and folding over to 9 o'clock, then 6 o'clock to 12 o'clock, and finally 9 o'clock to 3 o'clock. Flip the dough so the seams are face down. Run your hand around the edge of the dough, tucking it under until the dough has a round ball shape and enough strength to hold this shape (it will slowly flatten out again—don't stress). Wet your hand often as needed to prevent the dough from sticking to it during the "stretch and fold" process. Cover the dough ball again and let rest for 30 minutes. Perform a second "stretch and fold" series exactly as before. Cover the dough again and let rise for 1 hour, until just about doubled in size.

To shape the dough, turn it out onto a semolina-dusted surface. Perform a third "stretch and fold" series exactly as before. After you flip the dough seam-side down, use both hands to rotate the dough clockwise along an imaginary diagonal line that runs from the top left to the bottom right of your workspace. Tuck the edges of the dough as you rotate it clockwise along this imaginary diagonal line. Repeat this "rotate and tuck" three times, or until the dough holds its shape and looks like a smooth ball. Sprinkle a linen-lined proofing basket with semolina flour. Place the dough in the basket, smooth-side down. Cover the basket with a clean kitchen towel (sprinkle some semolina on the dough before covering it if you think the towel might stick). Let the dough rest for 35 to 45 minutes. (The dough doesn't always rise much during this final proofing stage before baking; it is more of an effort to let the dough relax than gain volume.)

Meanwhile, preheat the oven to 500°F (or higher, if possible—550°F is great). Position a rack low in the oven and place a pizza stone on the rack. Position a second oven rack right above the stone. Cover a large (8-quart or so) Dutch oven with its lid and place it on the rack above the pizza stone to preheat.

When the dough is ready to bake, cut a piece of parchment paper slightly larger than the size of the proofing basket. Place it on top of dough and, with one hand lightly pressing it into the dough, flip the basket to release the dough onto the parchment and place them on the counter. If desired, brush excess semolina from the top of the dough. Using a bread lame or a sharp knife, score a cross in the top of the dough (see Notes).

WEARING OVEN MITTS, remove the *hot* Dutch oven from the oven. Moving quickly, sprinkle semolina over the bottom of the Dutch oven. Using the edges of the parchment, lift the dough from the counter and place the parchment and dough into the Dutch oven. Cover with the lid (see Notes) and return the pot to the oven. Reduce the oven temperature to 500°F, if necessary, and bake for 18 minutes. Remove the lid and, if desired, remove the parchment from under the bread (be careful!). Bake, uncovered, for 25 minutes more. Knocking on the bottom of the bread should produce a dark hollow sound, indicating the bread is done. Carefully remove the bread from the Dutch oven and place on a wire rack to cool for at least 1 hour. Store in a sealed bag or airtight container at room temperature for up to 4 days. *Makes 1 loaf.*

NOTES *King Arthur whole wheat flour is a good grocery store option, but a locally sourced whole wheat would make the loaf special.*

Scoring the dough properly can be a learning curve. If you think your dough has risen a lot during the final rest, score a shallow cut. A shallow cut is preferred. However, if you think your dough could have risen more, you can score a deeper cut to allow it to "spring" more in the oven.

To create an even crispier crust and a focaccia-like consistency, lightly spray olive oil on top of the dough before covering the Dutch oven and baking.

The poolish is a type of starter made with a 1:1 ratio of water to flour. This is the trick to creating a sourdough-like loaf without having a true sourdough starter. The poolish ferments overnight, adding tremendous amounts of flavor, and helps create the crust that is so loved on a sourdough loaf.

STUFFED FRENCH TOAST

Eddie Sutton
Men's Basketball
Head Coach, 1974–1985

Butter, for greasing

1 (1-pound) loaf sourdough bread, crust trimmed off, cut into small cubes

1 (8-ounce) package cream cheese, cubed

12 large eggs

1½ cups whole milk

⅓ cup maple syrup, plus more for serving

1 teaspoon vanilla extract

1 teaspoon ground cinnamon

½ teaspoon ground nutmeg

Powdered sugar

Grease a 9 by 13-inch baking dish with butter.

Spread half the bread cubes over the bottom of the prepared baking dish. Distribute half the cream cheese cubes over the bread. Repeat with the remaining bread and cream cheese.

In a medium bowl, whisk together the eggs, milk, maple syrup, vanilla, cinnamon, and nutmeg and pour the egg mixture over the bread and cream cheese. Cover and refrigerate overnight.

The next day, preheat the oven to 350°F (see Note).

Bake, uncovered, for 30 to 40 minutes, until top is browned. Dust with powdered sugar and serve with additional maple syrup. *Makes 12 servings.*

NOTE *If using a glass baking dish, preheat the oven to 325°F instead.*

Eddie Sutton's favorite recipe was from Patsy Sutton's cookbook. Their grandchildren called Patsy "Honey," and she also called this recipe Honey's French Toast Casserole.

—Recipe submitted by Eddie's son Scott Sutton

TOMATO-ROSEMARY FOCACCIA BREAD

Joe Kleine
Men's Basketball
Center, 1982–1985

3⅔ cups bread flour

5 teaspoons instant yeast

1 teaspoon sugar

½ cup extra-virgin olive oil

1¾ teaspoons salt

1 pint cherry tomatoes, halved

Leaves from several rosemary sprigs

1 teaspoon dried oregano

¾ teaspoon ground black pepper

In the bowl of a stand mixer fitted with the dough hook, mix the flour, yeast, and sugar on medium speed until combined, about 30 seconds. With the mixer on low speed, drizzle in 2 cups cool to room-temperature water, then increase the speed to medium and mix until the ingredients form a very wet, smooth dough, about 5 minutes. Turn off the mixer, cover the bowl, and let stand for 10 minutes.

Meanwhile, coat a large bowl with 2 tablespoons of the olive oil.

Sprinkle 1 teaspoon of the salt over the dough, then knead on medium speed until smooth and elastic, about 5 minutes. The dough will be wet enough to cling to the sides of the bowl. Using a silicone spatula, scrape the dough into the oiled bowl. Dip your fingers into the oil pooled at the side of the bowl and dab the surface of the dough until completely coated with oil. Cover loosely with plastic wrap and let stand at room temperature for 5½ to 6 hours. During this time, the dough will double in volume, deflate, then rise again (but will not double in volume again).

After the dough has risen for 4½ hours, preheat the oven to 500°F. Place a baking steel or stone on the middle rack to preheat as well. Coat a 9 by 13-inch baking pan with cooking spray, then pour 2 tablespoons of the olive oil into the center of the pan.

When the dough is ready, gently pour it into the prepared pan, using a silicone spatula to loosen the dough from the sides of the bowl and trying to retain as much air in the dough as possible. Do not spread the dough with a spatula, as this will cause it to deflate—it will eventually settle into an even layer in the pan on its own. Set aside.

In a medium bowl, use a potato masher to lightly crush the tomatoes. Scatter the rosemary evenly over the dough, then do the same with the tomatoes, leaving the juice and seeds in the bowl. If the dough has not fully filled the corners of the pan, use your hands to lightly press down on the tomatoes to push the dough into the corners. Let stand, uncovered, at room temperature for 20 minutes.

Drizzle the dough with the remaining 4 tablespoons olive oil, making sure each tomato is coated. Sprinkle evenly with the oregano, the remaining ¾ teaspoon salt, and the pepper. Place the pan on the baking steel or stone and bake for 20 to 22 minutes, until the focaccia is golden brown and the sides have pulled away from the pan. Let cool in the pan on a wire rack for 5 minutes. Using a wide metal spatula, lift the focaccia from the pan and slide it onto the rack. Let cool for at least 30 minutes more before serving. *Makes 10 to 12 servings.*

This is a favorite recipe from Christopher Kimball's *Milk Street Magazine*. It's time-consuming, but delicious!

ZUCCHINI NUT BREAD

Deena Drossin Kastor
Women's Track & Field / Cross Country
5000m, 10,000m, 1991–1996

½ cup plain Greek yogurt

⅓ cup coconut oil, melted

1 large egg

2 teaspoons maple syrup

1½ teaspoons vanilla extract

1 ripe banana, mashed

½ cup coconut sugar or granulated sugar

1 cup all-purpose flour

½ cup oat flour

1 teaspoon baking soda

1 teaspoon ground cinnamon

¼ teaspoon salt

1 cup grated zucchini (about 1 medium), patted dry with paper towels

½ cup dark chocolate chips

½ cup walnuts

Preheat the oven to 375°F. Lightly grease a 9 by 5-inch loaf pan with baking spray.

In a large bowl, stir together the yogurt, melted coconut oil, egg, maple syrup, and vanilla. Add the banana and sugar and stir to combine. Add the all-purpose flour, oat flour, baking soda, cinnamon, and salt and stir to combine. Fold in the zucchini, chocolate, and walnuts. Pour the batter into the prepared loaf pan and bake for 40 to 50 minutes, until a toothpick inserted into the center comes out clean. *Makes 12 to 16 servings.*

I would make this bread on Sundays, and it offered a quick and nutritious snack after a workout or long run. Protein from the yogurt and nuts, vitamins from the banana and zucchini, and an endorphin boost from the chocolate come together for a satisfying and healthy refueling option.

SOUPS, SALADS, AND SANDWICHES

BLACK-EYED PEA SOUP

Tim Siegel
Men's Tennis
Player, 1982–1986

4 beef bouillon cubes

1 pound bulk sausage

1 pound ground beef

1 large onion, diced

¾ teaspoon minced garlic

3 (28-ounce) cans black-eyed peas, undrained

1 large (14.5-ounce) can diced tomatoes, undrained

1 large (10-ounce) can Ro*Tel diced tomatoes and green chiles, with their juices

1 (4-ounce) can diced green chiles, undrained

4 teaspoons molasses

1 teaspoon Worcestershire sauce

½ teaspoon salt

¼ teaspoon ground cumin

Place the bouillon cubes in a small microwave-safe bowl with ¼ cup water. Microwave for 2 to 3 minutes, then stir until the bouillon cubes have dissolved; set aside.

In a large pot, brown the sausage and ground beef over medium-high heat, breaking up the meat as it cooks, then drain the fat. Add the onion and cook until translucent. Add the garlic and stir for 2 to 3 minutes. Add the bouillon mixture, black-eyed peas, canned tomatoes, Ro*Tel, green chiles, molasses, Worcestershire, salt, cumin, and 4 cups water and stir to combine. Bring to a simmer and cook for 1 hour to let the flavors blend. *Makes 10 to 12 servings.*

My mother-in-law, Lindy, made the best black-eyed pea soup! We could count on having this every year on New Year's Day. It's great with cornbread.

Nobody loves the Razorbacks more than I!

BUBBA'S DEER CHILI

Bubba Carpenter
Baseball
First Base and Outfield, 1988–1991

3 pounds ground venison

2 yellow onions, chopped

2 jalapeños, diced

1 tablespoon minced garlic

2 (16-ounce) cans chili beans, drained

2 (16-ounce) cans pinto beans, drained

3 (14.5-ounce) cans petite diced tomatoes, with their juices

2 small (10.75-ounce) cans tomato puree

1 (1.25-ounce) packet hot chili seasoning (or substitute mild or original)

2 (1.25-ounce) packets original chili seasoning (I use McCormick original chili seasoning mix)

Salt and black pepper

Garlic powder

In a large skillet, combine the ground venison, onions, jalapeños, garlic, and salt and pepper to taste. Cook over medium-high heat until the meat is browned; be careful not to let it burn. Transfer the mixture to a slow cooker and add the chili beans, pinto beans, diced tomatoes, tomato puree, and chili seasonings. Season with salt, pepper, and garlic powder to taste. Stir well. Cover and cook on Low for at least 6 hours or up to 8 hours. The longer it cooks, the better it tastes! *Makes 12 to 16 servings.*

Believe it or not, the reason I chose this recipe and Bubba's Venison Tenderloin (page 71) for this book is really more about the memories associated with them than the actual food itself! Growing up in Brentwood, Arkansas, there were always two seasons I looked forward to with great anticipation. One was obviously opening day for the Razorback baseball season (both as a young country boy dreaming of being a Razorback and later as a Razorback player). The second was opening day of deer season, which meant lots of fun at deer camp. I hope y'all try these recipes and enjoy them with friends and family. The recipes have been tweaked over the years, but the memories last a lifetime! Go Hogs!

CHEESEBURGER SOUP

Mark Henry
Football
Offensive Line, Guard, and Center, 1988–1991

8 ounces ground beef

4 tablespoons (½ stick) salted butter

¾ cup chopped onion

¾ cup shredded carrots

¾ cup diced celery

1 teaspoon dried basil

1 teaspoon dried parsley flakes

3 cups chicken broth

4 cups diced peeled potatoes

¼ cup all-purpose flour

12 ounces Velveeta cheese

1½ cups whole milk

¾ teaspoon salt

½ teaspoon black pepper

¼ cup sour cream

French bread, for serving

In a 3-quart saucepan, brown the ground beef over medium heat, then drain the fat; transfer the meat to a bowl and set aside.

In the same saucepan, melt 1 tablespoon of the butter over medium heat. Add the onion, carrots, celery, basil, and parsley and cook until the vegetables are tender, about 10 minutes. Add the broth, potatoes, and ground beef and bring to a boil. Reduce the heat to low, cover, and simmer for 10 to 12 minutes, until the potatoes are tender.

In a small skillet, melt the remaining 3 tablespoons butter over medium heat. Add the flour and cook, stirring, for 2 minutes, then reduce the heat to low. Add the Velveeta, milk, salt, and pepper and cook, stirring, until the Velveeta melts and the soup is well combined. Remove from the heat and stir in the sour cream. Serve with French bread. *Makes 6 to 8 servings.*

CHEESY CREAM OF BROCCOLI SOUP

Harold Horton
Football
Defensive Back and Running Back, 1958–1961
Linebacker and Defensive Line Coach, 1968–1980

4 cups Swanson's chicken broth

2 cups chopped fresh or frozen broccoli

2 cups chopped ham

1 medium onion, chopped

1 cup chopped celery

1 medium potato, chopped

1 teaspoon dried basil

1 teaspoon black pepper

4 chicken bouillon cubes

½ to 1 teaspoon dried thyme leaves

½ teaspoon salt

1 cup whole milk

2 (10.5-ounce) cans condensed cream of chicken soup

½ (15-ounce) jar Cheez Whiz

Grated Parmesan or sharp cheddar cheese, for garnish

In a Dutch oven or large pot, combine the broth, broccoli, ham, onion, celery, potato, basil, pepper, bouillon cubes, thyme, and salt and bring to a boil over medium-high heat. Reduce the heat to maintain a simmer and cook, stirring occasionally, for 30 minutes, or until the broccoli is tender. If you want the soup to be smooth, carefully transfer all or a portion of it to a blender and blend, then return the soup to the pot. We prefer it with small chunks in it. Stir in the milk and Cheez Whiz and simmer for 30 minutes. Ladle into bowls, garnish each portion with Parmesan or cheddar, and serve. *Makes 8 to 10 servings.*

"Coach loves this soup!" —Betty Horton

CHEESY VEGETABLE SOUP

Martine Bercher Jr.
Football
Safety and Defensive Back, 1964–1966

3 tablespoons salted butter

2 small carrots, thinly sliced

2 small potatoes, diced

½ cup chopped celery

¼ cup chopped onion

3 tablespoons all-purpose flour

3 cups chicken broth

Black pepper

1 slice Velveeta cheese, about 1 inch thick, cubed

In a 2-quart saucepan, melt the butter over low heat. Add the carrots, potatoes, celery, and onion and cook, stirring occasionally, until the vegetables are tender, about 15 minutes. Add the flour and cook, stirring continuously, until well combined. While stirring, gradually pour in the broth. Cook, stirring continuously, until thick and bubbling, about 10 minutes. Season with pepper. Reduce the heat to maintain a simmer and cook for 10 minutes more. Add the Velveeta and stir until melted and well combined, then serve. *Makes 4 to 6 servings.*

—Recipe submitted by Carole Bercher

CHICKEN TACO SOUP

Scott Tabor
Baseball
Pitcher, 1979–1982

1 tablespoon olive oil

½ medium onion, diced

3 cups chicken broth (see Notes)

2 (10-ounce) cans Ro*Tel diced tomatoes and green chiles (see Notes), with their juices

1 (14-ounce) can black beans, drained and rinsed

1 (12-ounce) can corn, drained

½ red bell pepper, diced

1 tablespoon chili powder

1 teaspoon garlic powder

1 teaspoon ground cumin

1 teaspoon smoked paprika

1 (8-ounce) package cream cheese, cut into small pieces, at room temperature (see Notes)

2 cups cooked/rotisserie chicken, shredded

Salt and black pepper

Optional toppings: shredded Mexican-style cheese blend, avocado, cilantro, tortilla strips

In a large soup pot, heat the olive oil over medium-high heat. Add the onion and cook over medium-high heat, stirring, for 5 minutes. Add the broth, Ro*Tel, black beans, corn, bell pepper, chili powder, garlic powder, cumin, and paprika. Increase the heat to high and bring the soup to a boil. Reduce the heat to maintain a gentle simmer and cook, uncovered, for 5 minutes. Add the cream cheese to the soup and let it melt, stirring until it is fully incorporated. Stir in the chicken and cook until warmed through, 5 to 7 minutes. Ladle the soup into individual bowls, season with salt and pepper to taste, and add toppings of your choice. *Makes 8 to 10 servings.*

NOTES *The cream cheese should be super soft so it melts easily into the soup. I recommend taking it out of the refrigerator prior to starting the soup and microwaving it in 20- to 30-second intervals until it's very soft.*

If you have concerns with salt, use low-sodium broth.

*You can use regular canned diced tomatoes instead of the Ro*Tel, but if you do, I suggest adding a 4-ounce can or two of diced green chiles, as it makes a difference in the flavor.*

DEER CAMP CHILI

Kendall Trainor
Football and Baseball
Kicker and Punter, 1985–1988
Outfield, 1986–1988

2 pounds ground venison or lean ground beef

1 pound bulk venison sausage or pork sausage

2 teaspoons minced garlic

½ cup chopped onion

½ teaspoon black pepper

1½ teaspoons garlic salt

2 (2-ounce) packets Williams chili seasoning mix

2 tablespoons chili powder

½ to 1 cup diced jarred or fresh jalapeños

1 (10-ounce) can no-salt-added Ro*Tel diced tomatoes and green chiles, with their juices

1 (16-ounce) bag frozen three-pepper mix

1 (28-ounce) can crushed or diced tomatoes, with their juices

2 (15-ounce) cans Ranch Style pinto beans with jalapeños, undrained

2 (16-ounce) cans Bush's medium or hot chili beans, undrained

2 (14.5-ounce) cans low-sodium beef broth

FOR SERVING

Fritos

Grated cheddar cheese

Sour cream

In a large chili pot, combine the ground venison, sausage, onion, and garlic and season with black pepper. Cook over medium-high heat, stirring, until the meat is almost browned, then sprinkle in the garlic salt and cook until the meat is browned. Stir in the chili seasoning mix and add the chili powder across the top. Add the jalapeños (using more or less to taste) and cook, stirring occasionally, for 2 to 3 minutes. Add the Ro*Tel and the mixed peppers and stir well. Cook over medium-high heat, stirring occasionally, until the mixture begins to boil. Add the crushed tomatoes, Ranch Style beans, chili beans, and broth and stir well. Cook, stirring occasionally, until the mixture comes to a boil. Reduce the heat to low and stir until the boiling stops, then simmer for 1 hour to allow the flavors to blend. Serve over a bed of Fritos, topped with cheese and a little sour cream. *Makes 14 to 18 servings.*

This is a staple in our house and at the hunting lodge from late September through March here in Arkansas! Many Razorback football games have been enjoyed while having a bowl or three of this relatively healthy chili. Of course, the healthiness depends on what you serve it with, but that's completely up to y'all! Hope it becomes one your favorites, too. Go Hogs!

DEER CHILI

Richard LaFargue
Football
Center, 1972–1975

1 pound ground beef

1 pound ground venison

1 yellow onion, diced

1 tablespoon minced garlic

1 (1-ounce) packet Williams chili seasoning mix

1 (24-ounce) can chopped stewed tomatoes, undrained

1 (15-ounce) can dark kidney beans, undrained

1 (15-ounce) can light kidney beans, undrained

1 (15-ounce) can chili beans, undrained

1 (15-ounce) can black beans, undrained

Cooked rice, for serving

Shredded sharp cheddar cheese, for serving

In a large skillet, combine the ground beef, ground venison, onion, and garlic. Cook over medium-high heat, breaking up the meat as it cooks, until all the meat is browned, 18 to 24 minutes, then drain the fat.

Transfer the meat mixture to a large pot and add the chili seasoning, tomatoes, and all the beans with their liquid. Cook over low heat for 1 hour to allow it to slightly thicken and the flavors to blend. Serve over rice, topped with cheddar. *Makes 14 to 16 servings.*

HOG'S BREATH CHILI

Tony Cherico
Football
Nose Guard, 1984–1987

3 Anaheim chiles

3 poblano chiles

3 tablespoons bacon grease or canola oil

2 tablespoons unsalted butter

2 red bell peppers, diced

2 jalapeños, minced

2 yellow onions, diced

1 head garlic, cloves peeled and minced

1 pound boneless beef chuck, trimmed and cut into ¼-inch cubes

2 pounds coarse-ground beef

1 pound bulk hot or mild Italian sausage

3 tablespoons chili powder

2 teaspoons cayenne pepper

2 teaspoons ground coriander

2 teaspoons ground cumin

2 teaspoons granulated garlic

2 teaspoons granulated onion

2 teaspoons hot paprika

2 teaspoons kosher salt

2 teaspoons freshly ground black pepper

2 cups tomato sauce

1 cup tomato paste

12 ounces lager beer

1 cup chicken stock

2 (15.5-ounce) cans kidney beans, undrained

2 (15.5-ounce) cans pinto beans, undrained

FOR SERVING

Crackers of choice

Thinly sliced green onions

Shredded cheddar cheese

Preheat the broiler. Line a small baking sheet with foil.

Place the Anaheim and poblano chiles on the prepared baking sheet. Broil for 5 to 7 minutes, until most of the skin on top is charred. Flip the chiles and repeat to char the second side. Remove from the oven and place in a large zip-top bag. Seal the bag and let stand for 20 minutes to steam. One by one, remove the chiles from the bag and use your fingers to gently peel off the charred skin, then slice the chile open and scrape out the seeds with a spoon. Chop the flesh of the chiles and set aside.

In a large stockpot, melt the bacon grease and butter over high heat. Add the roasted Anaheim chiles and poblanos, the bell peppers, jalapeños, and onions and cook until browned, about 5 minutes. Add the garlic and cook for 1 minute more. Add the chuck and cook until browned, about 4 minutes. Add the ground beef and sausage and cook, stirring gently and trying not to break up the ground beef too much, until the meat is nicely browned and cooked through, 7 to 10 minutes. Add the chili powder, cayenne, coriander, cumin, granulated garlic, granulated onion, paprika, salt, and black pepper and cook until fragrant, about 1 minute. Add the tomato sauce and tomato paste and cook, stirring, until the tomato paste darkens, about 2 minutes. Stir in the beer and broth, then add the kidney and pinto beans with their liquid. Reduce the heat to maintain a simmer and cook for about 2 hours to allow the flavors to blend and to thicken the chili slightly. Serve the chili in bowls, topped with crackers, green onions, and cheddar. *Makes 12 to 14 servings.*

Once upon a time at the University of Arkansas, there were two football players named Tony Cherico and Ravin Caldwell. They were inseparable buddies, known for their humorous antics both on and off the field. Every game day, the dynamic duo had a special tradition: heading to Bowen's Restaurant for their pregame meal before taking on opponents in Little Rock.

On one eventful Friday night before a big game, Tony and Ravin excitedly walked into Bowen's Restaurant, ready to fuel up for the match ahead. They went through the line, loading up their plates with all the delicious offerings. Tony, a big fan of chicken legs, was delighted to see them on the menu and took a generous portion. Ravin, on the other hand, grabbed a mixture of various dishes, not paying much attention to what was on his plate. As they settled at a table and started to dig into their food, Tony noticed something odd about his chicken legs. They looked a bit peculiar and smelled . . . different. But he was so hungry and eager to eat that he didn't dwell on it for long. However, as soon as he took a bite, he couldn't help but make a face.

"Hey, Ravin, do your chicken legs taste funny?" Tony asked, looking a bit concerned. Ravin, who was busy munching on his own plate, looked up at Tony with a puzzled expression. "What chicken legs?"

Tony pointed to the food on Ravin's plate. "Those right there, man! They taste weird." Ravin took a closer look at his plate and started laughing heartily. "Haha, Tony, those aren't chicken legs! They're frog legs!" Tony's eyes widened in surprise and disbelief. "Frog legs? Are you serious?" Ravin nodded, still chuckling. "Yep, that's what they serve here sometimes. Guess you didn't pay much attention to what you were putting on your plate, huh?"

Tony couldn't believe it. He had unwittingly picked up a plate full of frog legs instead of his beloved chicken legs. The realization was so absurd that he couldn't help but join Ravin in laughter. "Well, I guess I'll be trying something new tonight!" The whole cafeteria seemed to be entertained by the spectacle of the two football stars feasting on frog legs. Tony and Ravin took it in stride, making jokes and laughing throughout the meal. They turned the frog leg mishap into a pregame ritual, believing that it would bring them good luck on the field the next day. And you know what? The following day, Tony and Ravin played the game of their lives. Maybe it was the frog legs, or maybe it was just their natural talent and camaraderie shining through. Either way, they helped lead the University of Arkansas to a glorious victory, and the legend of the frog leg pregame meal was born.

HUSBAND-PLEASIN' CHILI

Jeb Huckeba
Football
Defensive End, 2001–2004

2 pounds ground beef

Salt and black pepper

1 (2-ounce) packet Williams chili seasoning mix

1 (64-ounce) can tomato juice

1 (14.5-ounce) can diced tomatoes, with their juices

1 (10-ounce) can Ro*Tel diced tomatoes and green chiles (your choice: mild, original, or hot), with their juices

2 (15-ounce) cans black beans or kidney beans, drained and rinsed

Shredded cheddar cheese, for serving

Tortilla chips, for serving

In a large pot, brown the ground beef over medium heat, seasoning the meat with salt and pepper as it cooks. Drain the fat, then add the chili seasoning and stir. Add the tomato juice, diced tomatoes, Ro*Tel, and beans and stir to combine. Simmer for 20 to 30 minutes to allow the flavors to blend. This chili is even better if it sits overnight. Serve with cheese and chips. *Makes 10 to 12 servings.*

ITALIAN SAUSAGE AND ARTICHOKE SOUP

Bo Busby
Football
Safety, 1973–1976

1 (16-ounce) package bulk mild Italian sausage

¼ cup olive oil

1 to 2 onions, chopped

2 to 3 garlic cloves, minced or grated

1 (48-ounce) carton chicken broth

1 (28-ounce) can diced tomatoes, with their juices

2 (14-ounce) cans artichoke hearts in water, drained and chopped

1 teaspoon chopped fresh basil

1 teaspoon chopped fresh oregano

1 teaspoon chopped fresh parsley

Freshly shredded Parmesan cheese, for serving

In a Dutch oven, brown the sausage over medium-high heat, then drain the fat; transfer the meat to a bowl and set aside. Pour the olive oil into the Dutch oven and heat over medium heat, then add the onions and garlic and cook, stirring occasionally, until translucent, about 5 minutes. Return the sausage to the pot, then add the broth, tomatoes, artichokes, basil, oregano, and parsley. Bring to a boil, then reduce the heat to maintain a simmer and cook for 30 minutes to allow the flavors to blend. Serve in bowls, with Parmesan sprinkled on top. *Makes 4 to 6 servings.*

U. S. Reed

JAMAICAN OXTAIL STEW

U. S. Reed
Men's Basketball
Guard, 1977–1981

3 pounds sliced oxtails (see Note)

3 tablespoons Worcestershire sauce

3 tablespoons packed light brown sugar

1½ teaspoons salt

1 teaspoon black pepper

1 teaspoon ground allspice

2 tablespoons olive oil

1 large onion, chopped

4 garlic cloves, minced

4 carrots, cut into ½-inch-thick slices

2 bell peppers, chopped into 1-inch chunks

1 whole Scotch bonnet pepper

2 bay leaves

2 teaspoons chopped fresh thyme

2 tablespoons ketchup

1 tablespoon apple cider vinegar

2 cups beef broth

1 (16-ounce) can butter beans, drained

1 tablespoon cornstarch

½ cup chopped green onions, for serving

Place the oxtails in a large baking dish. Add the Worcestershire, brown sugar, salt, black pepper, and allspice. Toss well to coat the oxtails in the seasonings.

In a large (6- to 8-quart) saucepan, heat the olive oil over medium heat. When the oil is hot, place half the oxtails in the pot and cook until browned on both sides, 2 to 3 minutes per side. Move the oxtails around in the pot as they cook so the sugar doesn't burn on the bottom. Transfer the oxtails to a plate and repeat with the remaining oxtails.

Add the onion and garlic to the pot and cook, stirring, for 2 to 3 minutes, then return the browned oxtails to the pot and top them with the carrots, bell pepper, Scotch bonnet, bay leaves, thyme, ketchup, and vinegar. Pour the broth over the top. Cover and cook over medium-low heat until the oxtail meat is tender and the liquid has thickened to the consistency of gravy, 2 to 3 hours.

Drain the butter beans and toss them with the cornstarch. Stir the beans into the stew. Simmer for 5 to 10 minutes to thicken the stew. Serve warm in individual soup bowls, topped with green onions. *Makes 4 to 6 servings.*

NOTE *Oxtail can be purchased presliced in packages or ordered at the butcher counter.*

JOHNNY RAY'S CHILI

Johnny Ray
Baseball
Second Base, 1978–1979

1 pound ground beef

2 (16-ounce) cans pinto beans, undrained

1 (16-ounce) can jalapeño pinto beans, undrained

1 (14.5-ounce) can stewed tomatoes, with their juices

1 (15-ounce) can tomato sauce

2 small (6.5-ounce) cans tomato juice

1 (1-ounce) package chili seasoning mix

In a large skillet, brown the ground beef over medium-high heat, then drain the fat. Add the pinto beans, jalapeño pinto beans, stewed tomatoes, tomato sauce, tomato juice, and chili seasoning mix and stir. Cook for 10 minutes, then reduce the heat to maintain a simmer and cook until the mixture is slightly thickened, about 1 hour. *Makes 6 to 8 servings.*

MEXICAN CHICKEN CORN CHOWDER

Hunter Henry
Football
Tight End, 2013–2015

3 tablespoons salted butter

1½ pounds boneless, skinless chicken breasts, cut into 1-inch pieces

½ cup chopped onion

1 to 2 garlic cloves, minced

2 teaspoons chicken bouillon granules

½ to 1 teaspoon ground cumin

2 cups half-and-half

2 cups (8 ounces) shredded Monterey Jack cheese

Hunter Henry

1 (14.75-ounce) can cream-style corn

1 (4-ounce) can diced green chiles, undrained

¼ to 1 teaspoon hot pepper sauce

1 medium tomato, chopped

Minced fresh cilantro, for garnish (optional)

In a Dutch oven, melt the butter over medium heat. Add the chicken and onion and cook until the chicken is no longer pink inside. Add the garlic and cook for 1 minute more. Add the bouillon granules, cumin, and 1 cup hot water and bring to a boil over medium-high heat. Reduce the heat to maintain a simmer, cover, and cook for 5 minutes. Stir in the half-and-half, cheese, corn, green chiles, and hot pepper sauce. Cook over low heat, stirring, until the cheese has melted. Stir in the tomato and remove from the heat. Serve garnished with cilantro, if desired. *Makes 6 to 8 servings.*

MEXICAN SOUP

Hannah Gammill
Softball
Third Base, 2020–2024

2 pounds ground beef

1 cup diced onion

2 (15.5-ounce) cans pinto beans, undrained

1 (15.5-ounce) can whole kernel corn, undrained

2 (10-ounce) cans Ro*Tel diced tomatoes and green chiles, with their juices

2 (14.5-ounce) cans stewed tomatoes, with their juices

1 (1-ounce) packet taco seasoning mix

1 (1-ounce) packet Hidden Valley ranch seasoning mix

Tortilla chips and/or Fritos, for serving (optional)

Sour cream, for serving (optional)

In a large pot, combine the ground beef and onion and cook, breaking up the meat as it cooks, until the meat is browned and cooked through, about 15 minutes, then drain the fat. Add the pinto beans, corn, and Ro*Tel and the liquid from the cans. Add the stewed tomatoes with their juices, chopping the tomatoes into smaller portions with your spoon as you add them, if needed. Stir in the taco seasoning, ranch mix, and ¾ cup water. Simmer for 1 hour to allow the flavors to blend. Serve hot, in indivdual soup bowls, topped with tortilla chips, Fritos, and/or sour cream. *Makes 6 to 8 servings.*

NEW ENGLAND CLAM "CHOWDA"

Chris Bucknam
Men's Track & Field / Cross Country
Head Coach, 2008–present

2 or 3 slices bacon

½ cup (1 stick) salted butter

1 medium yellow onion, finely chopped

3 celery stalks, finely chopped

5 (6.5-ounce) cans chopped clams, undrained

3 potatoes, preferably Yukon Gold, peeled and cut into ½-inch cubes

2 to 3 cups half-and-half

Pinch of cayenne pepper (optional)

Salt and black pepper

1 (8-ounce) bottle clam juice

¼ cup all-purpose flour

Oyster crackers, for serving

In a large, heavy stockpot, cook the bacon over medium-high heat until cooked through, about 10 minutes. Transfer the bacon to a cutting board, leaving the rendered fat in the pot, and chop into small pieces.

Return the bacon to the pot with the fat and add the butter, onion, and celery. Cover and cook until the vegetables are tender, about 10 minutes. Add the clams and their liquid to the pot, then add the potatoes, 2 cups of the half-and-half (add the extra cup, if desired, for more creaminess), cayenne (if using), and salt and black pepper to taste.

In a 2-cup measuring cup, stir together the clam juice and flour. Add this mixture to the pot and stir (see Note). Cook over low heat (the liquid should be barely boiling), stirring occasionally so the potatoes don't stick to the bottom of the pot, until the potatoes are fork-tender, 20 to 30 minutes. Serve with oyster crackers. Great as leftovers the next day! *Makes 8 to 10 servings.*

NOTE *More flour can be added to thicken the chowder, or you can add milk to make it thinner, per your preference.*

It took a little over fifty years for me to make my way to Arkansas and join the Razorback family! I grew up in Beverly, Massachusetts, and as a student athlete, I ran track in the fall and spring. To keep my brothers and me busy in the winter, my dad would flood our backyard and let it freeze, and we'd play ice hockey with the neighborhood kids. The perfect ending to a day of skating was a bowl of my mom's clam chowder.

PASTA FAGIOLI SOUP

Ruth Cohoon
Women's Athletic Director, 1969–1989

1 pound ground beef

1 cup chopped white onion

1 teaspoon minced garlic

1 (30-ounce) jar Ragú chunky garden combination sauce

1 (10.5-ounce) can beef broth

1 cup chopped celery

1 teaspoon sugar

1 teaspoon salt

½ teaspoon black pepper

1 (10-ounce) can Ro*Tel diced tomatoes and green chiles

1 (15.5-ounce) can great northern beans, drained and rinsed

1 (15.5-ounce) can red kidney beans, drained and rinsed

Handful of matchstick-cut carrots

1 to 2 cups cooked elbow macaroni

Texas toast, for serving

Green salad, for serving

In a large Dutch oven, combine the ground beef, onion, and garlic and cook until the meat is browned, then drain the fat. Add the Ragú, broth, celery, sugar, salt, pepper, and 2 cups water. Bring to a boil over high heat, then reduce the heat to maintain a simmer and cook until the celery has softened, 20 minutes. Stir in the Ro*Tel, beans, carrots, and macaroni and cook until the beans and pasta are warmed through and the carrots have softened, about 30 minutes. *Makes 8 to 10 servings.*

This is a favorite recipe based on one from the February 5, 1997, edition of the *Tulsa World* newspaper. I serve it with Texas toast and a green salad.

POTATO SOUP

Dana McQuillin Dalke
Women's Gymnastics
Gymnast, 2003–2006

8 medium potatoes, peeled and chopped into small chunks

3 cups vegetable broth

4 garlic cloves, minced

3 tablespoons salted butter

1 tablespoon chopped fresh thyme leaves

Pinch of ground nutmeg

Pinch of paprika

Salt and black pepper

¾ cup shredded cheese (cheddar, smoked cheddar, or Parmesan work well)

3 green onions, chopped

Optional toppings: pepitas, chopped cooked bacon, chopped fresh parsley

Place the potatoes in a large pot with water to cover. Bring to a boil over medium-high heat and cook until the potatoes are soft, about 20 minutes. Drain and rinse to cool down. Transfer two-thirds of the cooked potatoes to a blender (set the remainder aside) and add 1 cup of the broth and 1 teaspoon of the garlic. Puree until smooth.

In the pot you used for the potatoes, melt the butter over medium heat. Add the remaining garlic and cook, stirring, for about 1 minute. Add the remaining 2 cups broth and the pureed potato mixture and cook until the mixture begins to bubble. Add the remaining cooked potatoes, the thyme, nutmeg, paprika, and salt and pepper to taste. Cook for a few more minutes, then remove from the heat and stir in ½ cup of the cheese. Ladle into bowls and garnish with the green onions, the remaining cheese, and any optional toppings just before serving. *Makes 8 to 10 servings.*

We have a variety of food allergies and preferences in our family, and this recipe still seems to work for everyone. Everybody loves it! If you want to make it vegan, just use vegan butter or olive oil in place of the butter and leave the cheese out at the end.

POZOLE VERDE

Tony Cherico
Football
Nose Guard, 1984–1987

VERDE SAUCE

1 pound tomatillos (about 12 golf ball–size tomatillos), husked and halved

1 large onion, roughly chopped

6 to 8 large garlic cloves, peeled

3 medium poblano chiles, seeded and sliced

1 jalapeño, halved and seeded (add 1 more to make it extra spicy)

1 tablespoon olive oil

POZOLE

8 cups flavorful chicken stock

1 teaspoon kosher salt

1 tablespoon ground coriander

1 tablespoon dried Mexican oregano

1 tablespoon dried epazote, or 2 bay leaves

2 teaspoons ground cumin

1 teaspoon freshly ground black pepper, plus more as needed

2 pounds boneless, skinless chicken breasts or thighs

1 bunch cilantro, leaves and tender stems (optional)

4 cups cooked hominy, or 3 (15-ounce) cans, drained and rinsed

Optional toppings: sour cream, sliced avocado, Mexican crema, lime wedges, crumbled queso fresco, chopped green onions, toasted pepitas, sliced radishes, thinly sliced red onion, chopped cilantro, shredded cabbage, diced tomatoes, tortilla chips, fresh corn kernels, black beans, hot sauce

Make the verde sauce: In a blender, combine the tomatillos, onion, garlic, poblanos, jalapeño, and 1 cup water. Blend until smooth, stopping and scraping down the sides if necessary.

In a large skillet, heat the olive oil over medium heat. Add the tomatillo mixture and cook, stirring occasionally, until the sauce turns a deep green, about 10 minutes.

Make the pozole: In a large heavy-bottomed pot or Dutch oven, combine the stock, salt, coriander, oregano, epazote, cumin, and pepper and bring to a boil over high heat. Add the chicken, reduce the heat to low, and cover. Simmer gently until the chicken is tender and cooked through, about 25 minutes. Transfer the chicken to a plate and shred the meat. Skim any fat from the surface and return the chicken to the pot.

Ladle 1 cup of the broth from the pot into the blender (it's okay if it's not rinsed) and add the cilantro (if using). Cover the lid tightly with a kitchen towel and blend until smooth. Add 1 cup of the hominy and blend again until smooth. If you need more liquid to get the blender going, just ladle some from the pot.

Pour the verde sauce into the pot. Add the remaining 3 cups hominy and bring the soup to a gentle simmer over medium heat—do not let the soup boil or you will lose the lovely color. Add the pureed mixture from the blender to the soup. Taste and season with salt and pepper (see Note) and cook until the soup is just heated through.

Serve the pozole in individual bowls, letting people add whatever toppings they want. *Makes 8 to 10 servings.*

NOTE *If soup lacks depth, add more salt, a couple of chicken bouillon cubes, a couple teaspoons of chicken bouillon paste, or even a splash of soy sauce. The goal is to get enough depth in the soup to balance out the tartness from the tomatillos and the heat from the chiles.*

TOMATO BASIL SOUP

Kendall Beth Sides

Softball

Center Field, 2021–2022

2 large (16-ounce) packages cherry tomatoes

1 sweet onion, coarsely chopped

1 head garlic, halved crosswise

1 red bell pepper, coarsely chopped

¼ cup olive oil

1 tablespoon Italian seasoning

1 tablespoon dried basil

Salt and black pepper

4 tablespoons (½ stick) salted butter

2 tablespoons sugar

½ (32-ounce) carton vegetable broth

1 cup heavy cream (optional)

Grated Parmesan cheese, for serving

Preheat the oven to 450°F.

Place the tomatoes, onion, garlic, and bell pepper on a baking sheet and drizzle with the olive oil. Season with Italian seasoning, basil, salt, and pepper (use a heavy hand—season with your heart and your eyes!). Roast for 45 minutes, or until the vegetables are tender. Remove from the oven. Squeeze the roasted garlic cloves out of their skins into a blender, add the the rest of the roasted vegetables, and blend until smooth.

In a large pot, combine the butter and sugar and heat over low heat until the butter melts, about 1 minute. Don't let the sugar caramelize! Add the tomato mixture and broth and even some heavy cream (optional, depending on your health goals!). Serve topped with Parmesan. *Makes 4 to 6 servings.*

My memories of this recipe are of making it in my apartment at the U of A during the times it snowed so much! Everything about Arkansas was wonderful memories for me. I miss all the wonderful people and the environment every single day. Fayetteville is one special place, and I am eternally grateful for Coach Deifel and staff.

TORTELLINI SOUP

Sandi Morris

Women's Track & Field / Cross Country

Pole Vault, 2012–2015

1 pound bulk pork sausage

1 onion, chopped

2 garlic cloves, minced

5 cups beef broth

½ cup dry red wine

2 (14.5-ounce) cans diced tomatoes with basil and oregano, with their juices

1 (8-ounce) can tomato sauce

1 cup thinly sliced carrots

½ teaspoon dried basil

½ teaspoon dried oregano

½ cup sliced zucchini

3 tablespoons dried parsley

1 medium green bell pepper, chopped

1 (12-ounce) package cheese tortellini

Grated Parmesan cheese, for topping

In a large saucepan, brown the sausage over medium-high heat, then drain the fat. Add the onion and garlic and cook until the onion is translucent. Add the broth, wine, diced tomatoes, tomato sauce, carrots, basil, oregano, and ½ cup water. Bring to a boil, then reduce the heat to maintain a simmer and cook for 30 minutes. Skim any fat from the surface and add the zucchini, parsley, and bell pepper. Simmer for 25 minutes more. Add the tortellini and simmer until soft, about 15 minutes more. Serve in bowls with Parmesan on top. *Makes 8 to 10 servings.*

A great memory about this soup recipe: My mom, Kerry Morris, made this soup for our family when I was growing up, and it was always one of my favorites. She is a wonderful cook and mother! I remember making it myself for the first time, planning to serve it to my now husband. I remember serving it up and thinking, *Hmm, something is missing*... THE TORTELLINI were missing from the tortellini soup. Well, the tortellini are the very last thing to go in after all the vegetables have cooked through, and OOPS ... I forgot them! My husband still makes jokes about it to this day. So, folks, don't forget the tortellini at the end! Otherwise, you will have yourself a delicious vegetable soup. (Although there's nothing wrong with that, either!)

VEGETABLE BEEF (OR VENISON) SOUP

Kendall Trainor

Football and Baseball

Kicker and Punter, 1985–1988

Outfield, 1986–1988

2 pounds lean ground beef or ground venison

¼ cup dried onion

1 teaspoon minced garlic

½ teaspoon garlic powder

½ teaspoon black pepper

1 large (28-ounce) can crushed tomatoes, with their juices

1 (10-ounce) can Ro*Tel diced tomatoes and green chiles (mild or hot—we like it spicy), undrained

1 large (16-ounce) bag your favorite frozen vegetables for soup

1 medium (10-ounce) bag frozen mixed vegetables

1 (14.5-ounce) can low-sodium beef broth

1 large (64-ounce) bottle low-sodium V-8 (original or hot)

In a large soup pot, combine the ground beef, dried onion, minced garlic, a dusting of garlic powder and pepper and cook over medium-high heat until the meat is browned. Add the crushed tomatoes, Ro*Tel, soup vegetables, and mixed vegetables and cook, stirring occasionally, for 5 minutes. Add the broth and V-8 and bring to a boil, stirring occasionally to keep the meat from sticking to the bottom of the pot. Reduce the heat to low and simmer for 1 hour, or until the vegetables are tender. It seems like the longer it simmers, the better it is. *Makes 8 to 10 servings.*

This soup is a staple at our home throughout the year. It freezes well, so we always make extra and store it in gallon-size freezer bags. Serve it with shredded cheese over cornbread. Enjoy! WPS!

VEGETARIAN CHILI

Raymond House

Football

Defensive End, 2000–2002

2 tablespoons olive oil

2 cups chopped white onions

2 tablespoons minced garlic

1 cup diced celery

1 jalapeño, diced (with seeds)

1 green bell pepper, diced

2 (14-ounce) cans diced tomatoes with basil, garlic, and oregano, with their juices

1 cup vegetable broth

1 (6-ounce) can tomato paste with basil, garlic, and oregano

⅓ cup Worcestershire sauce

1 (15-ounce) can pinto beans, drained and rinsed

1 (15-ounce) can kidney beans, drained and rinsed

2 tablespoons chili powder

Andrew Benintendi

1 tablespoon cumin

1 tablespoon Italian seasoning

½ teaspoon salt

½ teaspoon black pepper

Optional toppings and sides: cornbread, extra jalapeños, Fritos, sour cream, cheese, crackers

In a large pot, heat the olive oil over medium heat. Add the onions and garlic and cook until soft. Add the celery, jalapeño, and bell pepper and cook until soft. Add the diced tomatoes and their juices, broth, tomato paste, and Worcestershire. Stir to combine evenly and cook until the mixture is bubbling slightly. Add the beans, chili powder, cumin, Italian seasoning, salt, and black pepper and stir until combined. Reduce the heat to maintain a simmer and cook until the chili thickens, about 45 minutes. Serve with your choice of toppings and sides. *Makes 6 to 8 servings.*

When it is cold outside, my family loves soups and warm comfort foods. My wife loves my chili and requests it often, especially as we're cheering on the Hogs in the fall. It's packed with vegetables, and I add a kick of spice: a full jalapeño. This is a vegetarian recipe, but you can add meat if you choose.

WHITE BEAN, SPINACH, AND ITALIAN SAUSAGE SOUP

Andrew Benintendi
Baseball
Outfield, 2014–2015

4 ounces bulk hot or mild Italian sausage

1 tablespoon extra-virgin olive oil

½ cup chopped onion

1 garlic clove, finely chopped

3½ to 4 cups canned or cooked cannellini beans, undrained

3 cups unsalted or low-sodium chicken broth

1 cup chopped fresh tomatoes or drained canned tomatoes

½ cup dried pasta shells

1 (10-ounce) package fresh spinach

Freshly grated Parmesan cheese, for serving

In a large pot, brown the sausage over medium-high heat, breaking up the meat as it cooks, then drain the fat; transfer the meat to a bowl and set aside. In the same pot, heat the olive oil over medium heat. Add the onion and cook until soft. Add the garlic and cook for 1 minute, until fragrant. Return the sausage to the pot and stir in the beans, broth, and tomatoes. Add the pasta and bring the soup to a boil. Cook until the pasta is al dente, 7 to 9 minutes. Remove from the heat and stir in the spinach. Serve immediately, topped with Parmesan. *Makes 6 to 8 servings.*

WISCONSIN CHILI

Katherine Grable-Barnes
Women's Gymnastics
Gymnast, 2010–2014

3 tablespoons olive oil

1 large onion, chopped

3 pounds ground beef

2 (4-ounce) cans diced green chiles, undrained

1 (4-ounce) can chopped jalapeños, undrained

2 tablespoons chili powder

Salt and black pepper

2 teaspoons dried oregano

½ teaspoon cayenne pepper

2 (28-ounce) cans petite diced tomatoes, with their juices

2 (28-ounce) cans chili beans, undrained

1 (64-ounce) bottle V-8 juice

FOR SERVING

2 cups elbow macaroni, cooked and drained

Shredded cheddar cheese

Sour cream

Tortilla chips

In a large deep pot, heat the olive oil over medium heat. Add the onion and cook until translucent. Add the ground beef and cook, adding the green chiles and jalapeños after a minute or two, until the meat is browned and cooked through. Season to taste with chili powder, salt, black pepper, oregano, and cayenne. Add the tomatoes and beans, then pour in enough V-8 to cover the ingredients. Cover and simmer for 45 minutes to allow the flavors to blend.

To serve, combine the chili with your desired amount of macaroni and top with cheese, a dollop of sour cream, and chips. *Makes 14 to 16 servings.*

When I was growing up, we would make this chili to enjoy while we watched Green Bay Packers and college football games.

BING CHERRY SALAD

Jerry Jones
Football
Offensive Guard, 1960–1964

2 (15-ounce) cans Bing cherries, undrained

1 (20-ounce) can crushed pineapple, undrained

2 (6-ounce) packages cherry Jell-O mix

1 cup chopped pecans

1 large (8-ounce) package cream cheese, at room temperature

2 (8-ounce) cans Coke, chilled

Drain the juice from the cherries and pineapple into a measuring cup and add enough water to make 2½ cups of liquid total. Pour the liquid into a medium saucepan and bring to a boil over high heat. Remove from the heat, add the Jell-O, and stir to dissolve, about 2 minutes. Whisk in the cream cheese until combined, then add the drained cherries and pineapple, the pecans, and the Cokes. Pour the mixture into an 11 by 13-inch pan (or a Bundt pan, to make it pretty) and refrigerate overnight to set. If using a Bundt pan, unmold before serving. *Makes 16 to 20 servings.*

Jerry Jones

Jim Lindsey and I used to ride on the bus together down to Hot Springs. We'd stay there before we went over to Little Rock to play the next day. We'd ride along and talk about how we used to eat at home. Jim would give me these great meal descriptions that he had and then I'd have to roll out what Mom and Dad used to fix at home, because we were in the grocery business. We'd eat whatever the ripest and ready food we had was, which was the very best things you could eat in there. My dad was very creative and loved to cook, and we ate like kings.

Some of my greatest memories were from around our house with my sister and some of those creations that my dad put together with all the fresh stuff out of the grocery store. Eating was something that I had really gotten to a point where I didn't want more, though, towards the end of high school. I was only 150 pounds when I came out of my junior year at North Little Rock, but I wanted to be a Razorback so bad. I started drinking brewer's yeast and wheat germ and my mother and sister used to cook two extra meals for me every day. I went from 150 pounds to 220 pounds. And that's how I got my scholarship to the University of Arkansas. I thought, if I could ever get through this, and gain muscle and weight, I didn't ever want to see an ounce of food again.

I do think about food and cooking in context with my life and experiences with the Razorbacks. I got married to Gene when I was a junior, and we had Stephen. One of the very best parts of that was sitting over at our little apartment across from the practice fields and having dinner. It was a great change of scenery to be able to go back and eat those mashed potatoes and pork chops with them and try to keep my weight up for the Razorbacks.

CHICKEN CAESAR SALAD TRAYBAKE

Shelley Taylor-Smith
Women's Swimming & Diving
500yds, 100yds, 1650yds Freestyle
100yds and 200yds Backstroke and Open Water, 1982–1985

4 skin-on boneless chicken breasts

Salt and black pepper

Seasoning of choice, such as garlic powder, dried oregano, paprika (optional)

8 slices bacon

3½ tablespoons olive oil

2 ciabatta rolls or similar rolls, torn into pieces

1 head romaine lettuce, quartered lengthwise

CAESAR DRESSING

2 ounces Parmesan cheese, grated

½ cup mayonnaise

3 garlic cloves, crushed

1 teaspoon Dijon mustard

1 teaspoon Worcestershire sauce

2 tablespoons fresh lemon juice

4 anchovy fillets in oil, drained and finely chopped

Preheat the oven to 400°F.

Season the chicken breasts with salt and pepper and place them skin-side up on a large baking sheet. Place the bacon around the chicken and drizzle with 1 tablespoon of the olive oil. Bake for 10 minutes.

Meanwhile, place the bread in a large bowl, drizzle with 2 tablespoons of the olive oil, and season with salt and pepper. Add the bread to the baking sheet with the chicken and bake for 15 minutes more, or until the chicken is cooked through and the bacon is crisp.

Make the Caesar dressing: In a food processor, combine three-quarters of the Parmesan, the mayonnaise, garlic, pepper, mustard, Worcestershire, lemon juice, and anchovies. Process until smooth.

When chicken is cooked through, remove the baking sheet from the oven and switch the oven to broil. Add lettuce quarters to the baking sheet with the chicken and bread. Drizzle the remaining ½ tablespoon olive oil over the lettuce. Broil, watching closely, for 2 to 3 minutes, until the lettuce is lightly charred and the bread is crisp. Remove from the oven.

Drizzle with the Caesar dressing, season with more pepper, and top with the remaining Parmesan, then serve. *Makes 4 servings.*

CUCUMBER EDAMAME SALAD WITH CHICKEN

Suzie Fritz
Women's Volleyball
Associate Head Volleyball Coach, 2023–2024

DRESSING

3 tablespoons avocado oil or grapeseed oil

3 tablespoons rice vinegar

2 tablespoons toasted sesame oil

2 teaspoons low-sodium soy sauce

1½ teaspoons grated fresh ginger

1 garlic clove, minced

SALAD

1 pound English or Persian cucumbers, thinly sliced

1 cup shelled edamame

1 large avocado, cubed

½ cup thinly sliced green onions

2 cups fresh spinach

2 tablespoons toasted sesame seeds

Pinch of sea salt

Pinch of red pepper flakes or drizzle of chile oil

3 to 4 cooked chicken breasts, sliced or cubed

Make the dressing: In a large glass measuring cup, whisk together all the ingredients until well combined.

Make the salad: In a large salad bowl, combine the cucumber, edamame, avocado, green onions, spinach, chicken, and sesame seeds. Season with the salt. Add the dressing and toss to coat. Add the red pepper flakes or drizzle with chile oil to taste. Toss and serve topped with the chicken. *Makes 4 to 6 servings.*

FRAMILY SPINACH SALAD

Tony Bua
Football
Linebacker, 2000–2003

VINAIGRETTE

1 cup grapeseed oil

½ cup onion juice (see Note)

¼ cup distilled white vinegar

2 tablespoons sugar

1 tablespoon dry mustard

SALAD

1 (4-ounce) package prosciutto

2 (10-ounce) bags baby spinach

1 (8-ounce) block white cheddar cheese, grated

1 cup dried cranberries

½ cup toasted pine nuts

Make the vinaigrette: In a blender, combine the oil, onion juice, vinegar, sugar, and dry mustard and blend until well combined. (The vinaigrette can be stored in an airtight container in the refrigerator for up to 3 days. Shake well before use.)

Make the salad: Preheat the oven to 350°F.

Place the prosciutto slices on a baking sheet and toast in the oven for 7 to 10 minutes, until crispy, then chop.

Place the spinach in a serving bowl and add the prosciutto, cheese, dried cranberries, pine nuts, and vinaigrette. Toss to combine, then serve.
Makes 4 to 6 servings.

NOTE *To make onion juice, place an onion in a blender and puree, then strain the puree through a fine-mesh sieve into a bowl and discard the solids.*

LAYERED SALAD WITH PIGS ON TOP

Christy Smith
Women's Basketball
Point Guard, 1994–1998
Assistant Coach, 2014–2016

1 head lettuce, chopped

½ cup chopped celery

1 cup frozen baby sweet peas

½ cup chopped green onions

1 cup mayonnaise

1 teaspoon sugar

½ cup shredded cheddar cheese

¼ cup crumbled cooked bacon

2 or 3 large hard-boiled eggs, peeled and sliced

1 tomato, chopped

Layer the lettuce, celery, peas, and green onions in a 9 by 13-inch glass dish. In a small bowl, combine the mayonnaise and sugar, then spread the mayonnaise mixture over the lettuce mixture. Top with the cheese, bacon, and eggs. Cover and refrigerate until ready to serve. (It is best served within 1 to 2 days but will keep for up to 3 days.) Just before serving, top with the tomatoes (don't add them too early or they will make the salad watery). *Makes 4 to 6 servings.*

So many fun times as a Razorback. Really enjoyed the summers when all the athletes would stay at College Park while taking summer classes, and then heading to Beaver Lake on the weekends.

NAPA SALAD

Robert Cox
Men's Tennis
Player, 1976–1978
Head Coach, 1987–2013

TOPPINGS

4 tablespoons (½ stick) salted butter

½ cup sliced almonds

½ cup sunflower seeds

2 (3-ounce) packages oriental-flavor ramen noodles, smashed into small pieces, flavor packets reserved

DRESSING

½ cup sugar

½ cup oil

½ cup apple cider vinegar

2 tablespoons soy sauce

SALAD

1 head napa cabbage, coarsely chopped

3 green onions, finely chopped

Make the toppings: In a large skillet, melt the butter over low heat. Add the ramen noodles and their flavor packets, the almonds, and the sunflower seeds and stir. Cook until lightly browned, 10 to 15 minutes, then remove from the heat.

Make the dressing: In a 1-pint jar or other airtight container, combine the sugar, oil, vinegar, and soy sauce. Cover and shake to combine.

Assemble the salad: Just before serving, place the cabbage in a serving bowl. Add the green onions, toppings, and dressing and toss to combine. *Makes 10 to 12 servings.*

NOTE *The three components can be prepped up to 1 day ahead of time and stored in separate containers in the refrigerator until you're ready to assemble the salad. I use a Tupperware bowl for the cabbage and green onions, a zip-top bag for the toppings, and a glass jar for the dressing so you can shake it!*

My aunt Sug (pronounced like the beginning of the word "sugar") made this at a family reunion, and we were blown away! My wife, Meredith, has made it often ever since.

POTATO SALAD

Marc Brumble
Baseball
Outfield, 1976–1979

12 medium Yukon Gold potatoes, peeled

5 large hard-boiled eggs, peeled and chopped

¾ medium sweet onion, diced

3 sweet pickles, diced, plus ¼ cup brine from the jar

½ (30-ounce) jar Miracle Whip

3 squirts mustard

1 teaspoon salt

1 teaspoon celery salt

Place the potatoes in a large pot with water to cover. Bring to a boil over high heat and cook until the potatoes are tender, 15 to 20 minutes. Drain and chop the potatoes, then transfer them to a large bowl and add the eggs, onion, pickles and pickle brine, Miracle Whip, mustard, salt, and celery salt. Gently fold all the ingredients together with a large spoon and serve. Leftovers will keep, covered, in the refrigerator for up to 3 days. *Makes 8 to 10 servings.*

SOUR CREAM POTATO SALAD

Tommy Boyer
Men's Basketball
Forward and Guard, 1960–1964

7 medium red or Yukon Gold potatoes, peeled

⅓ cup clear Italian dressing

¾ cup sliced celery

⅓ cup sliced green onions

4 large hard-boiled eggs, peeled and chopped

1 cup mayonnaise

½ cup sour cream

Place the potatoes in a medium pot with water to cover. Bring to a boil over high heat and cook until the potatoes are tender, about 25 minutes. Drain the potatoes, then slice them and place in a large bowl. Pour the dressing over the warm potatoes and let stand for about 30 minutes. Add the celery, green onions, and eggs. In a small bowl, stir together the mayonnaise and sour cream. Add the mayonnaise mixture to the bowl with the potato mixture and fold to combine. Cover and refrigerate for at least 1 hour or up to 1 day before serving. *Makes 6 to 8 servings.*

TACO SALAD

Sam Pittman
Football
Assistant Head Coach / O-Line, 2013–2015
Head Coach, 2020–present

1½ pounds ground beef

1 (1-ounce) packet McCormick original taco seasoning

1 head lettuce, chopped

2 tomatoes, diced

1½ cups grated sharp cheddar cheese

1 (15.5-ounce) bag nacho cheese Doritos, broken up

1 (15-ounce) bottle Russian dressing

1 (16-ounce) bottle ranch dressing

Diet Coke, for serving

In a large skillet, brown the ground beef over medium-high heat, then drain the fat. Stir in the taco seasoning and ½ cup water and bring to a boil. Reduce the heat to maintain a simmer and cook, stirring occasionally, for 5 minutes. Transfer the seasoned meat to a large bowl. Add the lettuce, tomatoes, and cheese and stir to combine. Cover and refrigerate until ready to serve (it will keep for up to 2 days).

To serve, divide the salad among individual bowls and stir in the Doritos. Serve with Russian dressing and ranch dressing, with Diet Coke alongside. *Makes 4 to 6 servings.*

TANGY GREEN BEAN SALAD

Tommy Boyer
Men's Basketball
Forward and Guard, 1960–1964

1 (14-ounce) can French-cut green beans, drained

1 small (8.5-ounce) can English peas, drained

4 celery stalks, diced

1 medium onion, chopped

1 small green bell pepper, diced

1 small (4-ounce) jar chopped pimentos, drained

1 tablespoon salt

¾ cup sugar

½ cup distilled white vinegar

¼ cup vegetable oil

Paprika

In a medium bowl, combine the green bean, peas, celery, onion, bell pepper, and pimentos.

In a small bowl, combine the sugar, vinegar, oil, salt, 1 tablespoon water, and paprika to taste. Stir until the sugar has dissolved. Pour the vinegar mixture over the vegetables, cover, and marinate in the refrigerater for several hours before serving. *Makes 4 to 6 servings.*

GARY BLAIR SANDWICH

Gary Blair
Women's Basketball
Head Coach, 1993–2003

2 slices sourdough bread

4 slices American cheese

5 ounces sliced deli ham

2 extra-thick-cut slices bacon, cooked

1 lettuce leaf

2 slices tomato

1 tablespoon clarified butter

On a griddle, melt the butter over medium heat. Spread the melted butter evenly over the griddle, then lay the bread over the butter. Top each piece of bread with 2 slices of cheese. Quickly sauté the ham on the griddle, then place the ham on one piece of bread and top with the bacon. When the cheese has adequately melted, transfer both slices of bread to a clean cutting board. Top the ham and bacon with the lettuce and tomato and sandwich with the other piece of bread, cheese-side down. Slice the sandwich diagonally and enjoy. *Makes 1 serving.*

This is Coach Blair's favorite sandwich, as served at the Traditions Club in Bryan, Texas.

Pat Bradley

PEPPERONI PIZZA CALZONE

Pat Bradley
Men's Basketball
Guard, 1995–1999

1 pound pizza dough, homemade or store-bought

All-purpose flour

1 cup pizza sauce

8 ounces mozzarella cheese, shredded

1 stick pepperoni, sliced

1 egg yolk, beaten

Preheat the oven to 365°F.

On a floured surface, roll out the dough to a roughly 8 by 11-inch rectangle. Spread the sauce evenly over the dough. Spread the cheese evenly over sauce, followed by the pepperoni. Roll up the dough like a jelly roll to enclose the fillings and fold the ends under. Place the pizza roll seam-side down on a baking sheet or pizza pan. Brush the top of the roll with the egg yolk and poke a few holes in the dough to allow steam to escape. Bake for 40 minutes, or until golden brown and the dough is cooked through. *Makes 2 to 4 servings.*

This recipe is from my father, Rich Bradley.

PIGGY SLIDERS

James McCann

Baseball

Catcher, 2009–2011

Nonstick cooking spray

1 pound thin-sliced deli ham

1 (12-count) package Hawaiian rolls

8 slices Swiss cheese

½ cup (1 stick) unsalted butter, melted

1 tablespoon Worcestershire sauce

2 tablespoons yellow mustard

Sprinkle of garlic salt

Preheat the oven to 350°F. Line a 9 by 13-inch baking pan with foil and spray the foil with cooking spray.

Leaving the rolls attached to one another, slice them in half horizontally so you have a slab of tops and a slab of bottoms. Place the bottom slab in the prepared pan, layer the ham and cheese on top, then place the top slab over the ham and cheese.

In a small bowl, whisk together the melted butter, Worcestershire, mustard, and garlic salt. Pour the mixture over the rolls. Cover with foil and bake for 20 minutes, or until the cheese has melted. Uncover and bake for about 5 minutes more to toast the top. Slice into individual sliders and serve! *Makes 12 servings.*

SAM'S TUNA FISH SALAD

Sam Pittman

Football

Assistant Head Coach / O-Line, 2013–2015

Head Coach, 2020–present

2 (5-ounce) cans white albacore tuna in oil, drained

3 tablespoons Miracle Whip

2 tablespoons sweet pickle relish

1 tablespoon sugar

4 large hard-boiled eggs, peeled and chopped

Dash of mustard

Salt and black pepper

FOR SERVING (OPTIONAL)

Toasted bread

Ruffles potato chips

Ranch dressing

Diet Cokes

Place the tuna in a medium bowl and break it up with a fork. Add the Miracle Whip, relish, sugar, eggs, and mustard and stir to combine. Season with salt and pepper, then cover and refrigerate until ready to serve.

Serve on toast, with a side of Ruffles potato chips dipped in ranch dressing, and a cold Diet Coke, if you like. *Makes 4 servings.*

SLOPPY JOES

Marc Brumble

Baseball

Outfield, 1976–1979

2 pounds ground beef

1 onion, chopped

1 cup BBQ sauce

1 tablespoon Worcestershire sauce

1 tablespoon light brown sugar

1 tablespoon chili powder

1 tablespoon salt

½ teaspoon ground cinnamon

Buns, for serving

In a large skillet, brown the ground beef over medium-high heat, then drain the fat. Add the onion, BBQ sauce, Worcestershire, brown sugar, chili powder, salt, cinnamon, and ½ cup water and stir to combine. Cook over low heat for 1 hour to allow the flavors to blend and the sauce to thicken slightly. Serve on buns. *Makes 6 to 8 servings.*

SIDE DISHES

BAKED BEANS

Cliff Powell
Football
Linebacker, 1967–1969

3 tablespoons neutral oil

½ (14-ounce) package Hillshire Farm sausage links, sliced

1 large onion, chopped

½ red bell pepper, chopped

½ green bell pepper, chopped

1 pound ground beef

2 (15-ounce) cans Showboat pork and beans, undrained

8 ounces light brown sugar

Mustard

Worcestershire sauce

Preheat the oven to 350°F.

In a large skillet, heat the oil over medium heat. Add the sausage, onion, and bell peppers and cook until tender. Transfer to a large bowl and set aside.

In the same skillet, brown the ground beef over medium heat, then drain the fat. Transfer to the bowl with the sausage mixture. Add the beans and brown sugar, then add mustard and Worcestershire to taste. Transfer the mixture to a 9 by 13-inch baking dish and bake for 45 minutes to 1 hour to allow the flavors to meld and the sauce to thicken. *Makes 8 to 10 servings.*

BAKED CORN

Bettye Fiscus
Women's Basketball
Forward, 1981–1985

½ cup (1 stick) unsalted butter

1 heaping tablespoon all-purpose flour

2 (14.75-ounce) cans cream-style corn

½ cup sugar, or less as needed

½ cup PET evaporated milk

2 large eggs, beaten

1½ teaspoons baking powder

Salt and black pepper

Preheat the oven to 350°F.

In a large pan, melt the butter over medium heat. Add the flour and mix well. Remove from the heat and add the corn, sugar, evaporated milk, eggs, baking powder, and salt and pepper to taste. Stir to combine. Pour the mixture into a 2-quart casserole dish and bake for 40 to 45 minutes, until bubbling and set. *Makes 6 to 8 servings.*

NOTE *This recipe can be doubled; increase the baking time to 60 to 75 minutes.*

BARBECUED RICE

Harold Horton
Football
Defensive Back and Running Back, 1958–1961
Linebacker and Defensive Line Coach, 1968–1980

Nonstick cooking spray

½ cup (1 stick) margarine or unsalted butter

1 cup chopped celery

1 medium onion, chopped

2 cups condensed cream of chicken soup

1 cup chicken broth

2 teaspoons liquid smoke

Salt and black pepper

2 cups cooked rice

½ teaspoon garlic salt

Preheat the oven to 350°F. Coat an 8-inch-square casserole dish with cooking spray.

In a heavy medium skillet, melt the margarine over medium heat. Add the celery and onion and cook until translucent. Add the cream of chicken soup, broth, liquid smoke, and salt and pepper to taste. Bring to a boil, then pour the mixture into the prepared casserole dish. Add the rice and garlic salt and mix well. Bake for 30 minutes to allow the rice to soak up the flavors and absorb the liquid.
Makes 4 to 6 servings.

"This is the amount I make for my family, but when I take this dish to a potluck or make it for company, I double the recipe, and it makes a really full 9 by 13-inch casserole." —Betty Horton

BRUSSELS SPROUTS

Wallace Spearmon Jr.
Men's Track & Field / Cross Country
100m, 200m, 2003–2005

1 pound Brussels sprouts, trimmed and halved

2 teaspoons olive oil

1 garlic clove, thinly sliced

Salt and black pepper

2 teaspoons light brown sugar

4 slices unsalted butter

Preheat the oven to 350°F.

Place the Brussels sprouts on a large baking sheet. Drizzle with the olive oil and distribute the garlic slices evenly among the sprouts. Season with the salt and pepper and toss to coat. Sprinkle the brown sugar on top. Layer the slices of butter on top. Bake for 30 minutes, or until the sprouts are tender and slightly brown around the edges. *Makes 4 servings.*

This is my go-to when I am pressed for time and I need a quick, satisfying meal.

CHANTILLY POTATOES

Brad McMakin
Men's Golf
Head Coach, 2006–present

2 tablespoons unsalted butter, plus more for greasing

Salt

6 large Yukon Gold potatoes, scrubbed and peeled

¼ cup milk

Black pepper

½ cup heavy cream

¼ cup grated American cheese

Paprika

Preheat the oven to 350°F. Grease a casserole dish with butter.

Place the potatoes in a large pot with water to cover. Salt the water and bring to a boil over high heat. Cook until the potatoes are fork-tender, 12 to 15 minutes. Drain the potatoes and return them to the pot. Add the butter and milk and mash. Beat with a handheld mixer until light and fluffy, then taste and season with salt and pepper. Transfer the mashed potatoes to the prepared casserole dish.

In a large bowl using a handheld mixer, whip the cream until it holds stiff peaks. Cover the mashed potatoes with the whipped cream, then sprinkle with the cheese and some paprika. Bake for 20 to 30 minutes, until brown on top. *Makes 6 to 8 servings.*

CREAM CHEESE CORN IN THE SLOW COOKER

Lance Harter
Women's Track & Field / Cross Country
Head Coach, 1990–2023

3 pounds frozen corn kernels

1 (8-ounce) package cream cheese

½ cup (1 stick) salted butter

1 small (4-ounce) jar pimentos, drained

Handful of sugar

Combine the corn, cream cheese, butter, pimentos, and sugar in a slow cooker. Cover and cook on Low for 4 to 6 hours or on High for 2 to 3 hours, or until the cream cheese and butter have melted, stirring occasionally during the cooking time. *Makes 10 to 12 servings.*

It was absolutely the honor of a lifetime to be part of the Razorback family! But as a coach, I missed a lot of holidays and special occasions with my own family, so I tried to make the most of the times when we could all be together. This recipe is one of our holiday staples. It makes enough to serve our gang and is so effortless to start and let cook on its own while you're preparing other dishes.

CRISPY SMASHED POTATOES

Deane Pappas
Men's Golf
Golfer, 1989–1992

10 medium Yukon Gold or red potatoes, scrubbed and dried

¼ cup olive oil

1 (5.3-ounce) package garlic and herb Boursin cheese

¾ cup (1½ sticks) unsalted butter, at room temperature

2 tablespoons crushed garlic

1 cup grated Parmesan cheese

1 cup grated mozzarella cheese

Salt and black pepper

Preheat the oven to 385°F. Line a baking sheet with foil.

Rub the potatoes with olive oil, place on the prepared baking sheet, and bake for 45 to 60 minutes, until fork-tender.

Meanwhile, in a small bowl, stir together the Boursin, butter, and garlic.

Remove the potatoes from the oven and raise the oven temperature to 425°F. Use a potato masher or the bottom of a sturdy glass to smash the potatoes flat, ½ to ¾ inch thick. Spoon the Boursin mixture liberally over each potato and top evenly with the mozzarella and Parmesan. Season with salt and pepper and bake for 20 to 25 minutes, until golden brown and crispy. *Makes 10 servings.*

DIRTY RICE

Jim Lindsey
Football and Baseball
Wingback, 1963–1965
Outfield, 1964–1965

1 (6-ounce) box Ben's Original long grain and wild rice

2¼ cups chicken broth

2 tablespoons unsalted butter

1 pound fresh button mushrooms, sliced

2 bunches green onions, chopped

½ (8-ounce) can water chestnuts, drained and chopped

4 celery stalks, chopped

8 to 10 slices bacon, cooked until crisp and crumbled

Garlic powder

Cayenne pepper

Salt and black pepper

Cook the rice according to the package directions, using the broth for the liquid and adding 1 tablespoon of the butter to the pot when you add the broth.

In a large pan, melt the remaining 1 tablespoon butter over medium heat. Add the mushrooms, green onions, water chestnuts, and celery and cook until the mushrooms and celery are softened. Add the rice and bacon to the pan and stir to combine. Season with garlic powder, cayenne, salt, and black pepper to taste. *Makes 4 servings.*

My sister, Joyce Clark, started making this dirty rice recipe for Lindsey family holiday dinners. From the first time she made it, it was a family favorite and had to be included in all future dinners. Thank you, sister Joyce. I love you.

DOWELL LOGGAINS'S SWEET POTATO CASSEROLE

Dowell Loggains
Football
Quarterback, 2000–2004

Butter or oil, for greasing

FILLING

3 cups mashed cooked sweet potatoes

¾ cup granulated sugar

1 teaspoon vanilla extract

½ teaspoon salt

2 large eggs

4 tablespoons (½ stick) unsalted butter, melted

TOPPING

1 cup packed light brown sugar

1 cup crushed pecans

⅓ cup all-purpose flour

½ cup (1 stick) unsalted butter, melted

Preheat the oven to 350°F. Lightly grease a 11 by 7-inch baking dish with butter or oil.

Make the filling: In a large bowl, stir together the sweet potatoes, granulated sugar, vanilla, and salt. Add the eggs and melted butter and mix thoroughly. Pour the filling into the prepared baking dish.

Make the topping: In a medium bowl, stir together the brown sugar, pecans, flour, and melted butter to combine.

Dollop and spread the topping evenly over the filling. Bake for 30 minutes, or until the topping is lightly browned. Let cool for 30 minutes to set before serving. *Makes 6 to 8 servings.*

EASY CHEESY SUMMER SQUASH BAKE

Jim Barnes
Football
Offensive Guard, 1966–1968

Nonstick cooking spray

3 to 4 zucchini, sliced into half-moons

3 to 4 yellow squash, sliced into half-moons

2 or 3 green onions, thinly sliced

1 cup grated mozzarella cheese

½ cup coarsely grated Parmesan cheese, plus more if needed

2 to 4 teaspoons chopped fresh basil

¾ teaspoon garlic powder

½ teaspoon dried thyme

Salt and black pepper

Preheat the oven to 350°F. Coat a 8 by 11-inch baking dish with cooking spray.

In a large bowl, combine the zucchini, yellow squash, green onions, ½ cup of the mozzarella, the Parmesan, basil, garlic powder, and thyme. Season with salt and pepper and toss until the veggies are well coated with the herbs and cheese. Transfer the mixture to the prepared baking dish and bake, uncovered, for 25 to 30 minutes. Remove the baking dish from the oven and top with the remaining ½ cup mozzarella and more Parmesan, if desired. Bake for 10 to 15 minutes more, until the cheese is melted and lightly browned. *Makes 8 to 10 servings.*

A crowd-pleaser and family favorite!

GREEN BEAN BUNDLES

Brad McMakin
Men's Golf
Head Coach, 2006–present

1 cup packed light brown sugar

1 cup (2 sticks) unsalted butter, melted

½ teaspoon garlic salt

Dash of soy sauce

3 (15-ounce) cans vertical-packed green beans, drained

16 slices bacon, halved crosswise

In a medium bowl, stir together the brown sugar, melted butter, garlic salt, and soy sauce to make a marinade.

Gather 10 green beans into a bundle, wrap a piece of bacon around them, and secure with a toothpick. Place the bundles in a 9 by 13-inch casserole dish and pour the marinade over them. Cover and refrigerate overnight.

The next day, preheat the oven to 350°F.

Bake, uncovered, for about 30 minutes, until the bacon is thoroughly cooked. *Makes 16 to 20 servings.*

GREEN BEAN CASSEROLE

Logan Forsythe
Baseball
Third Base, 2006–2008

½ cup (1 stick) margarine or unsalted butter

12 ounces sharp cheddar cheese, cubed

2 (15-ounce) cans green beans, drained

1 (10.5-ounce) can condensed cream of mushroom soup

1 (8-ounce) can sliced water chestnuts, drained

1 medium onion, chopped

¾ cup almonds

1 teaspoon salt

¼ teaspoon black pepper

⅛ teaspoon Tabasco sauce

Preheat the oven to 275°F.

In a large saucepan, combine the margarine and cheese and cook over medium heat, stirring, until melted. Add the cream of mushroom soup and stir to combine. Fold in the green beans, water chestnuts, onion, almonds, salt, pepper, and Tabasco and stir. Transfer the mixture to a casserole dish and bake for 20 minutes, until hot and bubbling.
Makes 8 to 10 servings.

HANUKKAH POTATO LATKES

Phil Elson
Voice of the Razorbacks
Baseball, 2014–present
Women's Basketball, 2014–present

3 pounds russet potatoes

1 large yellow onion, grated

3 large eggs, beaten slightly

2 tablespoons matzo meal or all-purpose flour

Salt and black pepper

1 cup neutral oil, such as peanut, canola, or vegetable, for frying

Applesauce or sour cream, for serving

Peel the potatoes, then shred them coarsely on the large holes of a box grater. Place the shredded potatoes in a fine-mesh strainer and aggressively press on them to extract excess liquid, or wrap them in cheesecloth, twist the top closed, and squeeze to extract excess liquid.

Place two-thirds of the shredded potatoes in a large bowl and add the onion, eggs, matzo meal, and salt and pepper to taste. Stir to combine. Add the rest of the potatoes and mix very lightly.

Preheat the oven to 170°F. Line a baking sheet with paper towels.

In a large, heavy skillet, heat the oil over medium-high heat. To test if the oil is hot enough, drop in 1 tablespoon of the potato mixture; if it sizzles on contact, the oil is ready. Working in batches, scoop large spoonfuls of the potato mixture into the hot oil and press down on them with a spatula to form ¼- to ½-inch-thick pancakes. Cook until golden brown on the bottom, 4 to 6 minutes, then flip and cook until golden brown on the second side, 4 to 6 minutes more. Transfer the latkes to the prepared baking sheet to drain and place in the oven to keep warm. Repeat with the remaining potato mixture. Serve the latkes topped with applesauce or sour cream. *Makes 12 to 16 servings.*

HOG-APPLE BAKED BEANS

Robert Farrell
Football
Wide Receiver, 1976–1979

6 slices bacon, diced

1 medium onion, chopped

½ green bell pepper, chopped

1 (21-ounce) can apple pie filling

2 (28-ounce) cans pork and beans, undrained

1 pound homemade or store-bought smoked pork, chopped

½ cup BBQ sauce

½ cup packed light brown sugar

2 tablespoons Worcestershire sauce

2 tablespoons mustard

1 teaspoon BBQ rub

1 teaspoon cayenne pepper (optional)

Preheat the oven to 325°F.

In a large skillet, cook the bacon over medium heat until crisp and browned. Transfer to a paper towel to drain, leaving the rendered fat in the pan. Add the onion and bell pepper to the pan and cook until they are soft.

Place the apple pie filling in a large bowl and use a pastry cutter or potato masher to chop the apples. Add the bacon, onion and bell pepper, pork and beans, smoked pork, BBQ sauce, brown sugar, Worcestershire, mustard, BBQ rub, and cayenne and stir to combine. Transfer the mixture to a 9 by 13-inch casserole dish and bake for at least 1 hour, until bubbling and the sauce has thickened slightly. *Makes 12 to 14 servings.*

A fun memory was when we beat Texas in Little Rock in 1979. Before the last snap, Kevin Scanlon got under center and sang, "Turn out the lights, the party is over!"

LYNNETTE'S CAJUN STUFFED MIRLITONS

Dusty Hannahs
Men's Basketball
Guard, 2015–2017

Salt

6 fresh mirlitons (chayote)

1 tablespoon extra-virgin olive oil, plus more for drizzling

1 medium to large Vidalia or other sweet onion, chopped

1 small green or red bell pepper, chopped

3 to 4 garlic cloves, minced

2 tablespoons dried or fresh parsley

1 tablespoon dried thyme

1 tablespoon dried oregano

1 tablespoon Worcestershire sauce

1 tablespoon soy sauce

Black pepper

12 ounces medium wild-caught gulf shrimp, peeled, deveined, and cut into ½-inch pieces

½ cup to ¾ cup diced ham

2 tablespoons unsalted butter

1 cup crushed panko or unseasoned breadcrumbs

¼ cup grated Parmesan cheese

Preheat the oven to 350°F.

Fill a large cast-iron or other heavy pot with enough water to cover the mirlitons. Salt the water and bring to a boil over high heat. Drop the whole mirlitons into the water, cover, and reduce the heat to low. Simmer until the mirlitons are tender and easily pierced with a fork, about 45 minutes. Remove from the pot and set aside to cool. Halve the mirlitons lengthwise and remove the seeds. Scoop out the flesh, keeping the shells intact. Be gentle while scooping out flesh since the shells will be very soft and will tear easily. Set the shells aside; coarsely chop the flesh and set aside as well.

In a large skillet, heat the olive oil over medium heat. Add the onion, bell pepper, garlic, parsley, thyme, oregano, Worcestershire, soy sauce, and black pepper to taste and cook, stirring, for 5 minutes. Add the shrimp and ham and cook until the shrimp is just pink. Add the mirliton flesh, stir, and cook for 2 to 3 minutes. Add the butter and ½ cup of the panko and cook, stirring, until incorporated. Remove from the heat and let cool for a bit, then fill the reserved mirliton shells with shrimp mixture and place them in a casserole dish or jelly-roll pan.

In a small bowl, mix the remaining ½ cup panko with the Parmesan and sprinkle the mixture evenly over the stuffed mirlitons. Drizzle lightly with olive oil. Bake for about 30 minutes, until the tops are browned. Let cool, then enjoy. *Makes 12 servings.*

NOTES *Thawed frozen gulf shrimp can be used.*

Diced ham can be found by the bacon in your grocery store.

This stuffed mirliton recipe comes from a history of Cajun cooks in Dusty's family on his mother's side. From New Orleans to Lacombe to Slidell, Louisiana, all are excellent lower Louisiana cooks! Thanksgiving and Christmas holidays are always blessed with these delicious mirlitons. Enjoy!

PICNIC BAKED BEANS

Bill Bakewell
Baseball
Pitcher, 1977–1979

2 pounds ground beef

1 large onion, diced

1 large green bell pepper, diced

1½ cups KC Masterpiece BBQ sauce

¼ cup ketchup

2 tablespoons light brown sugar

2 tablespoons granulated sugar

4 teaspoons mustard

1 teaspoon chili powder

4 dill pickles, diced

4 (28-ounce) cans Bush's baked beans, partially drained

In a large skillet, combine the ground beef, onion, and bell pepper. Cook over medium-high heat until the meat is browned, then drain the fat.

In a large bowl, stir together the BBQ sauce, ketchup, brown sugar, granulated sugar, mustard, chili powder, and pickles until thoroughly combined, then add the baked beans and stir again to combine. Transfer the bean mixture to a slow cooker, add the beef mixture, and stir to combine. Cover and cook on Low for 2 to 3 hours. *Makes 24 servings.*

RED POTATO CASSEROLE

Denise Baez
Volleyball
Outside Hitter, 1994–1996

Butter, for greasing

8 to 10 large red potatoes, quartered

1 to 2 garlic cloves, peeled

1 cup ranch dressing

1 cup sour cream

1 cup shredded sharp cheddar cheese

⅓ cup crumbled crisp-cooked bacon

¼ cup chopped green onions

1 teaspoon salt

½ teaspoon black pepper

Preheat the oven to 350°F. Grease a 9 by 13-inch baking dish with butter.

Place the potatoes and garlic in a large pot with water to cover. Bring to a boil over medium-high heat and cook until fork-tender, 25 to 30 minutes.

Meanwhile, in a large bowl, stir together the ranch dressing, sour cream, ½ cup of the cheddar, the bacon, green onions, salt, and pepper. Drain the potatoes, discarding the garlic, and add them to the bowl. Mix well to coat the potatoes, then transfer the potatoes to the prepared baking dish and top evenly with the remaining ½ cup cheddar. Bake for 20 to 30 minutes, until mixture is bubbling, then switch the oven to broil. Broil until the top is golden—watch closely, as this usually takes no more than 5 minutes. Enjoy this casserole with BBQ ribs! *Makes 8 to 10 servings.*

I was an outside hitter on the women's volleyball team from 1994–1996. I was the first signed recruit and the first senior in program history.

SIDNEY'S FAVORITE SWEET POTATO CASSEROLE

Sidney Moncrief
Men's Basketball
Point Guard, 1976–1978

½ cup (1 stick) butter or margarine, at room temperature, plus more for greasing

1 (29-ounce) can sweet potatoes

½ cup granulated sugar

½ cup firmly packed light brown sugar

2 large eggs, lightly beaten

1 cup crushed cornflakes

1 cup chopped nuts (we like pecans)

Preheat the oven to 350°F. Grease a 2-quart casserole dish with butter.

In a large bowl, mash the sweet potatoes. Stir in the granulated sugar, brown sugar, eggs, and 6 tablespoons (¾ stick) of the butter. Spread the mixture in the prepared casserole dish.

In a small bowl, combine the remaining 2 tablespoons butter, the cornflakes, and the nuts. Mix well. Sprinkle the cornflake mixture over the sweet potatoes. Bake for 25 minutes, or until the topping is lightly browned. *Makes 4 to 6 servings.*

SWAMP DISH

Tim Lollar
Baseball
Pitcher, 1976–1978

2 (10-ounce) packages frozen spinach

1 (16-ounce) container cottage cheese

½ cup (1 stick) margarine, at room temperature

4 ounces Monterey Jack cheese, cubed

4 ounces American cheese, cubed

3 large eggs, beaten

3 tablespoons all-purpose flour

Preheat the oven to 350°F.

Cook the spinach as directed on the package, then drain it thoroughly and transfer it to a large bowl. Add the cottage cheese, margarine, Monterey Jack, American cheese, eggs, and flour and stir to combine. Pour the mixture into an 8-inch square casserole dish. Bake, uncovered, for 45 minutes, or until firm. *Makes 6 to 8 servings.*

SWEET POTATOES AND BRUSSELS SPROUTS

Christy Smith
Women's Basketball
Point Guard, 1994–1998
Assistant Coach, 2014–2016

2 sweet potatoes, peeled and chopped into ½- to 1-inch cubes

1 onion, chopped

2 tablespoons olive oil

8 ounces sliced pancetta or bacon

2 pounds Brussels sprouts, halved

Salt and black pepper

Preheat the oven to 350°F.

In a large skillet, combine the sweet potatoes, half the onion, and 1 tablespoon of the olive oil and heat over medium heat. Throw in half the pancetta and cook until the sweet potatoes start to brown, 10 to 15 minutes. Dump it all into a 9 by 13-inch baking dish and push it to one side to make room for the Brussels sprouts.

In the same skillet, combine the Brussels sprouts, the remaining 1 tablespoon olive oil, and the remaining onion and pancetta. Cook until the sprouts are browned, 10 to 15 minutes, then add them to the empty side of the baking dish with the sweet potatoes. Bake for 20 to 30 minutes, until the Brussels sprouts and potatoes are cooked to the desired tenderness. Taste and season with salt and pepper as desired. *Makes 8 to 10 servings.*

MAIN DISHES

AIR FRYER DUCK BREASTS

Joe Falcon
Men's Track & Field / Cross Country
1500m, 3000m, 5000m, 10,000m, 1984–1989

2 tablespoons garlic salt

4 mallard duck breasts, cut into 2-inch-thick strips

Buttermilk, for brining

1 (6-ounce) box Ben's Original long grain and wild rice

Zatarain's Fish Fri seafood breading mix

1 bunch asparagus

Oil spray

Badia all-purpose ranch seasoning

Fill a medium bowl with water and add the garlic salt. Submerge the duck breasts in the garlic water and refrigerate overnight. (This will help draw out blood and excess moisture and result in a more flavorful duck.)

The next day, drain the duck breasts, pat dry, and tenderize with a meat mallet. Place the duck breasts in a clean medium bowl, pour over enough buttermilk to fully cover them, and refrigerate overnight.

The next day, preheat an air fryer to 380°F.

Cook the rice according to the package directions.

Place some Fish Fri in a shallow bowl. Remove the duck breasts from the buttermilk and dredge them in the Fish Fri to coat, then air-fry for 10 minutes.

Meanwhile, spray the asparagus with oil to coat, then sprinkle with ranch seasoning.

Flip the duck breasts, place the asparagus on top of the breasts, and air-fry for 10 minutes more. Serve the duck breasts and asparagus over the rice. *Makes 2 to 4 servings.*

In the fall of 1984, I arrived on campus as a freshman and joined the Razorback family. That season, Coach John McDonnell guided our cross-country team to the National Championships at Penn State. That day our team was blessed to win the first cross-country National Championship for the university, and for John. After the race, we had a team dinner where we enjoyed a great meal to celebrate. What I will forever cherish was the humility exhibited by John that night. He reminded us that many great athletes had paved the way for our success, and now it was our responsibility to do likewise for those that would follow in our steps. What an honor and a privilege it was to be a Razorback athlete coached by John. Go Hogs!

ALABAMA WHITE SAUCE

Eddie Jackson
Football and Men's Track & Field
Defensive Back, 2000–2003
110m Hurdles, 2000–2003

¾ cup mayonnaise

¼ cup apple cider vinegar

¼ cup fresh lemon juice

1 tablespoon prepared horseradish

1 tablespoon coarsely ground black pepper

2½ teaspoons garlic powder

2½ teaspoons sugar

2 teaspoons kosher salt

1 teaspoon whole-grain mustard

1 teaspoon cayenne pepper

Game plan: In a small bowl, whisk together the mayonnaise, vinegar, lemon juice, horseradish, black pepper, garlic powder, sugar, salt, mustard, and cayenne. Serve right away or transfer to an airtight container and refrigerate for up to 7 days. Audibles: Use this sauce on burgers, chicken wings, and French fries. *Makes 1½ cups sauce.*

I know what you're thinking: *white barbecue sauce?* If you've never had white barbecue sauce on a piping-hot piece of smoked chicken, you don't know what you've been missing. A traditional condiment from Alabama, this tangy vinegar-based sauce is definitely one of my favorites, especially with the unexpected kick of heat from the prepared horseradish. Let's see if you feel the same after you give this recipe a try.

"ARKANSAS" POT ROAST

Troy Eklund
Baseball
Outfield, 1986–1989

1 (3-pound) chuck roast

1 (1-ounce) packet ranch dressing mix

1 (1-ounce) packet au jus gravy mix

½ cup (1 stick) unsalted butter

8 peperoncini peppers, plus ¼ cup brine from the jar

Place the roast in a slow cooker. Sprinkle the ranch and au jus seasonings over it. Place the butter and peperoncini on top. Pour the peperoncini brine along the bottom of the slow cooker. Cover and cook on Low for 7 to 8 hours, until the meat falls apart easily when pulled with a fork. *Makes 6 to 8 servings.*

The recipe was originally called the Mississippi Pot Roast, but we made a minor tweak and the name had to be changed. When you're "diehard" Razorback player and fan like those of us in the Eklund house, then it only seems appropriate to name our new favorite dish the "Arkansas" Pot Roast.

Joe Falcon

BAKED KIBBE

Jordyn Wieber
Women's Gymnastics
Head Coach, 2019–present

1 cup fine bulgur wheat

2 cups boiling water

1 pound ground beef or turkey (see Note)

1 medium onion, finely grated

1 tablespoon salt

1 teaspoon black pepper

1 teaspoon ground allspice

1 teaspoon ground cinnamon

Preheat the oven to 325°F.

Place the bulgur wheat in a medium bowl. Pour over the boiling water and let stand for 10 minutes, then drain the wheat, transfer it to a large bowl, and fluff it with a fork.

Add the ground beef, onion, salt, pepper, allspice, and cinnamon to the bowl with the bulgur wheat. Mix with clean hands to combine. Transfer the mixture to a 9 by 11-inch baking pan and pat it down evenly. Bake for about 45 minutes, until the meat is fully cooked. *Makes 6 to 8 servings.*

NOTE *If using ground turkey, add a little more salt, pepper, allspice, and cinnamon.*

This favorite recipe was handed down from my mother's Lebanese family.

BEEF BARBACOA

Robert Cox
Men's Tennis
Player, 1976–1978
Head Coach, 1987–2013

MARINADE

2 to 3 garlic cloves, peeled

2 canned chipotle peppers in adobe sauce

2 tablespoons apple cider vinegar

1 teaspoon salt

1 teaspoon ground cumin

1 teaspoon chili powder

½ cup beef broth

BEEF

2 tablespoons olive oil

1 (2½- to 3-pound) beef chuck roast, cut into 3 inchs chunks

Salt and black pepper

FOR SERVING (OPTIONAL)

Buns

BBQ sauce

Tortillas

Pico de gallo

Sliced radishes

Fresh cilantro

Lime wedges

Preheat the oven to 325°F.

Make the marinade: In a blender, combine all the marinade ingredients and blend until smooth; set aside.

Cook the beef: In a large skillet, heat the olive oil over medium heat. Season the beef with salt and pepper. Sear the beef until deep brown on each side, then transfer to a baking dish. Pour the marinade over the beef. Cover with foil and bake for 3 hours, then remove from the oven and shred the beef with two forks. If the meat has absorbed all the marinade, add a little water to keep it from drying out. Replace the foil and return the beef to the oven for about 1 hour. Serve on buns with BBQ sauce, or on tortillas with pico de gallo, radishes, cilantro, and lime wedges. *Makes 6 to 8 servings.*

BEEF ENCHILADAS

Bill Montgomery
Football, Baseball, and Men's Golf
Quarterback, 1968–1970
Golfer, 1971
First Base, 1975–1976

1 pound ground beef

1 yellow onion, chopped

1 (1-ounce) packet taco seasoning

3 tablespoons canola oil

12 corn tortillas

1 (28-ounce) can enchilada sauce

1 (12-ounce) bag shredded sharp cheddar cheese

1 (12-ounce) bag shredded Monterey Jack cheese

1 small (4-ounce) can diced green chiles, undrained

3 or 4 green onions, chopped (optional)

In a large skillet, combine the ground beef and ¼ cup of the yellow onion. Cook over medium heat until the meat is browned and fully cooked through. Stir in the taco seasoning, then transfer to a bowl and set aside.

In the same skillet, heat the canola oil over medium heat. Place a tortilla in the skillet and flip it quickly to soften, then place it on a paper towel to drain. Repeat with the remaining tortillas, stacking them on top of one another with a paper towel between each one; let cool.

Spread ½ cup of the enchilada sauce over the bottom of a 9 by 13-inch baking dish.

In a large bowl, combine the remaining yellow onion, cheddar, and all but ½ cup of the Monterey

Jordyn Wieber

Jack and mix. Divide the beef, cheese mixture, green chiles, and green onions (if using) evenly among the cooled tortillas. Roll the tortillas up tightly to enclose the filling and place the enchiladas seam-side down in the baking dish. Top with the remaining enchilada sauce; it should come two-thirds of the way up the sides of the enchiladas. Sprinkle the reserved ½ cup Monterey Jack over the top. Cover loosely with foil and bake for 18 to 22 minutes, until the cheese has melted and you can see bubbles in the sauce. Let stand for 5 minutes before serving, then enjoy! *Makes 6 to 8 servings.*

BEEF TIPS

Shane Collins
Football
Linebacker, 2000–2003

2 pounds beef stew meat, cubed

1 (1-ounce) packet brown gravy mix

1 (2-ounce) packet Lipton onion soup mix

1 tablespoon Worcestershire sauce

Onion powder

Garlic powder

Salt and black pepper

2 (10.5-ounce) cans condensed cream of mushroom soup

1 cup beef broth

½ cup ginger ale

1 (8-ounce) package Baby Bella mushrooms, sliced

1 tablespoon cornstarch (optional)

Cooked egg noodles or rice, for serving

Place the beef in a slow cooker and sprinkle with the gravy mix, onion soup mix, and Worcestershire, then season with onion powder, garlic powder, salt, and pepper to taste. Stir to make sure all the meat is seasoned. Add the cream of mushroom soup, broth, ginger ale, and mushrooms to the slow cooker and stir to combine. Cover and cook on High for 4 hours or on Low for 8 hours. If you'd like to thicken the sauce, whisk together the cornstarch and 2 tablespoons cold water in a small bowl and stir it into the sauce in the slow cooker, then cover and cook on High for 20 minutes more. Serve over egg noodles or rice. *Makes 4 to 6 servings.*

BRADY'S HAMBURGER STROGANOFF

Brady Toops
Baseball
Catcher, 2000–2004

1 pound ground beef

1 (10.5-ounce) can condensed cream of chicken soup

1 tablespoon beef bouillon powder

1 (12-ounce) package yolk-free egg noodles

2 tablespoons olive oil

1 small onion, chopped

1 (8-ounce) package sliced mushrooms

1 (15-ounce) can sweet corn, drained

1 (16-ounce) container sour cream

Salt and black pepper

In a large skillet, brown the ground beef over medium heat, then drain the fat. Stir in the cream of chicken soup and bouillon powder and simmer for 15 to 20 minutes.

Meanwhile, cook the egg noodles according to the package directions, then drain.

In a separate medium skillet, heat the olive oil over medium heat. Add the onion and mushrooms and cook, stirring, until the onion is translucent. In a small saucepan, heat the corn over medium heat until warmed through.

Just before serving, add the sour cream to the meat sauce and stir to combine, then cook until warmed through. Serve the sauce over the noodles, topped with the corn, onions, and mushrooms and season with salt and pepper. *Makes 4 servings.*

BRISKET STREET TACOS

Nick Schmidt
Baseball
Pitcher, 2005–2007

BRISKET SAUCE

2 cups sour cream

2 cups mayonnaise

1 cup BBQ sauce

1 tablespoon black pepper

1 tablespoon ranch dressing

1 tablespoon onion powder

1 tablespoon garlic powder

1 tablespoon sugar

1 tablespoon dried cilantro

3 tablespoons distilled white vinegar

1½ teaspoons salt

1 teaspoon red pepper flakes

TACOS

30 tortillas

4 pounds smoked brisket, sliced or chopped

Toppings: crushed nacho cheese Doritos, chopped fresh cilantro, chopped onions, chopped tomatoes, chopped jalapeños, shredded fiesta blend cheese, sliced or diced avocados

Make the sauce: In a medium bowl, stir together all the sauce ingredients to combine.

Assemble the tacos: Fill the tortillas with the smoked brisket and add the toppings. Drizzle the brisket sauce on top of the tacos and enjoy! *Makes 12 to 15 servings.*

A nod and tip of the cap to the Baum-B-Q squad and the many years they fed the Razorback baseball team. Woo Pig!

BUBBA'S VENISON TENDERLOIN

Bubba Carpenter
Baseball
First Base and Outfield, 1988–1991

¼ cup fresh lemon juice

¼ cup olive oil

5 garlic cloves, diced

1 tablespoon salt

1 tablespoon black pepper

1 pound venison tenderloin

6 to 8 slices bacon

In a large bowl or zip-top bag, combine the lemon juice, olive oil, garlic, salt, and pepper. Add the tenderloin and cover the bowl or seal the bag. Marinate in the refrigerator for at least 4 hours; overnight is best.

The next day, set up a smoker and heat to 225°F.

Remove the tenderloin from the marinade (discard the marinade) and wrap it in the bacon. Smoke for 1 to 2 hours. *Makes 2 or 3 servings.*

CAJUN SHRIMP ALFREDO PASTA

Jaylin Williams
Men's Basketball
Forward and Center, 2020–2022

8 ounces uncooked fettuccine

2 teaspoons olive oil

4 tablespoons (½ stick) unsalted butter

1 pound medium shrimp, peeled, deveined, and patted dry with a paper towel

1 tablespoon Tony Chachere's original (or spicy) Cajun seasoning

1 tablespoon minced garlic

3 tablespoons all-purpose flour

2 cups whole milk

1 cup freshly grated Parmesan cheese

1 teaspoon salt, plus more if needed

Black pepper (optional)

Baked garlic bread, for serving

Cook the fettuccine according to the package directions. Reserve 2 cups of the pasta cooking water, then drain the fettuccine, toss with 1 teaspoon of the olive oil and set aside.

In a large skillet, melt 1 tablespoon of the butter over medium heat, then add the remaining 1 teaspoon olive oil. Add the shrimp and sprinkle with the Cajun seasoning. Cook, stirring continuously, until the shrimp are opaque, 4 to 7 minutes. Transfer the shrimp to a dish and cover to keep warm.

In the same skillet, melt the remaining 3 tablespoons butter over medium heat. Stir in the garlic and cook for 1 minute. Stir in the flour and cook for another minute. Slowly whisk in the milk, then gradually whisk in the reserved pasta water. Add the Parmesan and salt and cook, stirring, until the Parmesan has fully melted. Taste and add more salt and pepper, if necessary. Add the fettuccine and the shrimp to the skillet and mix everything together well. Serve with garlic bread. *Makes 4 servings.*

CARNITAS TACOS

Greg Koch
Football
Guard and Tackle, 1973–1976

4 pounds pork shoulder (pork butt)

2½ teaspoons salt

1 teaspoon black pepper

1 tablespoon dried oregano

2 teaspoons ground cumin

1 teaspoon olive oil

1 onion, sliced

1 jalapeño, sliced

4 garlic cloves, minced

¾ cup fresh orange juice

Tortillas, for serving

Optional toppings: salsa, pico de gallo, guacamole, shredded cheese, chopped tomato, sour cream, etc.

Rinse and dry the pork shoulder, then rub it all over with the salt and pepper. In a small bowl, combine the oregano, cumin, and olive oil, then rub the mixture all over the pork. Place the pork in a slow cooker, fat-side up, top with the onion, jalapeño, and garlic, and pour over the orange juice. Cover and cook on Low for 10 hours or on High for 7 hours, until the pork is tender enough to shred. Remove the meat from the slow cooker and let cool it slightly, then shred with two forks. If desired, skim off and discard the fat from the juices remaining in the slow cooker. If you have much more than 2 cups of juice, pour it into a small saucepan and simmer over low heat until it has reduced to about 2 cups, then set aside.

To crisp the pork, in a large nonstick pan or well-seasoned cast-iron skillet, heat 1 teaspoon of oil over high heat. Working in batches, add about one-quarter of the pork, spread it out in the pan, and drizzle with some of the juices. Cook until the juices have evaporated and the bottom of the pork is golden brown and crusty, then flip the pork and quickly sear the other side. Remove from the skillet and repeat with the remaining pork.

Just before serving, drizzle the pork with more of the juices and serve hot, stuffed into tortillas and topped with your desired toppings. *Makes 8 to 10 servings.*

CHEESEBURGER MEATLOAF

Kenny Sandlin
Football
Center / Guard, 1997–2001

2 pounds ground beef

10 slices bacon, cooked and chopped, or 3 to 4 ounces real bacon bits

2 (8-ounce) packages shredded cheddar cheese

2 large eggs, lightly beaten

½ cup breadcrumbs

½ cup mayonnaise

2 tablespoons Worcestershire sauce

½ teaspoon salt

½ teaspoon black pepper

1 cup ketchup

4 tablespoons yellow mustard

Preheat the oven to 350°F.

In a large bowl, combine the ground beef, bacon, cheese, eggs, breadcrumbs, mayonnaise, Worcestershire, salt, and pepper and mix well with a large spoon or clean gloved hands.

In a small bowl, stir together the ketchup and mustard, then add ¾ cup of the ketchup mixture to the meat mixture and stir to combine; set the remaining ketchup mixture aside.

With gloved hands, press the meat mixture into the shape of a loaf and place it on the rack of a broiler pan (this allows the grease to drain into the pan). Spread the remaining ketchup mixture over the top of the loaf. Bake for 65 minutes, until the meatloaf is cooked through and reaches an internal temperature of 160°F. *Makes 4 to 6 servings.*

CHICKEN ADOBO

Tucker Clary
Women's Tennis
Head Coach, 2023–present

3 pounds boneless, skinless chicken thighs

2 tablespoons minced garlic

⅔ cup low-sodium soy sauce

⅓ cup distilled white vinegar

2 tablespoons black pepper

1 tablespoon garlic powder

1 to 3 bay leaves

2 tablespoons vegetable oil

Cooked white jasmine rice, for serving

Place the chicken thighs in a large bowl with the garlic, soy sauce, vinegar, pepper, garlic powder, and bay leaves and toss to coat. Marinate in the refrigerator for at least 4 hours or up to overnight.

In a large skillet, heat the oil over medium-high heat. Add the chicken (reserving marinade) and cook until browned, about 5 minutes on each side. Add the remaining marinade to the skillet and bring to a boil. Lower heat to medium and simmer, stirring occasionally, for 20 minutes until sauce begins to thicken and thighs reach an internal temperature of 165°F. Serve this Filipino dish with rice. *Makes 4 to 6 servings.*

CHICKEN AND DUMPLINGS

R. C. Thielemann
Football
Guard and Center, 1973–1976

2 bone-in, skin-on chicken breasts with ribs (see Note)

Low-sodium chicken broth, as needed

2 tablespoons Wyler's chicken bouillon powder

2¼ cups Bisquick baking mix

⅔ cup whole milk

Salt and black pepper

Place the chicken in a large stockpot and add 3 quarts water. Bring to a boil over high heat, then reduce the heat to maintain a simmer and cover the pot. Cook for 45 minutes, or until the chicken is cooked through. Transfer the chicken to a plate and set aside until cool enough to handle.

Meanwhile, pour the broth from the pot into a large storage container or pitcher and put it in the freezer for a few hours (but don't let it freeze!) or refrigerate it all day so the fat solidifies on top. Skim off and discard the fat from the top.

When the chicken has cooled, pick the meat from the bones; discard the skin and bones and shred meat. Store in an airtight container in the refrigerator until ready to use.

Pour the broth back into the stockpot and add store-bought broth as needed to make 3 to 4 quarts total. Slowly bring to a boil over medium-high heat. Add the bouillon powder, starting with 1 tablespoon and then adding more to taste.

Meanwhile, in a medium bowl, stir together 2 cups of the Bisquick and the milk until the dough comes together and forms a ball. Dust a large cutting board with about ¼ cup of the Bisquick and place the ball of dough on the cutting board. Knead the dough a few times, then roll it out to about ¼ inch thick and cut into small squares. Carefully drop the dumplings into the boiling broth by hand. For thicker stew, add a little of the Bisquick from the cutting board to the broth as well. Reduce the heat to medium-low, cover, and cook for 10 minutes. Uncover and cook for 10 minutes more, then reduce the heat to maintain a simmer and add the shredded chicken. Cook for 10 minutes to warm through, then remove from the heat and let cool for a few minutes. Season with salt and pepper before serving. *Makes 6 servings.*

NOTE *To save time, you can use one store-bought cooked chicken instead of cooking it from scratch.*

"This is a simple recipe using only a few ingredients, but R. C. loves when I make it, especially on cold nights. You can substitute store-bought chicken broth to reduce the cooking time." —Laura Thielemann

The Memory of Coach John McDonnell (1938–2021)

JOHN McDONNELL has the records and championships that created the Arkansas track and field dynasty that has prevailed since they won their first NCAA championship in 1984. After that first NCAA championship, his teams steamrolled to the top year after year and won a combined forty-two NCAA championships. The question was, how was Coach Mac able to lead his teams to win the most championships of any NCAA coach or any sport combined? It was simple. He clearly had the gift of coaching, but most important, he taught his athletes to believe in themselves and to reach more astonishing feats of greatness than they could have ever imagined before meeting Dad and his coaching staff. Dad always told his teams to hold each other up, no matter what happened, for the sake of the team. For example, if a few events didn't go as planned at a meet, or an athlete had a setback at a meet, the rest of the team knew it was time to step up and perform so they could all still bring home the team championship trophy. The Razorback track and field and cross country teams always lifted each other up, no matter the event, and performed for the sake of the team—day in and day out. Coach Mac's teams never competed against each other; they won together through discipline and helping each other every step of the way. Dad created an atmosphere that was so incredibly positive and beyond encouraging that it spread like wildfire to all his teams over his tenure. Dad also had and built so, so many leaders among his entire squads, year after year, that it brought a whole new meaning to "success within a system." His teams believed in themselves, they believed in the team, they believed in hard work, and they believed in each other, hence all the championships that were won. That's how John McDonnell created the Arkansas track and field dynasty. Coach McDonnell's memory, lessons, faith, success, and humbleness will continue to reach and inspire others worldwide for generations to come. His teams and staff were blessed to have him as a coach; his children, Heather and Sean, were blessed to have him as a father; his wife of fifty-four years, Ellen McDonnell, was blessed to be his wife. What a blessing and cherished memory of a blessed man who blessed others. Rest in peace, Coach John McDonnell.

John McDonnell

CHICKEN CASSEROLE

John McDonnell
Men's Track & Field / Cross Country
Head Coach, 1972–2008

2 (4-ounce) cans chicken, drained

1 (10.5-ounce) can condensed cream of mushroom soup

1 large (12-ounce) can Carnation evaporated milk

1 small (4-ounce) jar pimentos, undrained

1 cup uncooked Minute rice

1 tablespoon onion flakes

Sliced almonds, for topping (optional)

Shredded cheddar cheese, for serving

Preheat the oven to 325°F.

In a large bowl, stir together the chicken, mushroom soup, evaporated milk, pimentos, rice, and onion flakes. Transfer to a 9 by 13-inch baking dish and top with almonds, if desired. Bake for 1½ hours, or until the rice is cooked and the sauce is thickened and bubbling. Sprinkle cheddar on top while hot and serve. *Makes 6 to 8 servings.*

—Recipe and biography submitted by Heather McDonnell Hastings, John's daughter

CHICKEN DRESSING CASSEROLE

Ron Brewer Sr.
Men's Basketball
Guard, 1975–1978

Nonstick cooking spray

2 pounds boneless, skinless chicken breasts, chopped

Mrs. Dash onion and herb seasoning

2 (10.5-ounce) cans condensed cream of chicken soup

¼ cup whole milk

1 onion, chopped

1 celery stalk, chopped

1 (12-ounce) package Stove Top stuffing

2 cups chicken broth

1 cup (2 sticks) unsalted butter, melted

Preheat the oven to 375°F. Coat a 9 by 13-inch casserole dish with cooking spray.

Spread the chicken over the bottom of the prepared casserole dish and lightly sprinkle with Mrs. Dash seasoning.

In a medium bowl, stir together the cream of chicken soup, milk, onion, and celery. Pour the mixture evenly over the chicken. In the same bowl, stir together the contents of the Stove Top stuffing package, the broth, and the melted butter. Spread the stuffing gently over the soup mixture to cover the top. Bake for 40 minutes, or until bubbling. *Makes 5 to 7 servings.*

CHICKEN PARISIAN

Jeb Huckeba
Football
Defensive End, 2001–2004

1 (8-ounce) container sour cream

1 (10.5-ounce) can condensed cream of mushroom soup

2 small (4-ounce) cans mushrooms, undrained

5 or 6 boneless, skinless chicken breasts

Cooked rice, for serving

Preheat the oven to 350°F.

In a large bowl, stir together the sour cream, cream of mushroom soup, and mushrooms with their liquid. Add the chicken breasts and stir to coat. Transfer to a 9 by 13-inch baking dish and bake for 1 hour, or until the sauce is bubbling and the chicken is fully cooked through. Serve over rice. *Makes 6 servings.*

My mom fixed two meals when college coaches would come to our home to do their "in home visit" for the recruiting process: this one, and the chili (page 35). She did a wonderful job entertaining guests like Houston Nutt, Bobby Allen, John Thompson, and Chris Vaughn from Arkansas. Notable coaches from other schools were Bobby Bowden and Joe Kines from Florida State and Turner Gill from the University of Nebraska. After Coach Bowden came to our home, I was convinced I was going to be a Seminole, but I promised Coach Nutt I wouldn't make a decision until he and the Razorback staff visited. This gave my family more time to talk and pray, and by the time Coach Nutt came to our home, I had made up my mind to play for my home state and represent the University of Arkansas. I wanted to be a Razorback not only because of the coaching staff, but also to represent the great state of Arkansas in the SEC and for the platform I would have to share my faith and be a positive influence on many others.

Ron Brewer Sr.

CHICKEN PARMESAN

Bev Lewis

Head Coach, Women's Track and Cross Country, 1981–1989
Director of Women's Athletics, 1989–2008
Associate Vice Chancellor and Executive Associate Athletic Director, 2009–2014

¼ cup kosher salt

4 boneless, skinless chicken breasts

Nonstick cooking spray

1 tablespoon Greek seasoning

1 teaspoon garlic powder

1 (8-ounce) container sour cream

½ cup grated Parmesan cheese

In a large bowl, mix the salt with 4 cups water to make a brine. Place the chicken breasts in an airtight container, pour in the brine, cover, and refrigerate for 2 to 4 hours.

Preheat the oven to 350°F. Coat a 9 by 13-inch baking dish with cooking spray.

Drain and rinse the chicken, then pat it dry and place it in the prepared baking dish. Sprinkle the chicken with the Greek seasoning and garlic powder. Spread the sour cream over each chicken breast and top evenly with the Parmesan, then cover with a lid or foil. Bake for about 30 minutes, until the internal temperature of the breasts reaches 165°F, then uncover the chicken and switch the oven to broil. Broil the breasts for about 5 minutes, until lightly browned on top.

Serve the breasts whole or cut into smaller portions. Try to keep the sour cream mixture on the breasts when you plate them and pour the juices from the baking dish over the breasts before serving. *Makes 4 to 6 servings.*

BEV LEWIS served the University of Arkansas athletic department as a coach and administrator for over three decades. She served as the head women's track and cross country coach, director of women's athletics, and associate vice chancellor and executive associate athletic director. She has received many honors for her contributions, including the University of Arkansas Sports Hall of Honor and the Southwest Conference Hall of Fame. She was instrumental in the growth and success of women's sports and was pivotal in combining the men's and women's athletic departments into one unified program. As director of women's athletics, she oversaw the addition of women's sports teams and many new facilities, including a building named in her honor. Female athletic scholarships were tripled during her tenure. As a coach, she had six top 20 national finishes, the team's first national ranking and conference championship, coached Team USA, and was twice selected as Southwest Conference Coach of the year.

CHICKEN POTPIE BAKE

Ronnie Brewer Jr.
Men's Basketball
Shooting Guard and Small Forward, 2003–2006
Recruiting Coordinator, 2021–2023
Assistant Coach, 2023–present

Butter, for greasing

3 cups chopped cooked chicken

2 (10.5-ounce) cans condensed cream of chicken soup

1 (12-ounce) bag frozen veggies (3 cups)

2 cups shredded cheddar cheese

2 (5-count) cans Pillsbury biscuits

2 tablespoons salted butter, melted

Preheat the oven to 375°F. Grease a 9 by 13-inch baking pan with butter.

In a large bowl, stir together the chicken, cream of chicken soup, veggies, and cheese. Spread the mixture evenly in the prepared baking pan. Cut the biscuits into quarters, place in a large bowl, and toss with the melted butter. Spread the biscuit pieces evenly over the chicken mixture. Bake for 25 minutes, or until the tops of the biscuits are crispy and the mixture is bubbling. *Makes 6 to 8 servings.*

CHICKEN QUESADILLAS

Bev Lewis
Head Coach, Women's Track and Cross Country, 1981–1989
Director of Women's Athletics, 1989–2008
Associate Vice Chancellor and Executive Associate Athletic Director, 2009–2014

BRINED CHICKEN

1 cup boiling water

1 teaspoon soy sauce

1 teaspoon salt

1 teaspoon sugar

8 ounces boneless, skinless chicken breast

QUESADILLAS

2 tablespoons olive oil

½ cup diced onion

½ cup diced red bell pepper

8 fajita-size (6-inch) flour tortillas

Fajita seasoning

8 ounces finely shredded Mexican-style four-cheese blend

Salsa, for serving

Sour cream, for serving

Brine the chicken: In a 2-cup measuring cup, stir together the boiling water, soy sauce, salt, and sugar until the salt and sugar have dissolved. Add ice and stir until the ice melts and cools the liquid and the volume of liquid increases to 2 cups.

Place the chicken in a large glass bowl. Pour the brine over the chicken, cover, and refrigerate for 30 to 60 minutes.

Make the quesadillas: In a medium skillet, heat 1 tablespoon of the olive oil over medium heat. Add the onion and bell pepper and cook until softened, then set aside. In a dry skillet, heat only one side of each flour tortilla over medium-high heat until lightly browned. Set aside, remembering which side was cooked. (This keeps the inside of the quesadilla from getting soggy before it's ready to eat.)

Drain the chicken, discarding the brine. Pat the chicken dry and cut it into strips. Season with fajita seasoning. In a large skillet, heat the remaining 1 tablespoon olive oil over medium-high heat. Add the chicken and cook until cooked through (no pink inside), 8 to 10 minutes on each side. Cut the chicken into small bite-size pieces.

Build each quesadilla as follows: Place one tortilla uncooked-side down in a cold skillet. Sprinkle with cheese, top with about ⅓ cup of the chicken, sprinkle with one-quarter of the onion-pepper mixture, and cover with more cheese. Use enough cheese in the first and last layers (⅓ to ½ cup total) that it will hold the two tortillas together when it melts. Add a second tortilla, cooked-side down. Set the pan over medium heat and cook the quesadilla, flipping it carefully (several times, if needed), until both sides are lightly browned and crunchy, and the cheese has melted. Cut into wedges with a pizza cutter. Serve with salsa and sour cream. *Makes 4 servings.*

CHICKEN TETRAZZINI

Shauna Taylor
Women's Golf
Head Coach, 2007–present

Salt

1 (8-ounce) package spaghetti, broken into 2-inch pieces

4 tablespoons (½ stick) unsalted butter

3 tablespoons chopped onion

½ teaspoon celery salt

¼ teaspoon dried marjoram

Dash of cayenne pepper

1 (4-ounce) can mushrooms, drained, liquid reserved

1 (10.5-ounce) can condensed cream of chicken soup

1 (12-ounce) can Milnot evaporated milk

2 cups cubed boiled chicken (or use canned chicken)

2 tablespoons chopped pimentos

½ cup shredded mild cheddar cheese

¼ cup grated Parmesan cheese

Chicken broth, if needed

Preheat the oven to 350°F.

In a medium pot, bring 1½ quarts salted water to a boil over high heat. Add the spaghetti and cook until just tender, 9 minutes. Drain and rinse with hot water.

In a large skillet, melt the butter over medium heat. Add the onion and cook, stirring, until translucent. Add the celery salt, marjoram, and cayenne, then pour in the reserved mushroom liquid. Add the cream of chicken soup and stir until smooth, then gradually stir in the evaporated milk. Cook, stirring continuously, until smooth and thick.

In a large bowl, combine the spaghetti, mushrooms, chicken, and pimentos. Pour the sauce over the spaghetti mixture and mix well. Transfer to a 9 by 13-inch casserole dish and top with the cheddar and Parmesan. Bake for about 30 minutes, until lightly browned. Add broth to the casserole if needed to keep it from drying out as it bakes. *Makes 6 to 8 servings.*

A family-favorite recipe that I love. My husband's grandmother makes this every time we visit.

CHICKEN WITH LINGUINE

Martin Terry
Men's Basketball
Guard, 1971–1973

2 boneless, skinless chicken breasts, thinly sliced

Salt and black pepper

Garlic powder

¼ to ½ cup extra-virgin olive oil

2 garlic cloves, crushed

1 (16-ounce) box linguine

½ cup white cooking wine

2 tablespoons capers

Season the chicken breasts with salt, pepper, and garlic powder. In a large skillet, heat the olive oil over medium heat. Add the chicken and crushed garlic and cook, stirring occasionally, until the chicken is almost cooked through, about 20 minutes.

Meanwhile, cook the linguine according to the package directions. Drain and set aside.

Pour the wine into the pan with the chicken and add the capers. Reduce the heat to low and cook for 10 minutes more, until chicken is fully cooked through. Serve the chicken and wine sauce over the linguine. *Makes 2 to 4 servings.*

CHICKPEAS IN THE OVEN

Maria Pavlidou
Women's Tennis
Player, 1995–1999

1 pound dried chickpeas

2 medium onions, diced

2 (14-ounce) packages fully-cooked smoked sausages, cut into ½-inch-thick slices

½ cup olive oil

½ teaspoon dried oregano

Salt and black pepper

1 (15-ounce) can tomato sauce

Place the chickpeas in a large bowl with hot water to cover. Let stand overnight.

The next day, drain and rinse the chickpeas, then transfer them to a large pot and add water to cover by a few inches. Bring to a boil over high heat, then reduce the heat to maintain a simmer and cook until they are soft, 1½ to 2 hours. They are ready when they squish easily. Drain the chickpeas, reserving 1 cup of the hot cooking water.

Preheat the oven to 180°F.

Transfer the chickpeas to a 9 by 13-inch baking pan and add the reserved cooking water, the onions, sausages, olive oil, and oregano, salt, and pepper to taste. Pour in enough of the tomato sauce to cover the ingredients. Bake for 1 hour to allow the flavors to meld. You can cover the pan with foil to keep the chickpeas from burning on top. *Makes 6 to 8 servings.*

COUNTRY BOY COOKED RABBIT AND RICE

Darren McFadden
Football
Running Back, 2005–2007

1 rabbit, cleaned and cut into serving pieces

1 tablespoon ground black pepper

1¾ teaspoons sea salt

¼ cup vegetable oil

1 onion, chopped

1 cup vegetable broth

½ cup sliced mushrooms

½ cup diced bell pepper

1 garlic clove, chopped

1 (2-ounce) package Lipton onion mushroom soup mix

1 tablespoon Worcestershire sauce

Cooked rice, for serving

Preheat the oven to 350°F.

Season the rabbit pieces with the black pepper and salt. In a large skillet, heat the oil over medium-high heat. Add the rabbit and cook until browned on all sides. Transfer the rabbit to a 9 by 13-inch baking dish and set aside; pour the fat from the pan into a medium bowl. Add the onion, broth, mushrooms, bell pepper, garlic, onion soup mix, and Worcestershire and stir well, then pour the mixture over the rabbit. Bake, uncovered, for about 1 hour, until tender. Serve with rice. *Makes 4 to 6 servings.*

This rabbit recipe is from my dad. I always hunted with my dad growing up, and still do to this day. He first took me rabbit hunting when I was seven or eight years old, and I fell in love with it the first time I went. It's a joy to watch our dogs work and to hear them sing (bark) when they're chasing a rabbit. You must be quick and a pretty good shot to hit a rabbit moving at what seems like 100 miles per hour (lol). It's very relaxing to be in the woods spending time in fellowship with people you love. Being able to see the dogs work and hearing them run is something like no other. After a hunt, we always talk about the day as we sit around cleaning the game. My dad always taught me to eat what you kill and showed me how to cook rabbit. That's something I still do to this day, and I enjoy it. Not to mention that it tastes great.

COUNTRY FRIED CHICKEN

David Barrett
Football
Cornerback, 1996–1999

4 boneless, skinless chicken breasts

Vegetable oil, for frying

4 cups all-purpose flour

1 tablespoon salt

1 tablespoon black pepper

1 tablespoon paprika

1 tablespoon garlic powder

1 tablespoon onion powder

2 large eggs

½ cup whole milk

Your favorite sides, such as mashed potatoes, coleslaw, or biscuits, for serving

Place the chicken breasts between two sheets of plastic wrap and pound them to an even thickness, about ½ inch thick.

Fill a large skillet with about ¼ inch of oil and heat over medium heat.

In a shallow dish, mix the flour, salt, pepper, paprika, garlic powder, and onion powder. In another shallow dish, beat the eggs with the milk. Working in batches, dredge the chicken breasts in the flour mixture, then dip in the egg mixture, then back into the flour mixture, shaking off any excess between each step. Carefully place the coated chicken in the hot oil and fry until golden brown and cooked through, 5 to 6 minutes per side. Transfer the fried chicken to a paper towel–lined plate to drain and repeat to fry the remaining chicken. Serve hot, with your favorite sides—I prefer mashed potatoes or biscuits! *Makes 4 servings.*

CREAMY GARDEN ZUCCHINI PASTA

Joe Kleine
Men's Basketball
Center, 1982–1985

Kosher salt

1 pound dried medium pasta shells, cavatelli, or similar short-cut pasta

2 tablespoons extra-virgin olive oil

4 tablespoons (½ stick) unsalted butter

1 medium yellow onion, diced

6 garlic cloves, thinly sliced

½ teaspoon red pepper flakes

2½ pounds zucchini or yellow squash (or a mix), diced

½ cup cherry or grape tomatoes

Zest of 1 large lemon

2 cups plain full-fat Greek yogurt

Leaves from 1 small bunch basil, finely chopped

Leaves from 1 small bunch mint, finely chopped

Black pepper

Grated Parmesan or Pecorino Romano cheese (optional)

Bring a large pot of water to a boil over high heat and salt the water generously. Add the pasta and cook for 1 minute less than directed on the package.

Joe Kleine

Meanwhile, in a large, deep skillet, heat the olive oil and 2 tablespoons of the butter over medium heat. Add the onion and cook, stirring, until soft, 3 to 5 minutes. Add the garlic and red pepper flakes and cook until fragrant. Add the zucchini and tomatoes and season with a generous sprinkling of salt. Cook, stirring occasionally, until the zucchini is tender, the tomatoes have softened and burst, and the liquid has reduced, 5 to 7 minutes.

When the pasta is ready, reserve 1 cup of the cooking water, then drain the pasta and add it to the pan with the zucchini. Add half the lemon zest, the yogurt, the remaining 2 tablespoons butter, and ¼ cup of the reserved pasta water. Stir until all the ingredients are evenly distributed and the pasta is fully coated by the sauce. Add additional pasta water if the sauce is too thick. Stir in the basil, mint, and remaining lemon zest. Season with black pepper. Taste and adjust the seasoning if needed, with more salt, black pepper, lemon zest, or red pepper flakes. Remove from the heat and serve immediately, topped with cheese, if desired. *Makes 4 servings.*

Adapted from a recipe by *Today* show contributor Alejandra Ramos, this pasta has become a favorite in our family.

CREAMY TACOS

Mike Neighbors
Women's Basketball
Director of Operations, 1999
Assistant Coach, 2006
Head Coach, 2017–2025

1 (2-pound) block Velveeta cheese, cut into 1-inch cubes

1 (10-ounce) can Ro*Tel diced tomatoes and green chiles, undrained

1 (5-ounce) can evaporated milk

1½ pounds 80/20 ground beef

10 to 12 corn or flour tortillas or taco shells

Optional toppings: shredded lettuce, Fritos, crackers, diced tomatoes

In a large saucepan, combine the Velveeta and Ro*Tel and heat over low heat, stirring frequently, until the Velveeta has melted and the mixture is well combined, about 10 minutes.

Meanwhile, in a large skillet, cook the ground beef over medium-high heat until browned and fully cooked through, then drain the fat.

Stir the evaporated milk into the Velveeta mixture, then add the browned beef and stir to incorporate. Cover and simmer over low heat for 10 minutes. Uncover, remove from the heat, and let stand for 10 minutes; this allows the mixture to thicken to perfection. Reheat over low heat (see Note) and serve warm in tortillas or taco shells, with the toppings of your choice. *Makes 10 to 12 tacos.*

NOTE *The mixture should have the consistency of chili; it shouldn't be soupy. If it is, allow it to cool again, then rewarm.*

This really is one of those dishes that might be better as leftovers than at first serving. If you want to serve more, double the ingredients for every pound of meat you use.

CREOLE CHICKEN

Shane Collins
Football
Linebacker, 2000–2003

4 boneless, skinless chicken breasts, diced

2 tablespoons Cajun seasoning (we like Tony Chachere's)

1 tablespoon olive oil

1 (10.5-ounce) can condensed cream of chicken soup

Juice of 1 lime

1 (4-ounce) can diced green chiles, undrained

¼ cup sour cream

Cooked white rice, for serving

Season the chicken with the Cajun seasoning. In a large skillet, heat the olive oil over medium-high heat. Add the chicken and cook until browned on all sides. Add the cream of chicken soup, green chiles, lime juice, and ½ cup water and bring to a boil. Reduce the heat to low and cook until chicken is cooked through, about 5 minutes. Stir in the sour cream. Serve over rice. *Makes 4 servings.*

The greatest memory I have from my time at Arkansas is of the first game I played in my freshman year. Walking through the crowd to the stadium, the anticipation of waiting for the game to start, and getting to run through the "A" for the first time are all memories I'll never forget and will always appreciate.

CRUNCHY SALMON

Jordan Walsh
Basketball
Forward, 2022–2023

1 tablespoon Mrs. Dash salt-free chicken grilling blend

1½ teaspoons Italian seasoning

1 teaspoon paprika

1 teaspoon salt

½ teaspoon garlic powder

1 tablespoon olive oil

3 skinless salmon fillets

2 tablespoons unsalted butter

In a small bowl, stir together the Mrs. Dash, Italian seasoning, paprika, salt, and garlic powder. Drizzle both sides of each salmon fillet with olive oil. Sprinkle the seasoning mix all over both sides of the fillets, patting it in to adhere to the fish.

In a large skillet, melt the butter over medium-high heat. Place all the salmon fillets in the skillet and cook, undisturbed, for 3 to 4 minutes, then flip and cook for 4 minutes on the second side, until a crisp crunchy coating is formed. Remove from the heat and serve. *Makes 3 servings.*

DEANO'S LAMB CHOPS

Deane Pappas
Men's Golf
Golfer, 1989–1992

1 rack of New Zealand lamb (usually about 16 chops)

Cavender's all-purpose Greek seasoning

¾ cup extra-virgin olive oil

⅔ cup fresh mint leaves, finely chopped

⅓ cup fresh rosemary leaves, finely chopped

2 tablespoons fresh garlic

1 teaspoon salt

1 teaspoon cracked black pepper

Your favorite sides, for serving

Rinse the rack of lamb with cold water and pat dry. Cut the rack between the bones into individual chops about 1½ inches thick. Season with Cavender's seasoning.

In a small bowl, stir together the olive oil, mint, rosemary, garlic, salt, and pepper to make a thin paste. Rub the mixture liberally over the chops, cover, and refrigerate for at least 2 hours and preferably overnight.

When ready to cook the lamb, remove the chops from the refrigerator and let them come to room temperature. Heat a grill, setting up two zones: a medium-heat zone for cooking and a high-heat zone for searing.

Sear the lamb chops for 1 to 2 minutes on each side until nicely browned. Reduce the heat or move the lamb chops to the medium-heat zone of the grill. Grill until cooked to your desired level of doneness, another 5 minutes on each side for medium. (A meat thermometer is useful for ensuring the correct temperature; for medium, that's an internal temperature of 150°F.) Let rest for 10 minutes before serving. Serve with your favorite sides. *Makes 8 servings.*

We usually serve these lamb chops with smashed, mashed, or scalloped potatoes and fresh vegetables and/or a salad. Recommended wine pairing: 2018 Boekenhoutskloof The Chocolate Block red blend.

DEVILED CHICKEN

Neil Harper
Women's Swimming & Diving
Head Coach, 2016–present

4 boneless, skinless chicken breasts

¼ cup vegetable oil

¼ cup mango chutney

2 tablespoons apple cider vinegar

4 teaspoons Worcestershire sauce

4 teaspoons mustard

1 teaspoon Badia original complete seasoning

1 teaspoon salt

½ teaspoon curry powder

½ teaspoon paprika

Preheat the oven to 375°F.

Place the chicken in a 9 by 13-inch baking pan. In a small bowl, stir together the oil, chutney, vinegar, Worcestershire, mustard, Badia seasoning, salt, curry powder, and paprika. Pour the mixture over the chicken. Bake for 45 to 50 minutes, until the chicken is fully cooked through. *Makes 4 servings.*

This is a favorite recipe my mother makes in England. We serve it with baked potatoes and pour the sauce over the potatoes.

DUSTY'S MOM'S CHICKEN PICCATA

Dusty Hannahs
Men's Basketball
Guard, 2015–2017

¼ cup vegetable or canola oil

1 cup unbleached all-purpose flour

4 boneless, skinless chicken breasts (1½ pounds total), pounded to an even thickness

Salt and black pepper

½ cup white wine (optional)

1 cup chicken broth

½ lemon, cut into ¼-inch-thick slices

Juice of 1½ lemons

¼ cup capers, drained

3 tablespoons unsalted butter

2 tablespoons fresh or dried parsley

Cooked angel hair pasta, for serving

In a heavy skillet large enough to hold the chicken, heat the oil over medium heat.

Place the flour in a shallow bowl. Season both sides of the chicken cutlets with salt and pepper, then dredge in the flour to coat, shaking off any excess. Add the chicken to the pan and cook until lightly browned on both sides and fully cooked through, about 2½ minutes per side. Try not to move the chicken around too much while it cooks. Transfer the chicken to a platter and keep warm.

Increase the heat to high and add the wine (if using), broth, and lemon slices to the skillet. Stir with a wooden spoon, scraping up any browned bits from the bottom of the skillet. Simmer until the liquid has reduced to ⅓ cup, about 4 minutes. Add the lemon juice and capers and simmer until reduced to ⅓ cup, about 1 minute. Remove from the heat, add the butter, and stir until the butter has melted and the sauce thickens. Add the parsley and chicken breasts and stir to coat the chicken with the sauce. Serve the chicken and sauce over angel hair. *Makes 4 servings.*

EGG ROLL IN A BOWL

Eric Musselman
Men's Basketball
Head Coach, 2019–2024

1 pound ground chicken or turkey

1 teaspoon minced garlic

1 onion, chopped

1 (14-ounce) bag coleslaw mix

¼ cup low-sodium soy sauce, plus more if desired

2 tablespoons rice vinegar

1 teaspoon ground ginger

1 teaspoon sriracha, plus more if desired

1 teaspoon sesame oil

Cooked rice, for serving (optional)

In a large skillet, brown the ground chicken over medium heat. Add the garlic and cook, stirring, for 30 seconds. Add the onion and cook, stirring, for 2 to 3 minutes. Add the coleslaw mix, soy sauce, vinegar, ginger, sriracha, and sesame oil and cook until the coleslaw mix reaches the desired tenderness. Serve as is or over rice, with additional soy sauce and sriracha, if desired. *Makes 4 servings.*

We are so busy during the week that we like quick and easy meals that are also healthy. This one is our daughter's favorite, and I love that it's packed with protein and vegetables. We make it at least once a month.

ENCHILADA CASSEROLE

Ronn Reynolds
Baseball
Catcher, 1979–1980

Butter, for greasing

1½ pounds ground beef

1 onion, chopped

1 (10.5-ounce) can condensed cream of mushroom soup

1 (10-ounce) can enchilada sauce

1 (4-ounce) can diced green chiles, undrained

1 (15-ounce) can Ranch Style pinto beans, undrained

Crushed tortilla chips

Grated cheddar cheese

Preheat the oven to 350°F. Grease a 9 by 13-inch casserole dish with butter.

In a large skillet, combine the ground beef and onion and cook over medium heat until the meat is browned. Drain the fat, then add the cream of mushroom soup, enchilada sauce, green chiles, and beans, stir to combine, and cook until bubbling.

Cover the bottom of the prepared casserole dish with crushed tortilla chips. Pour the meat mixture over the chips and top with cheddar. Bake for about 30 minutes, until bubbling. *Makes 6 to 8 servings.*

FAJITAS

Colby Hale
Women's Soccer
Head Coach, 2011–present

MARINADE

Juice of 1 orange

Juice of 2 limes

¼ cup olive oil

2 garlic cloves, coarsely chopped

3 canned chipotle peppers in adobo sauce

3 tablespoons coarsely chopped fresh cilantro leaves

1 teaspoon ground cumin

1 teaspoon salt

FAJITAS

2¼ pounds skirt or flank steak, trimmed of fat and cut into thirds or 8-inch pieces

Salt and black pepper

2 red bell peppers, thinly sliced

1 large onion, thinly sliced

Olive oil

Lime juice

12 flour tortillas, warmed

Optional toppings: guacamole, sour cream, shredded cheese, salsa, etc.

Make the marinade: In a tall cup, combine all the marinade ingredients. Puree with an immersion blender until smooth. Transfer to a large zip-top bag.

Make the fajitas: Add the steak to the bag with the marinade. Seal the bag and shake to coat the meat. Refrigerate for 2 to 4 hours.

Heat a grill to medium-high.

Drain the beef and season the meat liberally with salt and pepper. Grill for about 4 minutes on each side, or to your desired doneness. Transfer to a cutting board and let rest while you grill the vegetables.

In a large bowl, combine the bell peppers and onion. Drizzle with olive oil and lime juice. Toss to coat, then grill the vegetables (or cook in a large skillet over medium-high heat) until just barely limp, 7 to 8 minutes.

Thinly slice the steak against the grain on a diagonal. Serve the steak and grilled vegetables on warmed tortillas with the toppings of your choice. *Makes 6 servings.*

FATHER'S DAY RIBS

Hunter Yurachek
Director of Athletics, 2017–present

6 cups beer

1 (16-ounce) box dark brown sugar

½ cup apple cider vinegar

1 tablespoon dry mustard

2 teaspoons salt

2 teaspoons red pepper flakes

1½ teaspoons chili powder

1½ teaspoons ground cumin

2 bay leaves

8 pounds baby back ribs, cut into 4-rib lengths, back membrane removed

In a large pan, stir together the beer, brown sugar, vinegar, dry mustard, salt, red pepper flakes, chili powder, cumin, and bay leaves. Bring to a boil over high heat. Add the ribs, cover, and simmer until tender, turning frequently; this may take an hour or more. Transfer the ribs to a platter. Continue to simmer the liquid until it has reduced to 3 cups and thickened to the consistency of sauce, about 40 minutes.

Heat a grill to medium-high.

Grill the ribs until they are nicely browned, basting with the sauce every 5 minutes. *Makes 8 to 12 servings.*

When we lived close to my wife Jennifer's mom, she always made these ribs for Father's Day. As we moved around the country, we continued the tradition.

Scott Bull

FAVORITE SHISH KEBABS

Colby Hale
Women's Soccer
Head Coach, 2011–present

½ cup soy sauce or coconut aminos

¼ cup olive oil

¼ cup packed light brown sugar

1 garlic clove, minced

½ teaspoon black pepper

½ teaspoon ground ginger

1½ pounds sirloin steak, cut into large chunks (about 1½ inches)

1 onion, cut into evenly sized chunks

1 bell pepper, any color, cut into evenly sized chunks

Pineapple chunks (optional)

In a large bowl or zip-top bag, combine the soy sauce, olive oil, brown sugar, garlic, black pepper, and ginger. Add the steak, onion, and bell pepper and cover or seal the bag. Toss to coat, then marinate in the refrigerator for at least 1 hour or up to 8 hours for more intense flavor.

Heat a grill to medium-high.

Remove the meat and vegetables from the marinade and thread them onto skewers, alternating with pineapple chunks, if desired. Grill the kebabs for 3 to 5 minutes, then flip and grill for 3 to 5 minutes more, until you've achieved your desired doneness. *Makes 4 to 6 servings.*

FIVE-HOUR STEW OR POT ROAST

Scott Bull
Football and Baseball
Quarterback, 1971–1975
Pitcher, 1972, 1976

2 to 3 pounds beef stew meat or pot roast

1 (22.6-ounce) can Campbell's condensed cream of mushroom soup

1 (22.6-ounce) can Campbell's condensed tomato soup

1 (10-ounce) package frozen peas

1 tablespoon dehydrated onion

1 (12-ounce) bag baby carrots, sliced

4 medium russet potatoes, peeled and chopped into bite-size pieces

2 bay leaves

Salt and black pepper

Garlic salt

Preheat the oven to 250°F.

In a large oven-safe pot, combine the stew meat, cream of mushroom soup, tomato soup, peas, onions, carrots, potatoes, and bay leaves. Season with salt, pepper, and garlic salt and stir to combine. Cover tightly with a lid or foil and bake for 5 hours, until the meat and vegetables are tender. *Makes 10 to 12 servings.*

My junior year at the U of A, we were playing Texas in Austin, and the coaches took us for a steak dinner at a very nice restaurant. Normally on the night before the game, we had a roast beef dinner, so this was a special treat. When my table filled up, no one sat on my right. As we were being served, the staff put down salad, steak, and dessert. The extra food was grabbed by my teammates at the table, but I put the plate of steak on my knees under the table to share later. Just as I put it there, Coach Broyles came in and sat down next to me. One by one, my fellow teammates left the table, leaving me with the steak balancing on my knees. Awkward! I visited with Coach Broyles until he finished his meal and left. But by then I had lost my appetite!

FRIED COD WITH MATZO MEAL

Steve Conley
Football
Outside Linebacker and Defensive End, 1992–1995

2 tablespoons olive oil or vegetable oil

4 skinless cod fillets

Salt and black pepper

2 large eggs, beaten

1 cup matzo meal

Lemon wedges, for serving

Preheat the oven to 350°F.

In a large skillet, heat the olive oil over medium-high heat. Season the cod fillets with salt and pepper on both sides.

Place the eggs in one shallow bowl and the matzo meal in a second. Dip each fillet in the eggs, letting the excess drip off, then coat thoroughly with matzo meal. Add the coated fillets to the hot oil and fry until golden brown on both sides and cooked through, 3 to 4 minutes per side. Transfer the fried cod to a paper towel–lined plate to drain, then transfer to a baking sheet and bake for 10 minutes. Serve hot, with lemon wedges on the side. *Makes 4 servings.*

FRIED FISH

Mike Loggins
Baseball
Outfield, 1982–1985

4 cups peanut oil or vegetable oil, for frying

2 cups yellow cornmeal

Season-All seasoned salt

2 pounds fish fillets, cleaned, cut to your desired size, and patted dry

Preheat the oven to 175°F.

In a deep fryer (I use the Presto GranPappy fryer) or large heavy-bottomed pot, heat the oil to 400°F.

In a shallow bowl, combine the cornmeal and Season-All to taste. Working in batches, dredge the fish in the cornmeal to coat both sides, then add to the hot oil and cook for 3½ minutes, or until the fish floats. Transfer to a paper towel–lined plate to drain and keep warm in the oven while you fry the remaining fish. *Makes 2 servings.*

Kevin McReynolds

GRILLED PORK STEAK

DeeDee Brown-Campbell

Women's Track & Field / Cross Country

Heptathlon, 100m Hurdles, High Jump, Long Jump, 1997–2002

½ to ¾ cup packed light brown sugar

1 tablespoon salt

1 tablespoon coarsely ground black pepper

1 tablespoon smoked paprika

1 tablespoon garlic powder

1 tablespoon onion powder

1 tablespoon Creole or Cajun seasoning

1 tablespoon Badia Complete Seasoning

1½ teaspoons ground cumin

1½ teaspoons chili powder

Chopped fresh herbs, or 1 to 2 tablespoons Italian seasoning

5 to 7 bone-in pork steaks

Mustard

BBQ sauce (optional)

Mashed potatoes and a vegetable side or traditional BBQ sides, for serving

In a small bowl, stir together the brown sugar, salt, black pepper, paprika, garlic powder, onion powder, Creole seasoning, Complete Seasoning, cumin, chili powder, and herbs.

Lightly coat both sides of the pork steaks with mustard. Generously sprinkle the seasoning mix on both sides of the steaks, patting it in to adhere. Place the steaks on a tray, cover, and marinate at room temperature for 30 minutes.

Heat a grill to medium-high. Add the steaks and cook for about 12 minutes on each side, turning once caramelization occurs. (Alternatively—and preferably—set up a smoker and heat to medium-low. Smoke the steaks low and slow for 30 minutes to 1 hour, turning them halfway through. Heat a charcoal grill, then grill the steaks until caramelized on both sides with some seemingly burnt-looking bits. That's just the sugar in the marinade doing its thing!) If you like, coat the steaks with BBQ sauce in the last 5 to 10 minutes of grilling.

Pull the steaks from the grill and enjoy with your choice of side. *Makes 5 to 7 servings.*

My brother, Darrell Jr. (a University of Arkansas Law School graduate), was able to find this recipe we have always loved already written down on some recipe cards that he and my father have collected for many years! Me, my brother, and our father, Darrell Brown Sr. (the first African American football player at the U of A and a U of A Law School graduate), made this dish a lot. It's my favorite recipe, and I request it anytime I am in Arkansas. We are definitely a "grilling" family, and this is one of our favorites. We love the Hogs to win, but we also love a grilled piece of pork ☺.

GRILLED PORK TENDERLOIN

Kevin McReynolds
Baseball
Outfield, 1979–1981

1½ cups plus 1 to 2 teaspoons soy sauce

2 heaping tablespoons minced garlic

2 pounds boneless pork loin

½ cup packed light brown sugar

½ teaspoon ground ginger

½ teaspoon ground cinnamon

Dash of ground cloves

In a 1-gallon zip-top bag, combine 1½ cups of the the soy sauce and the garlic. Add the pork, seal, and marinate in the refrigerator for a few hours.

Heat a grill to medium.

In a small bowl, stir together the brown sugar, remaining 1 to 2 teaspoons soy sauce, the ginger, cinnamon, and cloves to make a paste. Remove the pork from the marinade and rub the paste over the meat. Grill for about 12 minutes on each side, about 45 minutes altogether, or until the meat is fully cooked through. *Makes 2 to 4 servings.*

HERB-ROASTED PORK TENDERLOIN

Tim Horton
Football
Wide Receiver and Punt Returner, 1986–1989
Assistant Coach, 2007–2012

¼ cup soy sauce

¼ cup Lea & Perrins Worcestershire sauce

¼ cup vegetable oil

1 teaspoon dried marjoram

1 teaspoon dried thyme

1 teaspoon garlic powder

1 teaspoon ground ginger

1 teaspoon onion powder

1 teaspoon rubbed sage

1 teaspoon salt

1 teaspoon black pepper

1½ pounds pork tenderloin

In a shallow dish or heavy-duty zip-top bag, stir together the soy sauce, Worcestershire, oil, marjoram, thyme, garlic powder, ginger, onion powder, sage, salt, and pepper. Prick the pork with a fork a few times, place it in the marinade, and turn to coat. Cover the dish or seal the bag and marinate at room temperature for 30 minutes or in the refrigerator for 2 hours.

Preheat the oven to 350°F.

Remove the pork from the marinade and place it on a rack in a roasting pan; discard the marinade. Bake for 40 minutes, or until a meat thermometer inserted into the center reaches 145°F. Remove from the oven, tent with foil, and let rest for 10 minutes before slicing and serving. *Makes 4 servings.*

This is an easy, delicious recipe! It's adapted from one in *Southern Living* magazine.

Having been around Arkansas football for many years as a coach's kid, a player, and a coach, I have wonderful memories. Getting to play with some outstanding players on championship teams and getting to coach and recruit some of the best players in Razorback history will always be special, but the greatest joy in sports is in the relationships with teammates, coaches, and players. I often think of a former recruit and Hog tight end player, Garrett Uekman from Little Rock Catholic High School. Garrett was a standout three-sport athlete (baseball, basketball, and football) for the Rockets and had a great future in front of him when he unexpectedly died on November 11, 2011. He suffered from cardiomyopathy, a disease that weakens and enlarges the heart. I will always remember the evening before his death, the Hogs defeated Mississippi State 41–17 on CBS in War Memorial Stadium, with the redshirt freshman excelling in his hometown. I still remember seeing Garrett's parents, Danny and Michelle Uekman, and his older sister, Meagan, that evening before Garrett got on the bus to travel back to Fayetteville. Garrett had such a zest for life and loved being a Razorback. He was such a wonderful role model to those he was around each day. I feel thankful and blessed to have had a relationship with Garrett, one of my favorite Razorbacks.

IKE'S FAVORITE CHICKEN SPAGHETTI

Ike Forte

Football

Running Back, 1974–1976

1 large chicken

½ cup (1 stick) margarine

1 cup chopped celery

1 onion, chopped

1 (10.5-ounce) can condensed cream of chicken soup

1 (10-ounce) can Ro*Tel diced tomatoes and green chiles, with their juices

1 (32-ounce) package thin spaghetti

1 (8-ounce) box Velveeta cheese, cubed (optional)

1 (15-ounce) jar pitted salad olives (optional)

Shredded cheddar cheese, for serving (optional)

Place the chicken in a large pot with 3 quarts water. Cover and bring to a boil over medium-high heat, then reduce the heat to maintain a simmer and cook until the chicken is cooked through, about 90 minutes. Remove the chicken from the pot, reserving the broth, and let cool slightly, then remove the skin and pick the meat from the bones, discarding the skin and bones.

Preheat the oven to 325°F.

In a large skillet, melt the margarine over medium heat. Add the celery and onion and cook, stirring, until onion is translucent, then add the cream of chicken soup and the Ro*Tel and stir well. Remove from the heat and set aside.

Bring the reserved broth to a boil over high heat. Add the spaghetti and cook according to the package directions. Reduce the heat to medium, add the Velveeta (if using), and stir to melt and combine. Add the soup mixture, chicken, and olives (if using). Transfer to a large greased baking dish and bake until heated through, about 45 minutes, or transfer to a slow cooker, cover, and cook on Low for 1 hour. Top with cheddar, if desired, and serve. *Makes 16 to 20 servings.*

ITALIAN-SEASONED CHICKEN

Gary Adams

Football

Cornerback, 1965–1968

1 whole chicken, cut into serving pieces, or 8 mixed pieces bone-in, skin-on chicken

½ cup (1 stick) unsalted butter, melted

Juice of 1 lemon

2 (.7-ounce) packets Good Seasonings Italian dressing mix

Preheat the oven to 350°F.

Pat the chicken dry and place it in a baking dish in a single layer. Add the melted butter and roll the chicken to coat, then drizzle with the lemon juice. Sprinkle half the Italian dressing mix over the chicken, then flip the pieces and sprinkle with the remaining dressing mix. Flip the chicken skin-side up and bake, uncovered, for 1½ hours, or until fully tender. *Makes 4 to 6 servings.*

We raised our own chickens and seemed to have chicken three or four times a week!! I guess I didn't get burned out on it, because I have Popeyes twice a week now!

JAMBALAYA

Ken Hamlin
Football
Safety, 2000–2002

2 tablespoons peanut oil

10 ounces andouille sausage links, sliced into rounds

1 tablespoon Cajun seasoning

1 pound boneless, skinless chicken breasts, cut into 1-inch pieces

1 onion, diced

1 small green bell pepper, diced

2 celery stalks, diced

3 garlic cloves, minced

1 (16-ounce) can crushed Italian tomatoes, undrained

2 teaspoons Worcestershire sauce

1 teaspoon filé powder

1 teaspoon salt

½ teaspoon red pepper flakes

½ teaspoon ground black pepper

½ teaspoon hot pepper sauce

1¼ cups uncooked white rice

2½ cups chicken broth

In a large Dutch oven, heat 1 tablespoon of the peanut oil over medium heat. Season the sausage with half the Cajun seasoning, add it to the pot, and cook, stirring, until the sausage is browned. Remove with a slotted spoon and set aside. Add the remaining 1 tablespoon peanut oil to the pot. Season the chicken with the remaining Cajun seasoning and cook until lightly browned on all sides. Remove with a slotted spoon and set aside.

Add the onion, bell pepper, and celery to the pot and cook, stirring, for 2 minutes. Add the garlic and cook until the onion is translucent, 1 to 2 minutes more.

Add the crushed tomatoes to the pot and season with the Worcestershire, filé powder, salt, red pepper flakes, black pepper, and hot pepper sauce. Stir in the chicken and sausage. Cook for 10 minutes, stirring occasionally. Stir in the rice and broth. Bring to a boil, then reduce the heat to maintain a simmer, cover, and cook until the liquid has been absorbed, 20 to 25 minutes. Serve and enjoy! *Makes 4 to 6 servings.*

JERRY JONES'S FAVORITE MEATLOAF

Jerry Jones
Football
Offensive Guard, 1960–1964

1 tablespoon unsalted butter

¼ cup finely chopped celery

¼ cup finely chopped onion

2 tablespoons finely chopped carrot

3 or 4 slices bread, cubed

½ cup milk

2 large eggs

2 pounds ground beef

1 pound bulk ground pork sausage

Salt and black pepper

1 to 2 jalapeños, chopped (optional)

1 sleeve Premium saltine crackers (about 40 saltines), crushed into crumbs

Ketchup

½ cup boiling water

Preheat the oven to 400°F.

In a small skillet, melt the butter over medium heat. Add the celery, onion, and carrot and cook, stirring, until the onion is translucent. Set aside.

Place the cubed bread in a medium bowl, add the milk, and let stand for 5 minutes to allow bread to soften. In a small bowl, beat the eggs and pour them into the bowl with the bread and milk, then blend with a handheld mixer until combined.

In a large bowl, mix the ground beef and sausage together using gloved or very clean hands. Add the vegetables to the bowl with the meat and season with salt and pepper. Add the bread mixture to the bowl with the meat and vegetables and mix until everything is evenly distributed (the bread mixture will help hold everything together). For Southwest flair, add the jalapeños, if desired.

Place the cracker crumbs in a shallow dish. Divide the meat mixture in half and form into two loaves; roll each loaf in the cracker crumbs to coat, then place the loaves in a large rectangular casserole dish. Score the tops of the loaves with a wooden spoon handle; add ketchup to the scored areas.

Place the casserole dish on the oven rack and carefully pour the boiling water into the dish. Bake for 40 minutes, or until a meat thermometer inserted into the center of each loaf reads 155°F. Remove from the oven and let stand for 10 minutes before slicing and serving. *Makes 12 servings.*

JILL'S GRANDMA'S SPAGHETTI

Jill Gillen
Women's Volleyball
Outside Hitter, 2019–2023

1 pound ground beef

1 medium onion, minced

1 (8-ounce) can tomato sauce

1 (6-ounce) can tomato paste

2 tablespoons minced fresh parsley

1 teaspoon Worcestershire sauce

1 teaspoon salt

¼ teaspoon black pepper

8 drops of Tabasco sauce

Cooked spaghetti, for serving

In a large skillet, combine the ground beef and the onion and cook over medium heat until the meat is browned. Drain the excess fat from the pan, then add the tomato sauce, tomato paste, parsley, Worcestershire, salt, pepper, Tabasco, and ¾ cup water (use a little more water for thinner sauce, if preferred). Bring to a simmer, then cover and cook for 30 minutes to thicken the sauce and allow the flavors to blend. Serve over spaghetti. *Makes 2 to 4 servings.*

JOHN DALY STEAKS

John Daly
Men's Golf
Golfer, 1984–1987

10 rib eye steaks, cut into 4 to 6 strips each

1 cup whiskey of your choice (my choice is Crown Royal)

1 (16-ounce) bottle balsamic vinaigrette (I like Ken's)

¼ cup soy sauce

½ teaspoon garlic salt

½ teaspoon black pepper

½ teaspoon Montreal steak seasoning

FOR SERVING

Garlic mashed, baked, or scalloped potatoes

Salad with ranch dressing

Garlic bread

In a bowl, stir together the whiskey, vinaigrette, soy sauce, garlic salt, pepper, and steak seasoning to make a marinade; taste and adjust the marinade

John Daly

until you like the flavor (see Notes). Place the steak strips in a deep dish and pour over the marinade, submerging the strips. Marinate in the refrigerator for 3 to 6 hours—the longer you marinate, the better the flavor, so let the marinade work its magic. (Make sure to have some Good Boy John Dalys on hand so you have something to drink while you patiently wait!)

When you're ready to cook, get the grill as hot as you can.

Place the steaks on the grill (reserve that marinade!) and cook until you have a good sear, then flip and cook to your desired doneness. Immediately place the steaks back in the marinade and serve, with some garlic mashed, baked, or scalloped potatoes and a great salad with ranch dressing alongside, because that's what you pair with John Daly steaks! And don't forget the garlic bread! *Makes 20 servings.*

NOTES *The best way to test the marinade is with your finger. You'll know the taste is perfect when you can dip bread into it and it's perfect to the palate . . . Finger-licking good! Marinating John Daly Steaks adds a blast of flavor to the meat, and you won't taste the whiskey at all. Allowing the marinade to soak into the meat and fat makes the meat more tender and ensures each bite will be filled with layers of my amazing John Daly marinade flavor!*

I like to cook on a Blackstone propane griddle so the meat doesn't lose its flavor. I put the steaks on the griddle, smoke a cigarette, then flip them. Light up another cigarette, smoke it, and the steaks are done. You can also cook the steaks in a cast-iron skillet on the grill, but make sure the pan is piping hot before you add the meat!

Remember, good steaks are like good men . . . the best ones have a little fat on them! Go Hogs!

JOHNNY MARZETTI

Andrew Benintendi
Baseball
Outfield, 2013–2015

Butter, for greasing

12 ounces ground beef

12 ounces ground pork

1 large onion, chopped

1 (8-ounce) can mushrooms, drained, liquid reserved

1 (20-ounce) can diced tomatoes, undrained

2 (5-ounce) jars Old English cheese spread

1 (12-ounce) package egg noodles

Preheat the oven to 350°F. Grease a 9 by 13-inch casserole dish with butter.

In a large skillet, combine the ground beef, ground pork, onion, and mushrooms. Cook over medium heat until the meat is browned. Add the tomatoes and the reserved mushroom liquid and cook until warmed through.

Cook the egg noodles according to the package directions, then drain them and return them to the pot. Melt the cheese spread in the microwave, add it to the noodles, and stir to combine.

Add the noodle mixture and the meat mixture to the prepared casserole dish in alternating layers. Bake for 45 minutes, or until bubbling. *Makes 4 to 6 servings.*

JOHNNY'S FAMOUS BBQ SAUCE

John Pelphrey
Men's Basketball
Head Coach, 2007–2011

2 cups ketchup

½ cup packed light brown sugar

⅓ cup whiskey

⅓ cup apple cider vinegar

¼ cup finely diced onion

2 tablespoons honey

1 tablespoon Worcestershire sauce

1 tablespoon molasses

1 teaspoon hot sauce

1 teaspoon black pepper

1 teaspoon salt

1 teaspoon liquid smoke

Combine all the ingredients in a medium saucepan. Bring to a boil, then reduce the heat to low and simmer, stirring occasionally, for 30 minutes. Remove from the heat and let cool completely (the sauce will thicken as it cools), then transfer to an airtight container and store in the refrigerator for up to 7 days. *Makes 3 to 4 cups.*

KAREN'S CHICKEN AND DUMPLINGS

Scott Bull
Football and Baseball
Quarterback, 1971–1975
Pitcher, 1972, 1976

2 cups all-purpose flour, plus more for dusting

1 teaspoon salt

¼ teaspoon baking powder

2 tablespoons Crisco

2 (32-ounce) cartons chicken broth

Cooked meat from 1 whole chicken (see Note)

In large bowl, stir together the flour, salt, and baking powder. Add the Crisco and mash to combine, then stir in ⅔ cup of the broth. The mixture should have the consistency of pie dough; if it's too stiff, add more broth 1 teaspoon at a time (up to 4 teaspoons).

In a large pot, heat the remaining broth over high heat until simmering, but not boiling.

Flour your hands and divide the dough in half. On a generously floured surface, roll out one half of the dough to ¼ inch thick. Using a sharp knife or a pizza cutter, cut the dough into 1 by 2-inch strips. Drop them into the broth one at a time. Repeat with the remaining dough. Cover and cook over medium heat until dumplings float to the top, about 15 minutes. Add the chicken and cook for 5 minutes more, watching the pot and stirring occasionally so the dumplings won't stick, then serve. *Makes 8 to 10 servings.*

NOTE *There are several ways to get the chicken meat for the recipe. You can cook a whole chicken: Season it with salt and pepper, then place it in a large pot with chicken broth to cover; bring to a simmer over medium-low heat and cook for 1 hour, then let cool. Remove the skin and pick the meat from the bones; discard the skin and bones. Reserve the broth. Meat from a rotisserie chicken will work if you don't have time to cook a chicken at home, and if you really want to save time, Walmart now sells deboned cooked chicken meat.*

This recipe was given to my wife, Becky, by Karen Craig, wife of wide receiver Reggie Craig. Reggie and I played together at Arkansas before he played for the KC Chiefs. This is a comfort food that Karen's grandmother made for her family.

LASAGNA

Stacy Lewis
Women's Golf
Golfer, 2005–2008

1 pound ground beef

1 onion, chopped

1 garlic clove, minced

2 teaspoons salt

¼ teaspoon black pepper

½ teaspoon dried rosemary

2 (6-ounce) cans tomato paste

6 no-boil lasagna noodles

1 (8-ounce) container cottage cheese or ricotta cheese

1 (12-ounce) package shredded mozzarella cheese

Preheat the oven to 350°F.

In a large skillet, combine the ground beef, onion, garlic to taste, salt, rosemary, and pepper. Cook over medium heat until the meat is browned. Drain the fat. Add the tomato paste and 1½ cups hot water. Simmer for 5 minutes, then remove the sauce from the heat.

In an 8-inch square casserole dish, layer one-third of the sauce, half the noodles, another third of the sauce, all the cottage cheese, half the mozzarella, the rest of the noodles, the rest of the sauce, and the rest of the mozzarella. Bake for 30 minutes, or until bubbling and the cheese has melted. *Makes 4 servings.*

LINDA'S CHICKEN CURRY

Bill Burnett
Football
Running Back, 1968–1970

½ cup (1 stick) unsalted butter

1 cup diced apple

¼ cup chopped onion

2 garlic cloves, finely chopped

¼ cup all-purpose flour

1½ tablespoons curry powder, or more to taste

1 teaspoon salt

2 cups chicken broth

3 cups cubed cooked chicken

Cooked rice, for serving

Optional toppings: peanuts, coconut flakes, raisins, chopped bell peppers, chopped bacon, chopped bananas, chopped green onions, Major Grey's mango chutney

In a large saucepan, melt the butter over low heat. Add the apple, onion, and garlic and cook, stirring occasionally, until tender, about 10 minutes. Stir in the flour, curry powder, and salt. Cook, stirring occasionally, until the mixture is thick and bubbling, about 10 minutes. Gradually stir the broth into the curry. Add the chicken and cook for 5 minutes more, until heated through. Serve with rice and the toppings of your choice. *Makes 4 servings.*

LUCAS PASTA

Anthony Lucas
Football
Receiver, 1995–1999

1½ pounds lean ground beef

1 large onion, diced

1 green bell pepper, diced

1 garlic clove, minced

2 (6-ounce) cans tomato paste

1 (8-ounce) can tomato sauce

2 (14.5-ounce) cans stewed tomatoes with basil, garlic, and oregano, undrained

1 to 1½ tablespoons sugar, to taste

1 tablespoon Worcestershire sauce

1 tablespoon Italian seasoning

1 teaspoon salt

Cooked angel hair pasta, for serving

In a large, heavy pot, brown the ground beef over medium heat, then drain the fat. Add the onion and

Stacy Lewis

bell pepper and cook, stirring, until the onion is translucent, about 5 minutes. Push the meat and vegetables to the sides of the pot and add the garlic to the space in the middle. Cook, stirring, for 30 seconds, until the garlic becomes fragrant, then combine with the meat and vegetables. Add the tomato paste, tomato sauce, stewed tomatoes, sugar, Worcestershire, Italian seasoning, salt, and 1 cup water. Simmer for 30 minutes to allow flavors to blend. Serve over angel hair. Let leftover sauce cool to room temperature, then transfer to an airtight container and refrigerate for up to 3 days or freeze for up to 3 months. *Makes 4 to 6 servings.*

LYNDY'S MOM'S LASAGNA

Lyndy Lindsey

Football

Tight End, 1987–1991

1 pound lean ground beef

1 pound Jimmy Dean Italian sausage

1 (24-ounce) jar Ragú spaghetti sauce

1 tablespoon garlic powder

1 tablespoon sugar

1 (16-ounce) box lasagna noodles

1 (16-ounce) container ricotta cheese

1 large egg, beaten

1 tablespoon salt

1 tablespoon black pepper

2 pounds mozzarella cheese, shredded

8 ounces Parmesan or Pecorino Romano cheese, shredded or grated

Preheat the oven to 350°F.

In a large skillet, brown the ground beef and sausage over medium heat, then drain the fat. Add the spaghetti sauce, garlic powder, and sugar. Simmer over low heat while preparing the other ingredients.

Cook the lasagna noodles according to the package instructions, then drain.

In a medium bowl, stir together the ricotta, egg, salt, and pepper. Set aside.

Spread one-quarter of the meat sauce over the bottom of a large 3½-inch-deep rectangular casserole dish. Top with a layer of the noodles, then half the ricotta mixture, then half the mozzarella. Top with another layer of noodles and then another quarter of the meat sauce. Add a third layer of noodles and top with the remaining ricotta mixture, then the remaining mozzarella. Add another layer of noodles and top with another quarter of the meat sauce. Add a final layer of noodles and then the remaining meat sauce. Top evenly with the Parmesan. Bake for about 1 hour, until bubbling and heated through. Let cool for 10 to 15 minutes before serving. It is even better the next day. *Makes 12 to 16 servings.*

My favorite meal is my mom's famous lasagna. She learned to make this dish from the women she met in Minnesota during the days she and my dad, Jim, lived there and he played for the "Purple People Eaters," the Minnesota Vikings.

MEXICAN CASSEROLE

Kenny Sandlin

Football

Center / Guard, 1997–2001

Butter, for greasing

2 pounds ground beef

2 tablespoons minced onion

1 tablespoon garlic salt

4 (8-ounce) cans tomato sauce

2 to 4 (2.25-ounce) cans sliced black olives, drained

2 cups sour cream

2 cups cottage cheese

2 (4-ounce) cans diced green chiles, drained

2 (7-ounce) bags tortilla chips

4 cups grated Monterey Jack cheese

Preheat the oven to 350°F. Grease a 9 by 13-inch casserole dish (or similar size baking pan) with butter.

In a large skillet, brown the ground beef over medium heat, then drain the fat and transfer to a large bowl. Add the onion, garlic salt, tomato sauce, and olives and stir to combine.

In a medium bowl, stir together the sour cream, cottage cheese, and green chiles.

Crush the tortilla chips slightly and spread half the chips over the bottom of the prepared casserole dish. Top with half the meat mixture, then half the sour cream mixture, then half the Monterey Jack. Repeat the layers. Bake, uncovered, for 30 to 35 minutes, until bubbling. *Makes 8 to 10 servings.*

MEXICAN CHICKEN CASSEROLE

Matt Hemingway
Men's Track & Field / Cross Country
High Jump, 1991–1996

2 tablespoons unsalted butter

¾ cup chopped onion

2 (10.5-ounce) cans condensed cream of chicken soup

2 (4-ounce) cans diced green chiles, undrained

4 or 5 large chicken breasts, cooked and chopped

1 (14.5-ounce) bag nacho cheese Doritos, crushed

12 ounces grated sharp cheddar cheese

12 ounces grated jalapeño Jack cheese

Preheat the oven to 350°F.

In a large skillet, melt the butter over medium heat. Add the onion and cook, stirring, until translucent. Add the cream of chicken soup and green chiles. Add the chicken and cook until warmed through.

Spread half the crushed Doritos over the bottom of a large casserole dish, then top with half the chicken mixture, then half the cheddar and jalapeño Jack. Repeat the layers. Bake for 30 minutes, or until it's hot and bubbling and the cheese has melted. *Makes 6 to 8 servings.*

NOTE *If you like it spicier, add chopped fresh jalapeños.*

MOM'S SOUTH AFRICAN BOBOTIE

Alistair Cragg
Men's Track & Field / Cross Country
1500m, 3000m, 5000m, 10,000m, 2001–2004

2 tablespoons vegetable oil, plus more for greasing

2 onions, sliced

2¼ pounds good-quality lean ground beef

1 cup whole milk

1 thickish slice white bread

1 tablespoon medium curry powder, or hot for the hale and brave

1½ tablespoons sugar

2 teaspoons salt

½ teaspoon black pepper, or more to taste

¾ teaspoon ground turmeric

1½ tablespoons malt vinegar

½ cup raisins

2 tablespoons strong chutney, plus more for serving

2 bay leaves or fresh lemon leaves (if available)

2 medium eggs

Steamed rice (preferably yellow), for serving

Preheat the oven to 350°F. Grease a 9 by 13-inch baking dish with vegetable oil.

In a medium sauté pan, heat the oil over medium heat. Stir in the onions and cook until translucent. Add the ground beef and cook until lightly browned and

Mike Conley Sr.

crumbly. (Try not to dry out the beef mix too much; the custard mixture helps with keeping it moist).

Place ½ cup of the milk in a shallow bowl and soak the bread in the milk. Squeeze the excess milk back into the bowl, then place the bread on a small plate and mash with a fork. Combine the milk used for soaking with the remaining ½ cup milk and set aside.

Add the mashed bread to the meat mixture, then add the curry powder, sugar, salt, pepper, turmeric, vinegar, raisins, and chutney and stir to combine.

Spoon the meat mixture into the prepared baking dish and place the bay leaves on top. In a small bowl, beat the eggs and milk, then pour over the meat mixture. Bake for 25 to 30 minutes, until set. Serve with steamed rice (traditionally yellow rice!) and extra chutney. *Makes 6 to 8 servings.*

Pure South African comfort food! Especially nice in winter, or served cold with a salad in the summer. No self-respecting South African cook does not own (and treasure!) a favorite bobotie recipe.

MOM'S SPAGHETTI SAUCE

Mike Conley Sr.

Men's Track & Field / Cross Country

Triple Jump and Long Jump, 1981–1985

1 pound ground turkey

1 large white onion, chopped

2 garlic cloves, crushed

1 celery stalk, diced

½ bell pepper, chopped

1 (15-ounce) can tomato sauce

1 (6-ounce) can tomato paste

1 tablespoon ground oregano

1 teaspoon salt

¼ teaspoon ground black pepper

½ teaspoon seasoning salt

Cooked spaghetti, for serving

Grated Parmesan cheese, for serving

In a large skilllet, brown the ground turkey over medium-high heat, then drain the fat. Add the onion, garlic, celery, and bell pepper and cook until the onion is translucent and the celery and bell pepper have softened. Add the tomato sauce, tomato paste, oregano, salt, black pepper, and seasoning salt and simmer for 30 minutes to allow the flavors to blend. Add cooked spaghetti to the sauce or serve the sauce over spaghetti. Top with Parmesan. *Makes 4 servings.*

MOM'S STROGANOFF

Blake Parker

Baseball

Outfield, First Base, and Third Base, 2004–2006

4 tablespoons (½ stick) unsalted butter

1 pound ground beef

1 medium onion, chopped

8 ounces shiitake or Baby Bella mushrooms, sliced

1 garlic clove, minced

2 tablespoons all-purpose flour

1 teaspoon salt

¼ teaspoon black pepper

1 (10.5-ounce) can condensed cream of chicken soup

1 cup sour cream

2 cups hot cooked egg noodles, for serving

Snipped fresh parsley, for garnish

In a large skillet, melt the butter over medium heat. Add the ground beef and onion and cook, stirring, until the onion is tender. Stir in the mushrooms, garlic, flour, salt, and pepper. Cook, stirring continuously, for 5 minutes. Remove from the heat. Stir in the cream of chicken soup, return the pot to low heat, and bring to a simmer. Cook, uncovered, for 10 minutes, then stir in the sour cream and cook until heated through. Serve over the egg noodles, garnished with parsley. *Makes 4 to 6 servings.*

This recipe has always been a favorite of mine. It always feels like home. Whether I was just down the street at the university or playing around the country during the summer, this was always my first meal when I got home.

MOMMA PISANI'S MEATBALLS AND MARINARA SAUCE

Jaime Pisani Armbrust

Gymnastics

Gymnast, 2008–2012

Director of Operations, 2012–2014

Assistant Coach, 2014–2018

Associate Head Coach, 2018–2019

MARINARA SAUCE

1 tablespoon olive oil

1 pound Italian sausage links (optional)

1 whole head of garlic, cloves peeled and chopped

Handful of fresh flat-leaf parsley, chopped

2 (28-ounce) cans whole peeled tomatoes, squeeze by hand into little pieces

1 (6-ounce) can tomato paste

4 or 5 (29-ounce) cans tomato sauce

Salt and black pepper

Dried basil

Dried oregano

10 to 12 fresh basil leaves, chopped

MEATBALLS

8 slices brick-oven white bread

1 pound ground beef or ground sirloin

2 large eggs

1 cup grated Parmesan cheese, plus more if needed

Garlic powder

Onion powder

Dried basil

Dried oregano

Salt and black pepper

Italian breadcrumbs (optional)

1 tablespoon olive oil

Cooked pasta, for serving

Garlic bread, for serving

Make the marinara sauce: Heat a large saucepan over medium heat, then add a little olive oil to the hot pan. If using sausage links, brown them in the pan, then add the garlic, cook for about 40 seconds, and stir in the parsley. Immediately add the squeezed tomatoes and bring to a boil. Reduce the heat to maintain a simmer and cook for 45 minutes.

Stir in the tomato paste and the tomato sauce and bring to a low boil, reduce the heat to maintain a simmer and cook, stirring occasionally, for at least 8 hours or up to 10 hours (the longer it cooks, the better the flavor!). As the sauce cooks, season it with salt and pepper, a couple shakes of dried basil, and a dash of oregano. Toward the end of the cooking time, stir the fresh basil into the sauce.

About 4 to 6 hours before the sauce is done, make the meatballs: Two slices at a time, quickly run the bread under running water, then squeeze the bread to wring out any excess liquid. You just want to dampen the bread, not soak it. Place the dampened bread on parchment or wax paper and let stand for about 20 minutes, then crumble the bread into a large bowl and add the meat and eggs. Use clean hands to combine the mixture well. Add the Parmesan and season with garlic powder, onion powder, basil, a dash of oregano, salt, and pepper. Mix with your hands to combine.

Form the meat mixture into balls, adding a little Italian breadcrumbs and/or additional Parmesan as needed to get the right consistency for rolling.

In a large skillet, heat the olive oil over medium heat. Add the meatballs and cook until browned on all sides. Transfer them to paper towels to drain, then add them to the pot with the marinara sauce. Cook for 3 to 5 hours to let the meatballs really get flavorful and allow them to absorb the sauce so they're nice and soft!

Serve with your favorite pasta, homemade garlic bread, and a nice glass of red wine! *Makes 20 servings.*

This was my favorite pre-meet meal when my parents flew into Fayetteville from New Jersey to attend my gymnastics meets! Marinara sauce has no meat in it, but sometimes I cook Italian sausage links in it for flavor, depending on what I'm using the sauce for. You can also brown pork braciole with the sausage and cook it in sauce, then add the meatballs. I don't usually measure; I go by look and feel. You can double or triple the recipe for a large crowd or to have leftovers. Enjoy!

MORREALE MEATBALLS WITH ROSSI'S RED SAUCE

Rossi Morreale
Football
Wide Receiver, 1997–1999

MEATBALLS

Nonstick cooking spray

¼ cup milk

3 slices white bread

2 to 3 celery stalks, chopped

1 small onion, chopped

5 garlic cloves, chopped

1 pound ground beef

1 pound ground pork

1 pound bulk hot or mild Italian sausage

2 large eggs

¼ cup herbes de Provence

2 teaspoons black pepper

2 teaspoons dried oregano

2 teaspoons dried parsley

2 to 3 handfuls of grated Parmesan cheese

2 handfuls of breadcrumbs

Salt

RED SAUCE

2 (29-ounce) cans tomato sauce

½ green bell pepper, chopped

2 (12-ounce) cans tomato paste

5 garlic cloves, chopped

Olive oil

1 pound hot Italian sausage links

Italian seasoning

Red wine (optional)

FOR SERVING

Cooked rigatoni

Garlic bread

Salad

Make the meatballs: Preheat the oven to 350°F. Coat a baking sheet with cooking spray.

Place the bread in a shallow bowl. Pour the milk over the bread and let stand for 10 minutes, then remove the bread from the bowl and squeeze out the excess milk.

In a food processor, combine the celery, onion, and garlic and process to combine. Add the soaked bread and process again.

In a large bowl, combine the ground beef, ground pork, and sausage and mix with clean hands, then add the eggs and the mixture from the food processor. Add the herbes de Provence, pepper, oregano, parsley, Parmesan, and breadcrumbs. Mix it all together with your hands. Form the mixture into palm-size meatballs (or the size of your choice) and place them on the prepared baking sheet. Season with salt. Bake for 30 minutes or until fully cooked.

Make the red sauce: In a large skillet, cook the sausage links over medium-high heat until browned and cooked through, then drain the fat. Set aside.

Pour ½ can of the tomato sauce into a blender, add the bell pepper, and puree until smooth.

In a large saucepot, cook the garlic in olive oil over medium heat until golden. Pour in the pureed bell pepper mixture and stir, then add the remaining tomato sauce and the tomato paste. Fill the empty tomato paste cans with water, pour the water into the pot, and stir. Add Italian seasoning to taste. Bring the sauce to a simmer and cook for 15 minutes—stir a lot! Add a little red wine, if you want, and keep stirring! Add the cooked sausage to the sauce.

When the meatballs are cooked through, add them to the sauce as well and cook for a few minutes more, until everything is warmed through. Serve with rigatoni, garlic bread, and salad—and *finito! Makes 8 to 10 servings.*

It was October 31, 1998—Halloween. We were 7–0 and had an away game against Auburn. I was living with Clint Stoerner, Chad Jones, and John Rutledge. I threw out the idea of having a costume party at our house if we won. While we traveled to Auburn, our girlfriends decorated and got everything set up, including a DJ, and hoped for the best. At the game, we jumped out to an early lead, 17–7. In the second half, Auburn took a 21–17 lead, but we ended up scoring for the win, 24–21, to go 8–0. We flew back to Fayetteville to the most epic Halloween costume party of all time. After the cops came to the house for the third time and said we had to keep it down . . . I led all two hundred people in calling the Hogs as they walked away laughing.

MUSSELS IN WHITE WINE CREAM SAUCE

Corey Beck
Men's Basketball
Point Guard, 1993–1995

4 pounds fresh mussels, scrubbed and debearded, if necessary

1

Nolan Richardson

tablespoon sea salt, plus more as needed

1 (16-ounce) box linguine pasta

6 tablespoons (¾ stick) salted butter, cut into pieces

4 teaspoons minced garlic

1½ cups sauvignon blanc

1 (10-ounce) can Ro*Tel diced tomatoes and green chiles, undrained

1½ cups heavy cream

1 tablespoon freshly ground black pepper

Freshly grated Parmesan cheese

½ ounce fresh chives, chopped

Dispose of any mussels that are already opened or that have cracked shells. Bring a large pot of salted water to a boil over medium-high heat. Add the linguine and cook according to the package directions.

Meanwhile, in a large pot, melt the butter over medium heat. Add the garlic and cook, stirring, until golden but not browned, about 2 minutes. Raise the heat to high and add the wine and salt. Cook, stirring every minute or so, until the alcohol burns off, about 4 minutes. Add the Ro*Tel and mussels, then cover tightly. Steam the mussels until most open, about 4 minutes. Reduce the heat to maintain a simmer and cook for 2 minutes, then stir in the cream and pepper. Simmer slowly until all the mussels are open, 2 to 3 minutes more. Toss any stubborn mussels that refuse to open. Turn off the heat and sprinkle Parmesan over the mussels.

Divide the pasta among individual bowls and top with 10 mussels per bowl. Spoon over more of the white wine cream sauce and sprinkle with more Parmesan and the chives. Tip: Use an empty mussel shell as pincers to pull the meat from the other shells. *Makes 4 servings.*

My grandmother passed this recipe to my sister, who passed it on to me. It is my favorite!

NOLAN'S TACOS

Nolan Richardson
Men's Basketball
Head Coach, 1985–2002

1 small onion, finely chopped

2 garlic cloves, minced

2 pounds 80/20 ground beef

1 (16-ounce) can refried beans (see Note)

2 jalapeños, finely chopped (seed them first for less heat, if desired; see Note)

1 Roma (plum) tomato, diced

Vegetable oil, for frying

16 to 20 corn tortillas

Toppings: shredded lettuce, diced tomatoes, shredded cheese (I recommend Fiesta blend)

In a large pan, cook the onion over medium heat until translucent. Add the garlic and ground beef to the pan and cook, breaking up the meat with a wooden spoon as it cooks, until the beef is browned and cooked through. Stir in the refried beans, jalapeños, and tomato until well combined and cook until the all the ingredients are heated through.

Coat a small skillet with oil and heat over medium-high heat. Carefully add a tortilla to the hot oil. Using tongs, fold it in half to form the U-shape of a taco shell and fry to your desired crispness. For a softer shell, fry for less time; for a crispier shell, fry it a bit longer. Transfer the taco shell to paper towels to drain and repeat with the remaining tortillas.

Fill each taco shell with the beef and bean mixture. Top with lettuce, tomatoes, cheese, and any of your favorite taco toppings, like salsa or sour cream. *Makes 8 to 10 servings.*

NOTE *Add more refried beans or use less jalapeño if needed to balance the spice.*

A college basketball legend, **COACH RICHARDSON** led the Razorbacks to an overall record of 389–169, setting a school record for wins. He won many conference championships, both in the SWC and SEC. He took the Razorbacks to six Sweet 16s, four Elite Eights, three Final Fours, a national runner-up, and, in 1994, the first NCAA Basketball Championship in the school's history. Coach Richardson has been elected to the National Collegiate Basketball Hall of Fame, the Naismith Memorial Basketball Hall of Fame, the University of Arkansas Sports Hall of Honor, and the Arkansas Sports Hall of Fame. He is the only head coach in college basketball history to win a National Junior College Championship, NIT Championship, and NCAA Championship. In 2019, the court in Bud Walton Arena was named in honor of Coach Richardson and his contributions to the University of Arkansas, the state of Arkansas, and the United States of America.

O YEAH

Oliver Miller
Men's Basketball
Center, 1988–1992

1 (14-ounce) package Eckrich beef or turkey sausage

1 red bell pepper

1 orange bell pepper

1 yellow bell pepper

½ onion

Slap Ya Mama Cajun seasoning

Blackening seasoning

1 (16-ounce) bag frozen cooked peeled large shrimp, thawed

Old Bay seasoning

4 or 5 russet potatoes, chopped

4 skinless catfish, tilapia, or orange roughy fillets

Chop up ya sausage. Dice ya bell peppers and onion. Combine ya sausage, onion, and bell peppers in a zip-top bag and season them all with Slap Ya Mama and blackening seasoning. Put ya shrimp in another zip-top bag and season with Old Bay and Slap Ya Mama. Dice up ya potatoes and put them in another zip-top bag. Season ya fish fillets with Slap Ya Mama (the spicier you want the fish, use more Slap Ya Mama) and put them in a fourth zip-top bag. Put all the bags in the fridge and let it all marinate overnight.

The next day, put ya potatoes in a medium pot and add water to cover. Bring to a boil over medium-high heat and cook until ya potatoes are fork-tender, then drain.

In a large, deep skillet, cook ya sausage, bell peppers, and onion over medium heat until browned. Next, add ya shrimp on top, then put ya potatoes on top of ya shrimp. Lay ya fillets on top of ya potatoes, cover the skillet with a lid, and cook until ya fish is cooked through, opaque, and flakes easily with a fork, about 15 minutes. Enjoy! *Makes 4 to 6 servings.*

ONE-POT CHICKEN BACON ALFREDO PASTA

Hudson Henry
Football
Tight End, 2019–2021

8 ounces uncooked fettuccine

2 cups chicken broth

1½ cups diced or thinly sliced cooked chicken

1 cup grated Parmesan cheese

1 cup heavy cream

1 tablespoon minced garlic

Salt and black pepper

½ cup crumbled cooked bacon

2 tablespoons chopped fresh parsley

In an 11-inch sauté pan, combine the fettuccine, broth, chicken, Parmesan, cream, and garlic. Cover and bring to a boil over medium-high heat. Cook, stirring frequently, until the pasta is tender, 12 to 15 minutes. Season with salt and pepper. Stir in the bacon and garnish with the parsley. Enjoy! *Makes 2 servings.*

ONE-SKILLET CHICKEN WITH LEMON GARLIC SAUCE

Kenoy Kennedy
Football
Safety, 1996–1999

4 boneless, skinless chicken breasts

Salt and black pepper

1 cup chicken broth

2 tablespoons lemon juice

1 tablespoon minced garlic

½ teaspoon red pepper flakes, or more to taste

1 tablespoon olive oil

⅓ cup finely diced shallot or red onion

2 tablespoons salted butter

¼ cup heavy cream

2 tablespoons chopped fresh basil

Cooked rice or pasta, or sautéed veggies, for serving

Position a rack in the lower third of the oven and preheat the oven to 375°F.

Using a meat mallet, pound the chicken breasts to an even ½-inch thickness. Season both sides of each piece of chicken with a pinch each of salt and pepper.

In a 2-cup measuring cup or a small bowl, combine the broth, lemon juice, garlic, and red pepper flakes. In a large ovenproof skillet, heat the olive oil over medium-high heat. Add the chicken and cook until browned on both sides, 2 to 3 minutes per side. Don't worry if the chicken isn't cooked through; we'll finish it in the oven. Transfer the chicken to a plate and set aside.

Add the shallot and the broth mixture to the skillet and reduce the heat to medium. Stir with a whisk, scraping up all the browned bits from the bottom of the pan. Kick the heat back up to medium-high and bring the sauce to a simmer. Cook until the sauce has reduced to about ⅓ cup, 10 to 15 minutes. Remove from the heat, add the butter, and whisk until it melts completely. Add the cream and whisk to combine, then return the skillet to medium heat for just 30 seconds—DO NOT allow the sauce to boil. Remove from the heat, return the chicken to the pan, and drizzle the sauce over the chicken. Place the skillet in the oven and bake for 5 to 8 minutes, until the chicken is completely cooked through.

Top with the basil and lemon slices and serve warm, with rice, pasta, or veggies on the side. *Makes 4 servings.*

I like to double or triple the sauce to have plenty to put on my pasta!

OVEN BBQ CHICKEN WITH BAKED SWEET POTATOES

Heston Kjerstad
Baseball
Outfield, 2018–2020

4 boneless, skinless chicken breasts

1 cup Sweet Baby Ray's Sweet 'n Spicy BBQ sauce

2 garlic cloves, crushed or chopped

Salt and black pepper

4 medium sweet potatoes

Preheat the oven to 350°F.

Place the chicken breasts in a 9 by 13-inch baking dish. Cover with the BBQ sauce, sprinkle the garlic on top of the sauce, then season with salt and pepper. Cover with foil and bake for 1 hour, or until the chicken breasts are fully cooked through.

After the chicken is in the oven, place the sweet potatoes on a baking sheet and place it in the oven with the chicken. Bake until a fork easily slides in. The chicken and sweet potatoes should be done at the same time. *Makes 4 servings.*

One of the few meals I would cook while I was in college. Simple and easy to make.

PAPPY'S STEAK

Jim Mabry
Football
Offensive Lineman, 1985–1989

A great cut of meat

Dale's Steak Seasoning

Hickory-flavor liquid smoke

Garlic salt with parsley

McCormick's Hot Shot! black and red pepper blend

Hickory chips, for grilling

Place the steak in a baking dish. Pour in some Dale's and a little liquid smoke, place in the refrigerator, and let marinate for 5 hours, then flip and season the top of the steak with garlic salt and Hot Shot. Place back in the refrigerator and marinate for 5 hours more. When you're ready to cook, grill the steak over charcoal using hickory chips to your desired doneness. *Makes 1 to 2 servings.*

My father-in law, Jim Wilson, from Mena, Arkansas, loved grilling out steaks for his family on Sunday nights, and we all thought his steaks were the best! All the kids and grandkids would head over to his house on Sunday nights to talk about the latest Razorback game and eat some of his delicious steaks. If the schedule permitted, after dinner, we'd watch the Dallas Cowboy game (he was from Dallas originally). I still enjoy cooking this steak on weekends at my house, especially if there is a good ballgame on.

PENNE ALLA VODKA

Doc Sadler
Men's Basketball
Assistant Coach, 1982–1985

¾ teaspoon kosher salt, plus more as needed

2 tablespoons olive oil

1 medium yellow onion, finely chopped

3 garlic cloves, chopped

⅓ cup double-concentrated tomato paste

¼ teaspoon red pepper flakes

1 (28-ounce) can whole peeled tomatoes, such as San Marzanos, with their juices

½ cup vodka

1 pound dried penne pasta

Leaves from 4 basil sprigs, sliced

½ cup heavy cream

2 ounces Parmesan cheese, grated

Black pepper

Heston Kjerstad

Bring a large pot of salted water to a boil.

In a large skillet, heat the olive oil over medium-high heat. Add the onion and garlic and cook until garlic starts to turn light brown, about 4 minutes. Add the tomato paste and red pepper flakes and cook for about 2 minutes more. Add the tomatoes and their juices, the vodka, and the salt. Break up the tomatoes with a wooden spoon. Bring to a simmer and cook for about 15 minutes.

Add the pasta to the boiling water and cook for 9 to 11 minutes. Reserve 1 cup of the pasta cooking water and then drain the pasta.

Add the cream, basil, and pepper to the skillet with the tomato mixture and stir until combined. Add the pasta, Parmesan, and ½ cup of the reserved pasta water. Stir to combine, adding more pasta water if the sauce is too thick, then serve. *Makes 4 servings.*

PHILLY CHEESESTEAK MEATLOAF

Dave England

Assistant Athletic Trainer, 1984–1989
Head Athletic Trainer, 1989–2019
Director of Sports Medicine, 2019–2022

1 tablespoon avocado oil

1 onion, diced

1 bell pepper, diced

8 ounces mushrooms, diced

2 garlic cloves, chopped

2 pounds ground meat of your choice

1 teaspoon salt

1 teaspoon black pepper

1 cup panko breadcrumbs

½ cup Cheez Whiz (optional)

2 tablespoons ketchup

1 tablespoon Worcestershire sauce

2 eggs

8 slices provolone cheese, plus
1 (4-ounce) chunk provolone

Preheat the oven to 350°F.

In a large pan, heat the oil over medium heat. Add the onion, bell pepper, and mushrooms and cook, stirring, until tender, 7 to 10 minutes. Add the garlic and cook for 1 minute, then remove from the heat.

In a large bowl, combine the ground meat, salt, black pepper, panko, Cheez Whiz, ketchup, Worcestershire, eggs, and the cooked vegetable mixture and mix with gloved or clean hands to combine. Transfer half the meat mixture to a baking sheet or baking dish, put the chunk of provolone in the center, then put the rest of the meat mixture on top and seal the edges well, shaping the loaf as desired. Bake for 50 to 60 minutes, until cooked through. Remove from the oven and switch the oven to broil. Top the meatloaf with the provolone slices and broil for 2 to 4 minutes, until the cheese has melted. *Makes 6 to 8 servings.*

This is my favorite game-day dish!

POT ROAST

Heston Kjerstad
Baseball
Outfield, 2018–2020

2 pounds roast beef

1 pound baby carrots

1 pound small potatoes

1 (12-ounce) bag frozen pearl onions

4 garlic cloves, crushed or chopped

2 to 3 cups beef bone broth,
plus more as needed

2 bay leaves

2 tablespoons balsamic vinegar glaze

Salt and black pepper

Preheat the oven to 350°F.

Place the beef, carrots, potatoes, pearl onions, and garlic in a Dutch oven. Pour the broth over the vegetables. Add the bay leaves. Drizzle the balsamic glaze over the roast and season with salt and pepper. Cover with the lid and bake for about 3 hours, until the vegetables are tender and the meat is falling apart, checking the pot at 2 hours, as you may need to add more broth. Remove the bay leaves before serving. *Makes 4 to 6 servings.*

This was the meal I would always ask my mom to make when I went home for breaks during college.

POTATO GNOCCHI WITH CHICKEN TOMATO SAUCE

Maria Fassi
Women's Golf
Golfer, 2015–2019

POTATO GNOCCHI

1 pound white potatoes

¾ cup all-purpose flour

⅔ cup cornstarch

2 large egg yolks

Pinch of ground nutmeg

Salt and black pepper

Olive oil

Grated Parmesan cheese, for serving

CHICKEN TOMATO SAUCE

8 chicken thighs, 4 legs and thighs, or 2 chicken breasts, cut into 8 pieces

Salt and black pepper

3 tablespoons olive oil

2 onions, diced

½ green bell pepper, diced

½ red bell pepper, diced

1 teaspoon dried oregano

3 bay leaves

1 glass white wine

2 (14.5-ounce) cans diced tomatoes, with their juices

SPECIAL EQUIPMENT

Potato ricer

Gnocchi board (optional, though highly recommended)

Make the sauce: Season the chicken with salt and black pepper. In a large saucepan, heat the olive oil over medium heat. Add the chicken and cook until evenly browned on all sides, about 5 minutes on each side. Transfer the chicken to a plate and set aside.

Add the onions to the pan and cook over medium heat until translucent. Add the green and red bell peppers and cook until they soften. Stir in the oregano and bay leaves. Add the wine and stir for a few minutes until the alcohol evaporates. Add the tomatoes and stir. Return the chicken to the pan. Cover and cook for 30 minutes, then fill the wineglass with water and pour it into the pan. Cook, uncovered, for 10 minutes more, until the sauce thickens slightly.

While the sauce is cooking, make the gnocchi: Place the potatoes in a large pot and add water to cover. Bring to a boil over high heat, then cook until the potatoes are fork-tender. Drain the potatoes. While they're still hot, peel them and pass them through a potato ricer onto a clean flat work surface, creating a shallow mound.

Sift the flour and cornstarch together over the potatoes. Create a well in the middle of the mixture and add the egg yolks. Season with the nutmeg and salt and black pepper to taste. Using your hands, start incorporating the flour mixture and the potatoes into the egg yolks until the ingredients come together to form a dough; it shouldn't stick to your fingers. Knead the dough until it is smooth and homogeneous, but don't keep kneading it past that point! Resist the temptation to add flour unless it's absolutely necessary, or you'll end up with tough gnocchi.

Slice off a small piece of the dough. Sprinkle a bit of flour on the work surface and roll the piece of dough into a long rope about the diameter of a finger (about ⅔ inch). Cut the rope crosswise into ¾-inch-long gnocchi (a little longer is okay, but no shorter). Start rolling the gnocchi over the tines of a fork or a gnocchi board (see Note) to make ridges in the dough. Place the gnocchi on a lightly flour-dusted counter or tray, trying not to let them touch each other to keep them from sticking, and repeat with the remaining dough.

Boil the gnocchi sooner than later; if left sitting for too long, they can get sticky. Bring a large pot of water to a rolling boil over high heat. Salt the water and add a bit of olive oil. Add the gnocchi to the pot, gently dropping them in as quickly as possible without damaging them. They will cook quickly; as soon as they float to the top, they are ready. Do not let them boil for more than 1 minute after they float. You can taste one to make sure the water is salty enough and that the gnocchi are cooked through. As they are done, use a strainer to remove them from the pot and place them in a serving bowl. Stir in the sauce, sprinkle with Parmesan, and serve immediately. *Makes 4 servings.*

NOTE *If using a gnocchi board, be sure to dust the board with flour before rolling the gnocchi; use enough flour so the gnocchi don't stick. To press ridges into the dough, hold the board at a 45-degree angle with one hand and use your opposite thumb to push the gnocchi down the grooves in the board.*

PUMPKIN GNOCCHI WITH SPINACH AND SAUSAGE

Christin Wurth-Thomas
Women's Track & Field / Cross Country
800m, 1500m, 3000m, 5000m, 1999–2003

1 tablespoon olive oil

12 to 16 ounces bulk hot or mild Italian sausage

10 ounces gnocchi

1 cup heavy cream

▯ cup chicken broth

1 cup pure pumpkin puree

4 teaspoons minced garlic

4 ounces fresh spinach

Salt and black pepper

In a large skillet, heat the olive oil over medium heat. Add the sausage and cook, breaking up the meat as it cooks, until browned, then drain the fat. Add the gnocchi, cream, and broth. Bring to a boil over medium heat while stirring. Reduce the heat to maintain a gentle boil, cover, and cook for 5 minutes. Uncover and stir in the pumpkin and garlic. Add the spinach, raise the heat to medium, and bring to a boil. Reduce the heat to medium-low and cook for 5 minutes more, until the spinach wilts. Remove from the heat and season with salt and pepper. *Makes 4 servings.*

Christin Wurth-Thomas

RC'S (AKA DADDY'S) FAMOUS CHICKEN TENDERS

R. C. Thielemann
Football
Guard and Center, 1973–1976

1½ cups all-purpose flour

Salt and black pepper

1 large egg

1½ cups milk

Season-All seasoned salt

Canola oil

1 pound chicken breast tenderloins or thin chicken cutlets

Start with a beer of your preference (for you, not the chicken:), then put about 1 cup of the flour in a large dish and season the flour generously with salt and pepper to your standards.

Crack the egg into a separate large bowl and pour in the milk. Season generously with Season-All and stir it all together.

Fill a large skillet (preferably cast-iron) with ½ inch of canola oil and heat over medium-high heat. To test if the oil is hot enough, add a couple drops of water—if it sizzles a good bit, the oil is "cooking ready." (Please be careful, hot grease and water are like Arkansas vs. Texas in any sport!) Line a large plate with a few paper towels and have it handy next to the stove.

Working in batches of four or five, dip each piece of chicken in milk-egg mixture, let the excess drip off, and then dredge it in the flour to coat. Add the coated chicken to the hot oil (don't overcrowd the pan) and cover the skillet with a splatter guard. At this point, you are allowed one more beer of your preference while you keep an eye on the sizzling tenders. Cook until golden brown on the bottom (use a fork or tongs to roll one tender over to check), then flip and cook until golden brown on the second side. Take one out of the skillet and cut it in half to check for doneness—the chicken should be fully cooked inside, with no pink. Transfer the chicken tenders to the paper towel–lined plate and cover with more paper towels to pat off any grease. Repeat to fry the remaining tenders and enjoy! *Makes 2 to 3 servings.*

Have fun playing with the ingredients on your next batch—we're all a bit unique.

RICE AND BEANS

Martin Terry
Men's Basketball
Guard, 1971–1973

RICE

2½ cups uncooked long-grain white rice, rinsed and drained

2 tablespoons corn oil

⅔ teaspoon salt

BEANS

1 (15.5-ounce) can red kidney beans, undrained

¼ (15-ounce) can tomato sauce

½ (1.41-ounce) packet Sazón Goya seasoning

¼ small onion, chopped

5 green olives, pitted

1 teaspoon garlic powder

½ teaspoon corn oil

¼ teaspoon dried oregano

Several fresh cilantro leaves

Make the rice: Cook the rice in a 2-quart saucepan according to the package instructions, adding the salt and corn oil to the water before adding the rice.

Meanwhile, make the beans: Dump the beans into a 1-quart saucepan, then fill the empty can halfway with water and add it to the pot. Add the tomato sauce, Sazón Goya, onion, olives, garlic powder, oil, oregano, and cilantro and stir to combine. Cook over medium heat, stirring every 10 minutes, until the beans are hot and the flavors are blended, about 30 minutes. Serve the beans over the rice. *Makes 2 to 4 servings.*

RICE AND HAMBURGER HOT DISH

Norm DeBriyn
Baseball
Head Coach, 1970–2002

1 large onion, chopped

1 cup chopped celery

1 pound ground beef

1 (10.5-ounce) can condensed cream of mushroom soup

1 (10.5-ounce) can condensed chicken with rice soup

1 (4-ounce) can sliced mushrooms, undrained

½ cup uncooked long-grain white rice

1 tablespoon soy sauce

1 (5-ounce) can chow mein noodles

Preheat the oven to 325°F.

In a large skillet, cook the onion and celery over mdium heat until slightly browned, then transfer to a large bowl and set aside.

In the same skillet, brown the ground beef over medium heat, then add it to the bowl with the vegetables. Add the mushroom soup, chicken with rice soup, mushrooms, rice, soy sauce, and 1 cup water and stir to combine. Transfer the mixture to a large casserole dish. Bake for 1 hour or slightly longer, until the mixture is bubbling and the rice is tender. In the last 15 to 20 minutes, sprinkle the chow mein noodles over the top. *Makes 4 servings.*

ROAST AFTER THE ROUND

Taylor Moore
Men's Golf
Golfer, 2012–2016

1 (3- to 4-pound) chuck pot roast

Salt and black pepper

6 or 7 large Idaho potatoes, scrubbed, peeled, and halved

1 (16-ounce) bag baby carrots

A few slices of onion (optional)

A few slices of celery (optional)

Preheat the oven to 275°F. Line a 9 by 13-inch baking dish with two large pieces of foil, placing them perpendicular to each other and making sure there's enough foil overhanging the edges to wrap the roast with potatoes and carrots on top.

Generously season the chuck roast with salt and pepper on both sides. Place the roast in the middle of the prepared baking dish. Place the potatoes in the baking dish around the roast. Place the carrots on top of the roast, then add the onion and celery (if you desire the flavor). Generously season all the ingredients with salt and pepper. Bring the overhanging foil up and crimp the edges tightly to enclose the ingredients. Bake for 5 hours, or until the meat is fork-tender and the vegetables are tender. *Makes 6 to 8 servings.*

My mom taught me how to prepare and cook this roast so that I could pop it in the oven before golf practice or a practice round. Five hours later, it is ready to eat.

RUTH'S FAVORITE CHICKEN AND SPAGHETTI

Ruth Cohoon
Women's Athletic Director, 1972–1989

1 whole rotisserie chicken

1 (12-ounce) box or small package spaghetti

1 tablespoon vegetable oil

1 cup chopped white onion

½ cup chopped green bell pepper

½ cup chopped celery

1 (28-ounce) can crushed or diced tomatoes, undrained

1 (8-ounce) can tomato sauce

1 (4-ounce) can mushrooms stems and pieces, drained (optional)

2 garlic cloves, minced

3 tablespoons chili powder

1 teaspoon salt

½ teaspoon ground allspice

½ teaspoon black pepper

1 bay leaf

Ketchup (optional)

2 (14.5-ounce) cans chicken broth

1 cup grated Cracker Barrel sharp cheddar cheese, for topping

Grated Parmesan cheese, for serving

Preheat the oven to 350°F.

Pick the meat from the rotisserie chicken, discarding the skin and bones, and set aside.

Cook the spaghetti according to the package directions. Drain and set aside.

In a large skillet, heat the oil over medium heat. Add the onion, bell pepper, and celery and cook, stirring, until the onion is translucent and the bell pepper and celery have softened.

In a large roasting pan, stir together the crushed tomatoes, tomato sauce, mushrooms, garlic, chili powder, salt, allspice, pepper, bay leaf, and a dab of ketchup (if using). Stir in the chicken and 3 cups of the chicken broth, the onion mixture, and the spaghetti (see Note). Top with the cheddar. Bake for 1 hour, or until bubbling and the cheddar has melted. Sprinkle Parmesan on top and serve. *Makes 4 to 6 servings.*

NOTE *The ingredients may be prepared to this point several days ahead of time; cover and refrigerate until ready to bake, then add the cheddar just before baking.*

This favorite recipe is from Coach Mike Bender's wife, Gail, sometime in the 1970s. Over the years, a lot has changed in the can sizes and preparation. Originally, a large fryer chicken was cooked and deboned; today I buy a rotisserie chicken and debone it.

In the 1960s, the only opportunity for female students to participate in sports at the university was through physical education classes, intramurals, and occasionally "play days" and "sports days" and "extramurals" with other schools. Our female students requested more opportunities, so some of the women on the PE faculty volunteered to coach basketball, tennis, swimming, track, volleyball, gymnastics, and golf. Somebody had to fill out paperwork the university required to take students off campus, so I volunteered! Over time, Extramural Sports became Women's Intercollegiate Sports, then Women's Intercollegiate Athletics, and in 1972 Title IX became a federal law, and here we are! A few early administrators at that time supported women playing sports: those that helped the most were Dr. Fred Vorsanger, former U of A vice president for finance; and Dr. Fred Vescolani, former dean of the College of Education. They were instrumental in securing funding for the program (a whopping $5,000!). Women's sports were administrated through the Physical Education Department. (Teaching loads were reduced for those coaching women's sports and men's spring sports that were housed in the PE Department.) A LOT has changed since then in budgets, facilities, travel, and national competition. Dr. Troy Hendricks was head of the Physical Education Department. In those "old days," the Physical Education Department was separated into men's and women's programs. The women's program was meeting in what was called the "Little Gym," located in the basement of the Men's Gym (now the Faulkner Performing Arts Building). At that time, I did not teach three-hour lecture classes—I only taught twelve one-hour PEAC (physical education activity classes) classes per semester, which met Monday/Wednesday and Tuesday/Thursday. So I had no Friday classes to teach. I volunteered to handle the paperwork required by the department and the university! Simple as that. No big national searches, no interviews.

SALMON AND FARRO

Frank O'Mara

Men's Track & Field

1500m, 5000m, 1978–1983

Assistant Coach, 1983–1988

1 cup pearled farro

1 bunch broccolini

1 cup fresh or frozen peas

1 skinless salmon fillet

Salt and black pepper

¾ cup prepared pesto

½ cup crumbled feta cheese

Preheat the oven to 400°F.

In a medium saucepan, bring 2 cups water to a boil over high heat. Add the farro, reduce the heat to low or medium, and cook for 20 minutes. Add the broccolini and peas and cook until the farro is tender, 5 minutes more.

Meanwhile, season the salmon with salt and pepper. Heat a cast-iron pan over medium-high heat. Add the salmon and sear for 90 seconds on each side. Transfer the salmon to a medium baking pan and bake for 10 to 12 minutes, until the salmon flakes easily with a fork.

Transfer the farro and vegetables to a large bowl and add the pesto. Mix well. Add the feta and mix once more. Serve the salmon with the farro and vegetables alongside. *Makes 1 to 2 servings.*

Athletes consume a ton of carbohydrates, so another bowl of pasta or rice can be uninviting. Give farro a try instead. Combine it with fresh salmon, and you have a great meal in around 30 minutes. Of course, you could make the pesto from scratch, but what student athlete has time for that?

SAUSAGE GREEN BEAN POTATO CASSEROLE

Al Dillard
Men's Basketball
Guard, 1994–1995

Nonstick cooking spray

2 pounds baby creamer potatoes, halved

2 tablespoons vegetable oil

1 teaspoon Slap Ya Mama Cajun seasoning

1 teaspoon garlic powder

1 teaspoon black pepper

½ teaspoon red pepper flakes

1½ pounds kielbasa or other smoked sausage, thickly sliced

4 tablespoons (½ stick) unsalted butter

1 cup chopped onion

3 garlic cloves, minced

2 (15-ounce) cans green beans, drained

Preheat the oven to 400°F. Coat a 9 by 13-inch baking dish with cooking spray.

Place the potatoes in a 1-gallon zip-top bag. Add the oil, Cajun seasoning, garlic powder, black pepper, and red pepper flakes. Seal the bag and shake to coat.

Place the sausage in a large skillet with ¼ cup water. Cook over medium-high heat until the sausage is browned and most of the water has evaporated. Remove the sausage from the pan and let cool, then add it to the bag with the potatoes.

In the same skillet, melt the butter over medium heat. Add the onion and garlic and cook until the onion is translucent. Let cool for a few minutes, then add to the bag and shake to mix. Add the green beans to the bag and shake to mix, then empty the bag into the prepared baking dish. Cover with foil and bake for 40 minutes, or until the potatoes are tender. *Makes 6 servings.*

SCOTTY THURMAN'S LOUISIANA RED BEANS AND RICE

Scotty Thurman
Men's Basketball
Guard, 1992–1995

2 smoked ham hocks

2 tablespoons chicken broth, plus more as needed

3 or 4 serrano chiles, stemmed but left whole (optional, for spicy flavor)

1 garlic clove, minced

1 bay leaf

1 pound dried red kidney beans, soaked overnight and drained

1 (16-ounce) package andouille sausage, thinly sliced

1 tablespoon Cajun or Creole seasoning, plus more as needed

2 tablespoons unsalted butter

2 celery stalks, diced

1 green bell pepper, diced

1 medium sweet onion, diced

1 cup uncooked basmati rice

2 tablespoons chopped fresh parsley, for garnish

In a large pot, combine the ham hocks, broth, serranos (if using), garlic, bay leaf, and 8 to 10 cups water. Bring to a boil over high heat, then reduce the heat to low, cover, and simmer for 1 hour. Add the beans, andouille sausage, and Cajun seasoning. Taste the liquid and adjust, if needed, with additional broth and Cajun seasoning. Return to a simmer, cover, and cook for 30 minutes.

Meanwhile, in a large skillet, melt the butter over medium-high heat. Add the celery, bell pepper, and onion and cook, stirring, until softened, about 6 minutes. Add the vegetable mixture to the pot with the beans. Cover and cook for 1½ to 2 hours, until the beans are tender and the ham hocks are falling apart; the consistency of the broth should be thick and creamy.

Meanwhile, cook the rice according to the package directions.

Serve the red beans with a scoop of rice, garnished with the parsley. *Makes 4 servings.*

SHADDY'S SMOKED PORK TACOS WITH ROASTED POBLANOS

Carson Shaddy
Baseball
Second Base, 2015–2018

1 (8-pound) Boston butt

Olive oil

Ground cumin

Garlic powder

Adobo seasoning

5 tomatillos, husked and rinsed

1 yellow onion, coarsely chopped

¼ bunch cilantro

1 jalapeño, stemmed

2 cups chicken broth

4 poblano peppers

FOR SERVING

Corn tortillas

1 tomato, chopped

3 avocados, sliced

Prepare a smoker.

Coat the pork butt in olive oil and season generously with cumin, garlic powder, and adobo. Don't be shy.

Place the pork butt in the smoker and smoke until the internal temperature of the pork reaches 203°F. Take the pork butt out of the smoker and wrap it in foil. Place it in a small cooler with old towels on top, cover with the lid, and let steam for 1 to 4 hours.

Preheat the broiler or heat a grill.

Place the tomatillos on a baking sheet and broil for 6 to 12 minutes, until they are blotchy brown and tender, or place directly on the grill grates and cook for 7 to 10 minutes, until browned and softened. Let cool slightly (keep the broiler or grill on), then peel the tomatillos and place them in a blender. Add the onion, cilantro, jalapeño, and broth. Blend until smooth, then set aside.

Place the poblanos on a baking sheet and broil for 5 minutes on each side, until blackened, or place directly on the grill grates and cook for 3 to 4 minutes on each side, until blackened. Let cool slightly, then peel the poblanos, remove the stems and seeds, and dice the flesh.

Unwrap the pork and place in a large bowl. Shred the meat, then add the tomatillo sauce and the diced poblanos and stir to combine. Fill tortillas with the pork and top with tomato and sliced avocado. *Makes 20 to 30 tacos.*

SHRIMP AND GRITS

Clint McDaniel
Men's Basketball
Guard, 1992–1995

2½ cups chicken broth

2 cups whole milk

4 tablespoons (½ stick) unsalted butter

Salt

¾ cup stone-ground grits

1 pound jumbo shrimp, peeled and deveined

Black pepper

1 cup shredded sharp cheddar cheese

In a medium saucepan, combine 2 cups of the broth, the milk, 3 tablespoons of the butter, and a pinch of salt. Bring to a gentle boil over medium-high heat. Add the grits and whisk to combine. Simmer, whisking every few minutes, until thickened and creamy, 10 to 15 minutes.

Meanwhile, rinse the shrimp with cold water and pat them dry. Season with salt and pepper. In a large skillet, melt the remaining 1 tablespoon butter over medium heat. Add the shrimp and cook until pink and cooked through, about 2 minutes per side. Add the remaining ½ cup broth to the shrimp and cook just until the broth is warm, then remove from the heat.

Add the cheese to the pot with the grits and stir until melted.

To serve, scoop some grits into individual bowls and spoon the shrimp mixture over the grits. *Makes 4 servings.*

SHRIMP AND PASTA IN CREAM SAUCE

Ralph Kraus
Baseball
Outfield and First Base, 1983–1986

8 to 12 ounces dried rigatoni

2 tablespoons olive oil

2 tablespoons salted butter

1 teaspoon red pepper flakes

1 teaspoon minced garlic

8 ounces large (21–25 count) shrimp (see Note)

1½ cups heavy cream

Cayenne pepper

Grated Parmesan cheese

Cook the rigatoni according to the package directions, then drain and set aside.

In a large skillet, heat the olive oil, butter, red pepper flakes, and garlic over medium heat. Add the shrimp and cook until cooked through, 3 to 4 minutes per side. Remove the shrimp from the pan and set aside. Add the cream to the pan and season with cayenne and Parmesan to taste. Add the rigatoni and shrimp to the cream and stir. Remove from the heat and serve. *Makes 2 servings.*

NOTE *You can substitute salmon for the shrimp, if you like.*

This is our go-to winter meal. The cream sauce is best spicy! It's Pacific Northwest meets Italian.

SIDNEY'S FAVORITE CHICKEN SPAGHETTI

Sidney Moncrief
Men's Basketball
Point Guard, 1976–1978

2 whole chickens

4 tablespoons (½ stick) unsalted butter, plus more for greasing

2 large onions, very finely chopped

4 celery stalks, very finely chopped

1 green bell pepper, very finely chopped

6 ounces vermicelli noodles

2 tablespoons chili powder

2 tablespoons chopped fresh parsley

1 (4-ounce) jar chopped pimentos, undrained

2 (10.5-ounce) cans condensed cream of mushroom soup

8 ounces cheddar cheese, shredded

Place the chickens in a large pot and add water to cover by 1 inch. Bring to a boil over medium-high heat, then reduce the heat to maintain a simmer. Cook until the meat starts to fall off the bone, about 90 minutes. Remove the chicken from the pot, reserving the broth, and let cool slightly, then remove the skin and pick the meat from the bones, discarding the skin and bones.

In a large skillet, melt the butter over medium heat. Add the onions, celery, and bell pepper and cook, stirring, until soft.

In a large pot, bring the reserved broth to a boil over high heat. Add the vermicelli and cook according to the package directions. Drain and transfer to a large baking pan. Add the chicken, onion mixture, chili powder, parsley, pimentos, and cream of mushroom soup. Mix thoroughly. Cover and refrigerate for 24 hours.

Preheat the oven to 350°F. Grease a 9 by 13-inch casserole dish with butter.

Transfer the chicken mixture to the prepared casserole dish and sprinkle with the cheese. Bake for 1 hour, or until bubbling and the cheese has melted. *Makes 8 servings.*

NOTE *Leftover chicken spaghetti may be frozen in an airtight container or freezer bag for up to 3 months.*

SLOW COOKER QUESO CHICKEN TACOS

Darin Phelan
Men's Tennis
Player, 1995–1998
Assistant Coach, 2002–2007

Nonstick cooking spray

2 pounds boneless, skinless chicken breasts

1 (1-ounce) packet taco seasoning

1 (10-ounce) can Ro*Tel diced tomatoes and green chiles, undrained

1 (4-ounce) can diced green chiles (optional)

½ cup chicken broth

¾ cup prepared salsa con queso

Taco shells or tortillas, for serving

Optional toppings: shredded lettuce, diced tomato, diced onions, shredded cheddar cheese, diced jalapeños, guacamole, sour cream, fresh lime juice, chopped cilantro, queso

Lightly coat a slow cooker with cooking spray. Place the chicken in the slow cooker in a single layer and sprinkle with the taco seasoning.

In medium bowl, stir together the Ro*Tel, green chiles, and broth. Pour the mixture evenly over the chicken. Cover and cook on Low for 6 to 8 hours or on High for 4 to 6 hours. Drain the excess liquid from the slow cooker, leaving a little behind. Shred the chicken, spoon the salsa con queso on top, and stir to combine. Cover and cook on Low for about 20 minutes more, then serve in taco shells or tortillas with the toppings of your choice. *Makes 4 servings.*

SLOW COOKER STEAK WITH GRAVY

Dave Van Horn
Baseball
Second Base, 1981–1982
Graduate Assistant Coach, 1985–1988
Head Coach, 2002–present

Olive oil, for greasing

5 filet mignon steaks

Montreal steak seasoning

1 (1-ounce) packet ranch dressing mix

1 (1-ounce) packet brown gravy mix

½ cup (1 stick) salted butter

1 small onion, chopped

3 tablespoons Worcestershire sauce

2 teaspoons minced garlic

5 peperoncini peppers, plus ¼ cup brine from the jar (if desired)

1 (32-ounce) carton beef stock

2 (10.5-ounce) cans condensed cream of mushroom soup

Mashed potatoes, for serving

Coat a large skillet with oil and heat over high heat. Season the steaks well with Montreal steak seasoning,

then place in the skillet and sear until browned on both sides. Transfer the steaks to a slow cooker. Sprinkle with the ranch mix and brown gravy mix, then place the butter on top. Sprinkle the onion around the edges of the steaks, along with the pep-eroncini peppers, Worcestershire, and garlic. Pour in the peperoncini brine for extra spice, if you like. Pour 3 cups of the stock into the slow cooker, cover, and cook on Low for 8 hours.

Gently remove the steaks from slow cooker and stir in the cream of mushroom soup and remaining 1 cup stock. Return the steaks to the slow cooker and separate the meat into big chunks or shred it. Serve over hot mashed potatoes. *Makes 6 to 8 servings.*

SMOKIN' HOG BABY BACK RIBS

Jay Udwadia
Men's Tennis
Player, 1993–1997
Head Coach, 2022–present

2 racks baby back ribs, membrane removed

Olive oil

Santa Maria seasoning

Wright's Barbecue Meat Rub

Apple cider vinegar or apple juice

Your favorite BBQ sauce (we prefer Traeger Show Me the Honey or Pit Boss Sweet Heat)

Set up a smoker (or grill) and heat to 225°F.

Cover the ribs with a combination of Santa Maria and Wright's BBQ seasoning. Spread a thin layer of olive oil all over the ribs. Fill a 4-ounce spray bottle halfway with vinegar or apple juice, then add water to fill it to the top. Spray the ribs with the vinegar mixture, then place them in the smoker. Cook for 3 hours, flip the ribs and spraying them with the vinegar mixture every 45 minutes. During the last 25 minutes, brush a layer of BBQ sauce over the ribs and increase the heat to 275°F to caramelize the sauce.

◂ Dave Van Horn

Remove the ribs from the smoker and let them sit for 5 to 10 minutes before serving. *Makes 4 to 6 servings.*

A family and friends' favorite! My son, Dash, will even eat them the next day for breakfast.

SMOTHERED PORK STEAK

Mike Anderson
Men's Basketball
Assistant Coach, 1985–2002
Head Coach, 2011–2019

2 pork steaks

Salt and black pepper

3 tablespoons olive oil

1 (10.5-ounce) can Campbell's condensed cream of mushroom soup

½ cup milk

Cooked rice or mashed potatoes, for serving

Preheat the oven to 400°F.

Lightly season the pork steaks with salt and pepper. In a large skillet, heat the olive oil over high heat until the skillet is hot, then reduce the heat to low. Place the pork steaks in the skillet and cook until lightly browned on both sides. Transfer the pork steaks to a medium baking pan.

In the same skillet, warm the mushroom soup and the milk over medium heat. Pour the mushroom soup mixture over the steaks, cover with foil, and place in the oven. Reduce the oven temperature to 350°F and bake for 30 minutes. Serve the pork steaks over rice or mashed potatoes, with the sauce spooned over the top. *Makes 2 servings.*

"Serve this with fresh green beans sautéed in avocado oil or olive oil, adding butter, salt, and pepper to taste, and you will have Coach A's favorite meal. When Coach A has a hard day at the office, this is the meal I prepare for him. It is one of his favorite heartwarming meals to eat." —Marcheita Anderson

SNOW ON THE MOUNTAIN

Mike Kirkland
Football and Baseball
Quarterback, Kicker, and Punter, 1972–1975
Third Base, 1973–1974

1 cup (2 sticks) unsalted butter

1 cup all-purpose flour

6 cups whole milk

2 cups chicken broth

Lawry's seasoned salt

Celery salt

Spice Islands Beau Monde seasoning

Ground white pepper

Dried parsley

4 cups cubed cooked chicken breasts

Cooked white rice, for serving

Optional toppings: chopped tomatoes, chopped onions, toasted almonds, shredded cheddar, chopped black olives, chopped celery, crushed pineapple, chow mein noodles, sweetened shredded coconut

In a large saucepan, melt the butter over medium heat. Whisk in the flour until combined, then whisk in the milk and broth. Cook over medium heat until the sauce has thickened. Season to taste with Lawry's, celery salt, Beau Monde seasoning, white pepper, and parsley, then stir in the chicken and cook until heated through. Serve the sauce and chicken over white rice and let guests sprinkle the toppings of their choice on top of the seasoned creamed chicken. *Makes 6 to 8 servings.*

"We first had this dish when Mike was a rookie for the Baltimore Colts. The offensive-line wives hosted a 'Snow on the Mountain' dinner, and we loved the fun meal. We served it back in Arkansas for many years. The 'snow' on the mountain is the coconut on top! Feel free to add other toppings." —Kerry Kirkland

SOUL FOOD SUPPER

Muskie Harris
Football
Defensive Back, 1973–1977

10 pounds neck bones

Small red potatoes

Small ears of corn

1 bushel mustard greens

1 bushel turnip greens

6 ham hocks

4 pounds sweet potatoes, peeled and cut into fork-size small pieces

Shake-Shake (see Note)

Neutral oil, for greasing

Aunt Jemima self-rising buttermilk cornmeal mix

4 (0.15-ounce) packets Kool-Aid, flavor of your choice

4 cups sugar, for the Kool-Aid

Put the neck bones in a large roaster and add water to the pan touching the neck bones; don't submerge the bones in water. Set the pan on the stovetop over low heat and simmer for 3 hours. Add the potatoes to the pan and continue simmering. Add the corn to pan and simmer some more, until the neck bones are fork-tender, the potatoes are tender, and the corn is ready to eat.

Wash the greens well to remove sand from the leaves. Put the ham hocks in a large pot and add water to cover. Bring to a boil, then start adding the greens until all are in the pot. Let the greens cook until you can smell them.

Preheat the oven to 350°F.

Put the sweet potatoes in a large roasting pan. Add the Shake-Shake and toss to coat. Bake the sweet potatoes for 1½ hours.

Grease a cast-iron skillet with oil to keep the cornbread from sticking. My mother always emphasized to follow the directions on the package, so mix up and bake the cornbread batter just like they say. Never be in a hurry cooking!

Divide the Kool-Aid mix between two large (1-gallon) pitchers, pouring 2 packets into each pitcher. Add 2 cups of sugar to each pitcher. Pour 1 quart of hot water into each pitcher and stir until the sugar and Kool-Aid mix have dissolved. Add 3 quarts cold water to each pitcher and stir until mixed. Refrigerate for 2 hours to cool completely before serving (or serve immediately, over ice).

Serve the neck bones, potatoes, and corn with the greens, cornbread, and glasses of Kool-Aid alongside. *Makes 12 servings.*

NOTE *The ingredients for Shake-Shake are 2 cups sugar, 3 tablespoons ground cinnamon, 3 tablespoons ground nutmeg, and 3 tablespoons ground allspice; stir them all together in a medium bowl before using.*

My parents were waiting for Coach Broyles, Coach Matthews, and Borys Malczycki to arrive for the signing of my letter of intent to the U of A. My mother was so excited that these coaches were coming that she prepared dinner for them. My dad and I were sitting on the porch when they pulled up, and he was so excited, he ran and opened the car door before Coach Matthews could open it. Coach and my dad hugged each other. Borys got out and told my parents Coach Broyles couldn't make it, but that he had sent Coach Matthews to handle the signing. We went into the house. Borys introduced Coach Matthews to my mom. They hugged each other and Mom told them how she had prepared dinner from them. Everyone sat down at the table to eat. The food was ready, Dad said a prayer, and we ate. Coach Matthews told my mom that the meal reminded him of growing up in Atkins, Arkansas. Coach then asked if he came through Little Rock again, would she have dinner available? Mom replied, "Give me a heads-up warning so greens won't be cold, and the neck bones will have an extra bottle of Louisiana hot sauce." Coach Matthews told Mom how he travels with a bottle of Louisiana hot sauce and that this meal was what he grew up on. Then he said, "I want Muskie to bring me a skillet of cornbread, a bucket of greens, and a pan of neck bones when he comes to Fayetteville." Borys and I delivered on May 16, 1973!

SOUTHERN CHICKEN SPAGHETTI

Darren McFadden
Football
Running Back, 2005–2007

1 pound chicken breasts

1 (14-ounce) package frozen bell peppers and onions

Onion powder

Garlic powder

Salt and black pepper

1 pound spaghetti

1 (16-ounce) regular or spicy Velveeta cheese, cubed

1 (10.5-ounce) can condensed cream of chicken or mushroom soup

1 (14.5-ounce) can petite diced tomatoes, undrained

3 cups shredded cheddar cheese

Preheat the oven to 375°F.

Place the chicken and the bell peppers and onions in a large saucepan. Season with onion powder, garlic powder, salt, and pepper, then add water to cover and bring to a boil over medium-high heat. Boil for about 30 minutes, until the chicken is cooked through. Remove the chicken from the water (leave the water boiling) and let cool slightly, then dice the chicken. Add the spaghetti to the boiling water and cook according to the package directions until almost done, a minute or two from al dente. Don't fully cook the noodles because they will cook further in the oven. Drain the water, leaving just enough to cover the spaghetti. Add the Velveeta, cream of chicken soup, and tomatoes and stir well. Stir in the chicken.

Pour the mixture into a casserole dish and sprinkle the cheddar evenly over the top. Bake for about 20 minutes, until the cheese is melted and golden brown. *Makes 6 to 8 servings.*

This Southern chicken spaghetti recipe is from my mom.

SPAGHETTI ALLA CARBONARA

Ron Calcagni
Football
Quarterback, 1975–1978

Salt

14 ounces spaghetti

4 large eggs

¼ cup heavy cream

½ cup grated Parmesan cheese

½ cup grated Pecorino Romano cheese

Black pepper

1 tablespoon unsalted butter

6 ounces pancetta, finely diced

Bring a large pot of lightly salted water to a boil over medium-high heat. Add the pasta and cook according to the package instructions until al dente.

Meanwhile, in a medium bowl, stir together the eggs, cream, Parmesan, and pecorino. Season with salt and pepper; set aside.

In a large pan, melt the butter over medium heat. Add the pancetta and fry until crispy. Drain the spaghetti and add it to the pan while still dripping wet. Pour the cheese mixture over the pasta and remove the pan from the heat. Toss the pasta in the sauce until the sauce begins to thicken but is still creamy. Serve on a warmed plate, sprinkled with more pepper. *Makes 4 to 6 servings.*

SPAGHETTI PIE

Shawn Andrews
Football
Offensive Line, 2001–2003

Nonstick cooking spray

6 ounces uncooked spaghetti

2 tablespoons unsalted butter

1 large egg

¼ cup grated Parmesan cheese

1 (8-ounce) container whipped cream cheese

1 (8-ounce) container sour cream

1 teaspoon Italian seasoning

8 ounces lean ground beef

1 (24-ounce) jar marinara sauce

2 cups shredded mozzarella cheese

Chopped fresh basil, for garnish (optional)

Preheat the oven to 350°F. Coat a 9-inch pie dish with cooking spray.

Cook the spaghetti according to the package directions, then drain and return it to the pot. Add the butter and toss with the spaghetti until melted. Add the egg and Parmesan and stir until combined. Press the spaghetti mixture into the bottom and up the sides of the prepared pie dish.

In a medium bowl, stir together the cream cheese, sour cream, and Italian seasoning. Spread the mixture on top of the pasta.

In a medium skillet, brown the ground beef over medium-high heat, breaking it up as it cooks. Stir in the marinara sauce. Spread the meat mixture on top of the cream cheese mixture, then top evenly with the mozzarella.

Bake for 20 to 25 minutes, until golden and bubbling. Serve garnished with basil, if desired. *Makes 6 servings.*

SPAGHETTI SECRET SAUCE

Lindsey Davis
Women's Swimming & Diving
1m and 3m, 1975–1979

4 tablespoons (½ stick) unsalted butter

¼ cup grease drippings

1 to 1½ large onions, finely chopped

Celery flakes

1 pound ground beef

4 chicken livers, or 2 gizzards, finely ground

2 (6-ounce) cans tomato paste

4 (15-ounce) cans tomato puree

3 garlic cloves, minced, or ¾ teaspoon garlic powder

Salt and black pepper

Cooked spaghetti, for serving

In a large heavy skillet, melt the butter and the drippings over medium heat. Add the onions and cook for a few minutes, until beginning to soften. Don't let them get too brown. Add the ground beef and chicken livers and cook slowly over low heat until the meat is browned and thoroughly cooked through. Add some celery flakes. Add the tomato paste, then fill the empty cans with water and add that as well; add a third can's worth of water to further thin the tomato paste. Add the tomato puree and stir well. Add the garlic, season with salt and pepper, and stir to combine. Cook for at least 1 hour to allow the flavors to blend. The longer it cooks, the better the flavor. Serve the sauce over spaghetti. *Makes 10 to 12 servings.*

NOTES *You can use dehydrated onions flakes that have been thoroughly soaked in water. Do not add dehydrated onions until after browning meat.*

This sauce is even better if made in the morning and cooked in a covered slow cooker on Low all day.

In 1975, I was a diver at the University of Arkansas. Fedosky was the swim coach at the time, and we really did not have a diving coach! My high school diving coach was Mike Bailey. I was a graduate of Little Rock Hall High with Super Sidney Moncrief! In 1980, I was slated to compete in the Olympics when Jimmy Carter and the US boycotted the Moscow Olympics. I live in Tontitown now and help every year with our church Grape Festival! My favorite recipe is the spaghetti dinner from the Grape Festival.

SPAGHETTI WITH CHICKEN SAUSAGE

Steve Conley
Football
Outside Linebacker and Defensive End, 1992–1995

8 ounces uncooked spaghetti

2 tablespoons olive oil

2 garlic cloves, minced

1 small onion, diced

4 chicken sausages, sliced

1 (14.5-ounce) can diced tomatoes, with their juices

1 (24-ounce) jar spaghetti sauce, such as Rao's or Bertolli

Salt and black pepper

Fresh basil leaves, for garnish (optional)

Grated Parmesan cheese, for serving (optional)

Cook the spaghetti according to the package directions until al dente. Drain and set aside.

In a large skillet, heat the olive oil over medium heat. Add the garlic and onion and cook, stirring, until the onion is translucent. Add sausage to the skillet and cook until browned. Pour in the tomatoes with their juices and the spaghetti sauce. Stir to combine. Season with salt and pepper. Simmer the sauce for 5 to 7 minutes. Add the cooked spaghetti to the skillet and toss until evenly coated with the sauce. Serve hot, garnished with basil and Parmesan, if desired. *Makes 2 servings.*

STEAK AND RICE

Matt Jones
Football and Basketball
Quarterback, 2001–2004
Forward, 2001, 2003

1½ tablespoons vegetable oil

1½ pounds boneless beef round steak, tenderized with a meat mallet and cut into thin strips

2 large onions, cut in ½-inch-thick slices and slices separated

1 (10¾-ounce) can condensed cream of mushroom soup

½ cup dry sherry

1½ teaspoons garlic salt or garlic powder

1 (4-ounce) sliced mushrooms, drained, liquid reserved

3 cups hot cooked rice, for serving

In a large skillet (ovenproof, if desired), heat the vegetable oil over high heat. Add the steak strips and cook until browned. Add the onions and cook, stirring, until tender-crisp.

In a medium bowl, stir together the cream of mushroom soup, sherry, garlic salt, and the liquid from the can of mushrooms. Pour the mixture over the steak, then add the mushrooms. Reduce the heat to low, cover, and simmer for 1 hour, or until the steak is tender. (Alternatively, cover with foil and bake at 350°F for 45 minutes to 1 hour, until tender.) Serve over a bed of fluffy rice. *Makes 4 servings.*

"This is a favorite recipe from Matt's grandmother Lorene Watie." —Paula Jones

STIR-FRIED CHICKEN AND STEAMED BROCCOLI

Steve Korte
Football
Defensive Lineman and Right Guard, 1978–1982

3 tablespoons olive oil

¼ cup teriyaki sauce

3 large boneless, skinless chicken breasts, cut into long, thin pieces

Steamed fresh broccoli florets or green beans, for serving

In a large saucepan or wok, heat the olive oil and teriyaki sauce over medium-high heat. Stir the sauce and add the chicken. Cook, stirring, until the chicken is fully cooked through, 7 to 9 minutes on each side. Serve with steamed broccoli (or green beans, if you are broccoli shy). *Makes 2 to 3 servings.*

SUN-DRIED TOMATO SAUCE

John Calipari
Men's Basketball
Head Coach, 2024–present

2 tablespoons unsalted butter

2 garlic cloves, peeled, minced

½ cup dry-pack sun-dried tomatoes

1 cup chicken broth

1 cup heavy cream

1 pound uncooked pasta

Salt and black pepper

Fresh parsley

Fresh basil

In a large skillet, melt the butter over low heat. Add the garlic and cook, stirring occasionally, for about 2 minutes. Add the sun-dried tomatoes and broth. Raise the heat to medium-high and bring to a boil, then reduce the heat to maintain a simmer and cook, uncovered, for 10 minutes. Remove the tomatoes with a slotted spoon, chop them, and return them to skillet. (This can all be done early in the day. Let the mixture cool, then cover and refrigerate until ready to use; reheat before continuing.)

Stir in the cream. Bring to a boil over medium-high heat, then reduce the heat to maintain a simmer and cook until slightly thickened, about 20 minutes.

Meanwhile, cook the pasta according to the package directions, then drain.

Taste the sauce and season with salt and pepper. Pour the sauce over the pasta and mix well. Sprinkle parsley and basil on top and serve. *Makes 4 servings.*

"A favorite recipe we got from a neighbor when we lived in New Jersey." —Ellen Calipari

SWEETIE ROASTED RED PEPPER PIZZA

April Steiner Bennett
Women's Track & Field / Cross Country
Pole Vault, 2000–2003

2 naan flatbreads or other flatbreads

¼ cup olive oil

½ cup marinara sauce

2 ounces roasted red peppers, coarsely chopped

1 teaspoon Italian seasoning

1 cup shredded cooked chicken or ham (optional)

2 ounces crumbled feta cheese

2 or 3 slices Fontina cheese, broken into small pieces

2 ounces shredded mozzarella cheese

½ red bell pepper, chopped

½ red onion, chopped

½ teaspoon red pepper flakes, plus more if needed

2 tablespoons honey

Preheat the oven to 400°F.

Brush the flatbreads with the olive oil and place on a baking sheet. Bake for 3 to 5 minutes—do not bake them too long, unless you like them crispy! Carefully transfer the flatbreads to a cutting board or plate; keep the oven on. Top each flatbread with the marinara, roasted red peppers, and Italian seasoning, and chicken (if using), dividing them evenly. Then top evenly with the feta, Fontina, and mozzarella, followed by the bell pepper, onion, and red pepper flakes. Return the flatbreads to the baking sheet and bake for 5 to 8 minutes, until the cheese has melted. Remove from the oven, drizzle honey lightly all over, and add more red pepper flakes if you like it spicy. Enjoy! *Makes 2 servings.*

My memories of my time as an athlete at U of A are flooded with learning and experiencing Southern hospitality, the kindness and respect always given in conversation but paired with the fire and the competitiveness of the SEC! The track and field fans are incredible, and the love of the Razorbacks is deep-seated. Coming from Arizona, I had to look at a map to know exactly where in the middle of the country Arkansas was. I found myself in an exciting culture shock, with the green trees, the loud buzzing of the trees from spring through fall, the llama farm on the way to Northwest Arkansas National Airport, and the size of the rivers around the state. It was incredible to feel so welcome in a place so different from where I grew up, and the university was majestic to me. There is an unmatched energy on Dickson Street, and the nostalgia that fills me when walking among Old Main's beautiful trees is unexplainable. To me, Coach Bryan Compton is the most memorable thing about U of A. And without him, and his belief and commitment to me and our goals, I would never have reached my dreams. I had no idea what I was about to experience and be opened to. The University of Arkansas awakened a section of my heart. I learned new ways to work hard, to be disciplined and respectful, and to lead with excitement, fire, and spice but have kindness and grace at the core.

TACO POTATO CASSEROLE

Ron Brewer Sr.
Men's Basketball
Guard, 1975–1978

1 pound ground beef

2 pounds hash brown potatoes

1 yellow onion, chopped

1 (10.5-ounce) can cheddar cheese soup

1 (10-ounce) can Ro*Tel diced tomatoes and green chiles, undrained

2 cups shredded Colby Jack cheese

2 cups shredded sharp cheddar cheese

½ cup sour cream

1 (1-ounce) packet taco seasoning

1 teaspoon Kinder's The Blend seasoning

1 teaspoon garlic powder

In a large skillet, brown the ground beef over medium-high heat. Drain the fat, then transfer the beef to a slow cooker and add the hash browns, onion, cheddar soup, Ro*Tel, Colby Jack, cheddar, sour cream, taco seasoning, Kinder's seasoning, and garlic. Stir to combine, then cover and cook on High for 2 hours. *Makes 5 to 7 servings.*

My mom would cook this taco potato casserole for us as kids. This was my go-to when we would have friends over to our apartment because it was easy—and it was all I knew how to cook. So every time we had a get-together with our teammates, everyone knew that I was going to bring this dish. I brought it to our get-togethers for three years!

TAYLOR'S LASAGNA

Tony Bua
Football
Linebacker, 2000–2003

2 pounds ground beef

2 pounds bulk mild Italian sausage

1 large white onion, chopped

2 garlic cloves, minced

3 (15-ounce) cans tomato sauce

2 (14-ounce) cans diced tomatoes with basil and oregano, undrained

1 (6-ounce) can tomato paste

1 tablespoon Worcestershire sauce, or to taste

2 teaspoons dried oregano

2 teaspoons dried basil

½ teaspoon garlic salt, or to taste

½ teaspoon garlic powder, or to taste

½ teaspoon onion powder, or to taste

½ teaspoon salt

½ teaspoon black pepper

1 (16-ounce) box lasagna noodles (not no-boil)

3 cups cottage cheese

10 ounces grated Parmesan cheese

¼ cup fresh parsley, chopped

4 large eggs

1 (16-ounce) block mozzarella cheese, shredded

Preheat the oven to 350°F.

In a large pot, combine the beef, sausage, onion, and garlic and cook over medium heat until the meat is browned. Drain the fat, then return the mixture to the pot and add the tomato sauce, diced tomatoes, tomato paste, Worcestershire, oregano, basil, garlic salt, garlic powder, onion powder, salt, and pepper. Stir to combine. Bring to a boil over medium heat, then reduce the heat to maintain a simmer and cook for 30 to 45 minutes, until the sauce slightly thickens and the flavors blend.

Meanwhile, cook the noodles according to the package directions, then drain.

In a medium bowl, stir together the cottage cheese, Parmesan, parsley, and eggs until combined.

Spread a layer of the sauce over the bottom of a 9 by 13-inch baking dish and top with a layer of 3 noodles. Spread half the cottage cheese mixture over the noodles, top with a third of the mozzarella, then repeat layers again. Top with a final layer of noodles, then the remaining sauce, and sprinkle with the rest of the mozzarella. Bake for 45 minutes, or until bubbling. *Makes 12 servings.*

Some of my most favorite memories as a Razorback are the team dinners the night before the game. For two years, I couldn't wait to be a senior because senior tables got called first to make their plates. The first four games of the season, I was able to have the server cut off the burnt ends of the brisket. Coach Nutt always got his plate after the seniors, but after those four games, he finally asked, "Who keeps taking all the burnt ends?" Everybody pointed at me, and Coach Nutt said, "That figures!" For the rest of the season, he went first. The conversations and camaraderie of eating together with the team are some of my best memories as a Razorback.

TERIYAKI CHICKEN

Kevin Kopps
Baseball
Pitcher, 2017–2021

1 cup ketchup

½ cup packed light brown sugar

½ cup soy sauce

¼ cup vegetable oil

¼ cup cooking sherry

6 large boneless, skinless chicken breasts

In a small bowl, stir together the ketchup, brown sugar, soy sauce, oil, and sherry. Place the chicken in a shallow dish and pour over the marinade. Let marinate for 30 minutes or more. Discard the marinade and cook the chicken in a skillet or on the grill, however you prefer, until the chicken is fully cooked through and the internal temperature reaches 165°F, 16 to 18 minutes. *Makes 6 servings.*

I was on a meal plan for a lot of my U of A career. My father cooked this chicken all the time back at home, and he would even send pounds of it back with me whenever I left for school so I would be able to have it. It's a recipe I could eat every day, and it never gets old.

TERIYAKI TOFU WITH THAI NOODLES

Ron Hightower
Men's Tennis
Player, 1976–1980

1 (14-ounce) package firm tofu, drained and cubed

Teriyaki sauce

2 tablespoons vegetable broth, plus more if needed

1 (16-ounce) bag frozen stir-fry vegetables or fresh vegetables

2 (7-ounce) packages precooked Thai wheat noodles

Soy sauce

Sriracha sauce

Place the tofu in a medium bowl and pour over teriyaki sauce to cover. Set aside to marinate for 30 minutes.

In a large skillet, heat the broth over medium-high heat until warmed, about 5 minutes. Add the stir-fry vegetables (see Note) and cook, stirring, for about 6 minutes. Add the marinated tofu and teriyaki sauce to taste and stir to combine. Cook for 5 minutes, then add the noodles and cook until heated through, about 5 minutes more. Stir in soy sauce and sriracha to your preference. *Makes 4 servings.*

NOTE *When adding the stir-fry vegetables, you can also add minced garlic, chopped onion, or anything you like.*

This is my favorite oil-free meatless meal. Enjoy!

TIM LOLLAR'S FAVORITE SPAGHETTI CARBONARA

Tim Lollar
Baseball
Pitcher, 1976–1978

5 hot or mild Italian sausage links

1 (10-ounce) package sliced cooked ham, cubed

3 large eggs, beaten

1 (16-ounce) package spaghetti

1 (10-ounce) package frozen peas

1 cup grated Monterey Jack cheese

¾ cup grated Parmesan cheese

¾ cup (1½ sticks) margarine

3 tablespoons fresh parsley or parsley flakes

In a large deep saucepan, melt 4 tablespoons (½ stick) of the margarine over medium heat. Add the sausage and ham and cook until heated through, about 10 minutes.

Meanwhile, cook the spaghetti according to the package directions. Cook the peas according to the package directions as well.

In a small bowl, combine the Monterey Jack and Parmesan.

In a small skillet, melt the remaining ½ cup (1 stick) margarine with the parsley over medium heat.

Drain the spaghetti and add it to the pan with the sausage and ham; mix well. Add the melted margarine and mix well. Immediately add the eggs and quickly lift the spaghetti with tongs to coat it well with the eggs. Add the peas, then sprinkle half the cheese mixture over the top and mix. Add the remaining cheese to the spaghetti, toss, and serve. *Makes 4 to 6 servings.*

TOM'S PORK BUTT

Tom Pagnozzi
Baseball
Catcher, 1982–1983

8 to 10 pounds pork butt

¼ cup apple juice

¼ cup BBQ sauce (Tom's favorite is Head Country Apple Habanero)

¼ cup Tony Chachere's Creole-style injectable butter

BBQ seasoning (Tom's favorite is Head Country Apple Habanero)

In a small bowl, mix the apple juice, BBQ sauce, and Creole butter. Inject the mixture into the pork butt in five places in front and five places in back for even distribution. You should have enough mixture to evenly inject all ten places. Season the top, bottom, sides, and ends of the pork butt with BBQ seasoning. Place the pork in a foil pan, cover, and refrigerate overnight.

The next day, set up a smoker and heat to 250°F.

Place the pork in the smoker fat-side up and smoke until the internal temperature reaches 165°F, 3 to 4 hours. Remove the pork and wrap it in foil, then return it to the smoker and smoke until the internal temperature

Kevin Kopps ▸

reaches 205°F, 2 to 3 hours more. Transfer the foil-wrapped pork to a cooler, cover with the lid, and let rest for 2 to 3 hours before serving. *Makes 16 to 20 servings.*

This is a staple of our cooking team, which consists of myself, Blake Ketchum, and Kelly Sharp. We use these for tailgating at football and baseball games, as well as at friends' weddings and parties. When we cook our butts, we are usually cooking thirty-six to seventy-two at a time. The only difference in what we do and the above recipe is that we keep the butts in the cooler for 10 to 12 hours. When we open them 10 to 12 hours later, the butts still have an internal temperature between 170° and 180°F. We then pull off the fat, remove the bone, and pull the meat apart using gloved hands.

TURKEY SPINACH ENCHILADAS

Dwight Stewart
Men's Basketball
Center, 1993–1995

1 pound ground turkey

¼ cup chopped onion

4 garlic cloves, minced

2 cups picante sauce

1 (10-ounce) package chopped frozen spinach

1 (4-ounce) can diced green chiles

2 teaspoons ground cumin

½ teaspoon salt

½ teaspoon black pepper

1 (8-ounce) package cream cheese

1 (14.5-ounce) can diced tomatoes, with their juices

12 flour tortillas, warmed

1 cup shredded cheddar cheese

1 (4-ounce) can black olives, drained (optional)

Preheat the oven to 350°F.

In a large skillet, combine the ground turkey, onion, and garlic and cook over medium heat until the meat is browned. Drain the fat, then add 1 cup of the picante sauce, the spinach, and the chiles and bring to a simmer. Stir in 1 teaspoon of the cumin, the salt, and the pepper. Add the cream cheese and stir until melted and combined.

In a medium bowl, stir together the diced tomatoes, remaining 1 cup picante sauce, and remaining 1 teaspoon cumin and set aside.

Spoon about 2 tablespoons of the turkey filling into each tortilla. Roll up the tortillas to enclose the filling and place them seam-side down in a 9 by 13-inch baking pan. Pour the tomato mixture over the top. Bake for 20 minutes. Sprinkle the cheddar on top and bake for 5 minutes more, until the cheese has melted. Sprinkle with the olives before serving, if desired. *Makes 6 servings.*

UNSTUFFED PEPPERS

Brooke Schultz
Women's Swimming & Diving
1m and 3m springboard, 2017–2021

3 tablespoons olive oil

4 bell peppers (red, yellow, or orange), diced

¼ cup chopped onion

2 garlic cloves, minced, or 1 teaspoon garlic powder

4 kale leaves, leaves stemmed and finely chopped

1 pound ground turkey or ground meat of choice

2 tablespoons tomato paste

½ teaspoon salt

¼ teaspoon ground cumin

¼ teaspoon chili powder

¼ teaspoon black pepper

1 cup frozen butternut squash or finely chopped peeled fresh squash

In a large skillet, heat the olive oil over medium heat. Add the bell peppers and cook, stirring, until tender, about 10 minutes, then remove from the pan and set aside. Add the onion to the skillet and cook, stirring, until translucent. Add the garlic and cook until fragrant, about 1 minute. Add the kale and cook, stirring, for 1 minute. Add the ground turkey and cook for 10 to 15 minutes, breaking up the meat with a spatula and stirring it into the vegetables as it cooks. Stir in the tomato paste, salt, cumin, chili powder, and black pepper. Stir in the squash and cook until softened, 15 to 20 minutes. Return the bell pepper to the pan and stir to combine, then cook just until all the ingredients are heated through. Serve hot in individual bowls. *Makes 4 servings.*

A few times during my freshman year, the entire dive team would get together and cook. This recipe is based on a stuffed pepper recipe sent to one of my teammates by her mom. She found it in a magazine and snapped a photo. I keep the original photo in my Favorites folder on my phone and go back to it often. I changed it up to make it with the exact ingredients I prefer and so it's easier to make and eat as a one-pan, one-bowl meal.

ZAC PAINTER'S CHICKEN SPAGHETTI

Zac Painter
Football
Defensive Back, 1995–1998

1 (16-ounce) package dried spaghetti

1 (10.5-ounce) can condensed cream of chicken soup

1 (10.5-ounce) can condensed cream of mushroom soup

1 (15-ounce) can peas, drained

1 (15-ounce) can corn kernels, drained

White meat from 1 rotisserie chicken, picked from the bones

1 (10-ounce) can Ro*Tel diced tomatoes and green chiles, undrained

1 (8-ounce) block Velveeta, cubed

Preheat the oven to 350°F.

Cook the spaghetti according to the package directions, then drain.

In a large bowl, stir together the cream of chicken soup, cream of mushroom soup, peas, corn, chicken, and spaghetti; set aside.

In a medium glass bowl, combine the Ro*Tel and Velveeta and microwave on high for 30 seconds, then stir and continue microwaving in 30-second intervals until melted and well combined. Add the cheese sauce to the bowl with the spaghetti mixture and mix well. Transfer to a large baking dish and cover with foil. Bake for 25 minutes, then uncover and cook for 5 minutes more to crisp the top. *Makes 8 servings.*

My favorite dish! Bon appétit!

ZIPLOCK SHRIMP

Mike Neighbors
Women's Basketball
Director of Operations, 1999
Assistant Coach, 2006
Head Coach, 2017–2025

1 pound raw shrimp (the bigger the better), peeled and deveined

2 tablespoons olive oil

SEASONINGS (SEE NOTE)

½ teaspoon paprika

½ teaspoon chili powder

½ teaspoon salt

½ teaspoon black pepper

½ teaspoon onion powder

½ teaspoon ground mustard

½ teaspoon dried basil

½ teaspoon dried oregano

½ teaspoon dried sage

½ teaspoon dried tarragon

½ teaspoon dried dill

½ teaspoon dried chives

½ teaspoon dried parsley

½ teaspoon dried chervil

½ teaspoon dried lemon peel

Place the shrimp in a bowl, add the olive oil, and stir to coat the shrimp. Cover and refrigerate for about 1 hour.

Combine the seasonings in a large zip-top bag. Add the shrimp to the bag, seal, and shake to coat.

Heat a griddle or cast-iron skillet over the highest heat you can achieve (or heat a grill to high). Arrange the shrimp on the griddle in a single layer and season the top with half the spices left in the bag. Cook until pink to orange on the bottom, then flip and season the cooked side with the remaining spices from the bag. Cook until lightly crispy on the second side to ensure shellfish-cooking success! Serve hot or warm. *Makes 2 to 4 servings.*

NOTE *If you prefer, use a mix of paprika, chili powder, and Morton Season-All seasoning mix instead of all fifteen seasonings listed.*

Big key here is flipping the shrimp only once. Perfect over a bed of rice but good on their own as well! I feel like we secured multiple commitments from prospects with this dish over the years!!

DESSERTS

ALMOND BARK

Courtney Deifel
Softball
Head Coach, 2015–present

1 pound (4 sticks) unsalted butter, plus more for greasing

2 cups sugar

3 cups sliced almonds, plus chopped almonds for topping

2 cups chocolate chips or chopped bar chocolate

Grease a 13 by 18-inch baking sheet with butter.

In a large saucepan, melt the butter over medium heat. Clip a candy thermometer to the side, then slowly stir in the sugar. Cook, stirring continuously, until the mixture reaches 315°F. Stir in the sliced almonds, then immediately pour the mixture onto the prepared baking sheet and use a silicone spatula to quickly spread it to the edges of the pan. Sprinkle the chocolate over the top and let it begin to melt, then spread it evenly over the sliced almond mixture. Top with chopped almonds. Let cool and harden. Break into pieces to serve. *Makes 2½ pounds toffee.*

APPLE CRISP

James McCann
Baseball
Catcher, 2009–2011

9 tablespoons unsalted butter, at room temperature, plus more for greasing

5 or 6 Granny Smith apples, peeled and sliced

1½ cups sugar

1½ cups all-purpose flour

3 tablespoons ground cinnamon

Preheat the oven to 350°F. Grease an 8-inch square baking pan with butter.

Arrange the apple slices over the bottom of the prepared pan. Sprinkle ½ cup hot water over the apples.

In a small bowl, stir together the sugar, flour, butter, and cinnamon to combine. Crumble the sugar mixture over the apples. Bake for 40 minutes, or until the apples are tender. *Makes 6 servings.*

AUNT EGIE'S PEANUT BRITTLE

Bo Busby
Football
Safety, 1973–1976

1 tablespoon unsalted butter, plus more for greasing

4 cups sugar

1 cup light corn syrup

4 cups raw peanuts

2 teaspoons baking soda

Grease two large sheet cake pans with butter.

In a large heavy saucepan, stir together the sugar, corn syrup, and 2 cups water. Clip a candy thermometer to the side of the pot and heat over medium heat, stirring, until the sugar has dissolved, then cook, without stirring, until the syrup reaches the soft-ball stage (234° to 240°F on the candy thermometer). Add the peanuts and mix well to combine. Cook, stirring occasionally, until the syrup turns a golden color and the peanuts have a parched smell. Remove from the heat, add the butter and baking soda, and stir until well combined (the mixture will foam). Divide the mixture evenly between the prepared pans and use a silicone spatula to spread it into a thin, even layer. Let cool and harden. Break up the brittle into pieces to serve. Store in an airtight container at room temperature for 4 to 6 weeks. *Makes 16 to 20 servings.*

"When Bo was one of the owners of Prairie Wings duck club, several of the coaches came to hunt, including Coaches Horton, Hatfield, DeBriyn, and Van Horn. Aunt Egie cooked for a few years at the camp, and her peanut brittle was a favorite with the

Courtney Deifel

coaches. One of her favorite memories was seeing Coach Horton asleep in the recliner with a piece of peanut brittle still in his hand!" —Nena Busby

BANANA BREAD CHOCOLATE CHIP COOKIES

David Walling
Baseball
Pitcher, 1998–1999

½ cup (1 stick) unsalted butter, at room temperature

½ cup packed light brown sugar

¼ cup granulated sugar

1 small ripe banana, mashed

1 teaspoon ground cinnamon

½ teaspoon vanilla extract

1 cup plus 1⅓ tablespoons all-purpose flour

⅔ cup rolled oats

½ teaspoon baking powder

½ teaspoon baking soda

½ teaspoon salt

¾ cup semisweet chocolate discs or chips or chopped bar chocolate

Preheat the oven to 350°F. Line a baking sheet with parchment paper.

In a large bowl, combine the butter, brown sugar, granulated sugar, banana, cinnamon, and vanilla and beat with a handheld mixer to combine.

In a separate medium bowl, stir together the flour, rolled oats, baking powder, baking soda, and salt. Add the flour mixture to the butter mixture and mix by hand to combine, then fold in the chocolate. Place the bowl in the freezer for 30 minutes to chill the dough.

Roll 2-tablespoon portions of the chilled cookie dough into balls and place them on the prepared baking sheet, spacing them 2 inches apart. Bake for 10 minutes, then remove from the oven and let cool on the pan for 5 minutes before transferring to a wire rack to cool completely. *Makes 24 cookies.*

NOTE *Best made with very ripe bananas for sweeter cookies. Feel free to add extra chocolate chips!*

BANANA PUDDING

Hagen Smith

Baseball

Pitcher, 2022–2024

1 (14-ounce) can sweetened condensed milk

1 (3.4-ounce) box instant vanilla pudding mix

3 cups good-quality heavy cream

4 to 5 cups sliced slightly underripe bananas (about 5 large)

1 (12-ounce) box Nilla wafers

In the bowl of a stand mixer fitted with the whisk attachment, or in a large bowl using a whisk, whisk together the condensed milk and 1½ cups cold water until combined. Add the pudding mix and beat until the mixture is smooth and all the pudding mix has dissolved. Cover and refrigerate the pudding for 3 to 4 hours, until set. (The pudding can be refrigerated for up to 2 days before use.)

In a large bowl, whip the cream with a handheld mixer, starting on low speed and gradually increasing to high, until it holds stiff peaks, 3 to 4 minutes. Using a spatula, fold the whipped cream into the pudding until no streaks of pudding remain. (Don't beat them together with a mixer! Just gently fold them together so the whipped cream doesn't deflate.)

To assemble, spoon a little less than half the pudding into the bottom of a serving bowl, then layer half the banana slices on top, followed by a layer of Nilla wafers. Repeat these layers again, ending with a little of the pudding on top. Cover and refrigerate for 4 to 8 hours before serving. *Makes 10 to 12 servings.*

NOTE *Plan ahead! The vanilla pudding needs a full 3 to 4 hours to set properly, and the assembled dessert will need another 4 to 8 hours to chill before serving.*

BANANA PUDDING PIE

Dave Van Horn

Baseball

Second Base, 1981–1982

Graduate Assistant Coach, 1985–1988

Head Coach, 2002–present

1 (14-ounce) can sweetened condensed milk

1¾ cups whole milk

1 (8-ounce) container whipped topping, thawed (see Note)

2 Keebler shortbread piecrusts

4 large bananas, thickly sliced

1 (5.1-ounce) package instant vanilla pudding mix

1 (11-ounce) box mini Nilla wafers

In a large bowl, combine the condensed milk and the whole milk. Add the pudding mix and beat well to combine. Place the bowl in the freezer for 10 minutes to chill the pudding, then fold in the whipped topping.

Divide the banana slices evenly between the piecrusts, arranging them flat in a layer over the bottom of the crusts. Pour the pudding mixture over the bananas, filling the piecrusts. Decorate the top of the filling with mini vanilla wafers. Place the pies in the refrigerator to set for 6 to 8 hours or up to overnight before serving. *Makes 2 pies.*

NOTE *Thaw the whipped topping in the refrigerator for 4 to 6 hours.*

Growing up in Kansas City, I always wanted to be a Razorback. I was fortunate to play and coach under my mentor, Coach Norm DeBriyn. In 2002, Frank Broyles gave me the opportunity to come back and coach at my alma mater, the one place I always wanted to coach. I have many fond memories of playing, coaching as a graduate assistant, and coming back as head coach. My relationships with all the players and coaches have been a blessing to me. What an honor to be able to play and coach at the University of Arkansas.

BANANA SPLIT SURPRISE

Ravin Caldwell Jr.

Football

Linebacker, 1982–1985

2 cups graham cracker crumbs

½ cup granulated sugar

½ cup (1 stick) unsalted butter, at room temperature or melted

3 cups milk

2 (5.1-ounce) boxes instant vanilla pudding mix (see Note)

½ cup powdered sugar

8 to 10 ripe bananas, sliced

1 (8-ounce) can crushed pineapple, drained (optional)

Chopped pecans (optional)

1 (11-ounce) box vanilla wafers or chessman cookies

2 (16-ounce) tubs Cool Whip, thawed for 30 minutes

Maraschino cherries

In a medium bowl, stir together the graham cracker crumbs, granulated sugar, and butter until well combined. Scrape the crumb mixture into a 9 by 13-inch baking pan and use a fork to press it into an even layer over the bottom of the pan.

In a large bowl, stir together the milk, pudding, and powdered sugar. Mix well until it thickens. Pour the pudding over the graham cracker crust. Arrange the bananas over the pudding. Spread the pineapple (if using) over the bananas. Sprinkle with pecans (if using). Layer the vanilla wafers over the pecans, then spread the Cool Whip over the wafers. Top the Cool Whip with cherries and additional pecans (if using). Place in the refrigerator to keep it cold until ready to serve. *Makes 10 to 12 servings.*

NOTE *You can substitute banana pudding or cheesecake pudding (or mix one box of each) for the vanilla.*

BEV'S CHRISTMAS FUDGE

Bev Lewis

Head Coach, Women's Track and Cross Country, 1981–1989

Director of Women's Athletics, 1989–2008

Associate Vice Chancellor and Executive Associate Athletic Director, 2009–2014

1 cup cubed Velveeta cheese

1 cup (2 sticks) salted butter, cut into small pieces

½ cup Hershey's unsweetened cocoa powder

¾ teaspoon pure vanilla extract

2 pounds powdered sugar

1 cup chopped nuts (optional)

In a large skillet, melt the butter over low heat; do not let it get so hot that it boils. Add the Velveeta and cook, stirring as it melts, until the mixture is smooth and well combined. Stir in the cocoa powder. Add the powdered sugar (and nuts, if desired) and mix well. Transfer the mixture to a serving dish and spread it evenly. Score the top of the fudge with a knife into 48 squares (this will make it easier to cut later) and refrigerate for several hours before slicing along the scored lines and serving. *Makes 48 pieces.*

BLACKBERRY COBBLER LITE

Jim Counce
Men's Basketball
Forward, 1974–1978

3 tablespoons unsalted butter, plus more for greasing

3 to 4 cups fresh blackberries

1 large egg

⅔ cup sugar

1 Pillsbury refrigerated piecrust

Lightly grease a 9-inch glass pie plate with butter. Place the blackberries in the prepared pie plate and dot with 1 tablespoon of the butter. Beat the egg and ⅓ cup of the sugar together. Pour the sugar-egg mixture evenly over the berries.

Unroll the piecrust and lay it over the berry mixture in the pie plate. Crimp the edges as desired. Cut the remaining 2 tablespoons butter into small pieces and dot them over the top of the crust. Sprinkle the remaining ⅓ cup sugar over the crust. Cut air vents in the top. Bake until the filling is bubbling and the crust is crust golden brown, about 45 minutes, depending on how cold the berries are and how brown and crispy you like it. *Makes 6 to 8 servings.*

This recipe has been revised many times, reducing the sugar and butter to make a very light cobbler. Best served with a scoop of your favorite vanilla bean ice cream.

BROOKE'S CHOCOLATE PUDDING CAKE

Brooke Matthews
Women's Golf
Golfer, 2017–2021

Nonstick baking spray

1 (15.25-ounce) box Duncan Hines yellow cake mix

¾ cup vegetable oil

3 large eggs

1 teaspoon vanilla extract

1 (3.4-ounce) box instant chocolate pudding mix

8 ounces sour cream

6 ounces chocolate chips, or more as desired

Preheat the oven to 350°F. Grease a 10-inch Bundt pan with baking spray.

In a large bowl, combine the cake mix, oil, eggs, vanilla, pudding mix, sour cream, and ¾ cup water and beat with a handheld mixer on medium speed for 3 minutes. Add the chocolate chips and mix just to incorporate. Pour the batter into the prepared Bundt pan. Bake for 45 minutes to 1 hour, until a toothpick inserted into the center comes out clean. Remove from oven and let cool for 10 minutes, then invert onto a serving platter and continue to cool. *Makes 12 servings.*

BRUCE MAXWELL'S FAVORITE COCONUT PIE

Bruce Maxwell
Football
Fullback, 1966–1969

PIE

1 piecrust

½ cup all-purpose flour

3 large egg yolks, beaten

2½ cups milk

1½ cups sugar

2 cups sweetened shredded coconut

⅔ stick margarine

1 teaspoon vanilla extract

MERINGUE

3 large egg whites

¼ teaspoon cream of tartar

1 teaspoon vanilla extract

6 tablespoons sugar

¼ cup sweetened shredded coconut, for topping

Preheat the oven to 350°F.

Prebake the piecrust and let cool.

In a medium saucepan, combine the flour and ½ cup water to make a paste. Add the egg yolks and beat well. Add the milk and sugar, set the pan over low heat, and cook, stirring continuously, until thickened. Remove from the heat and add the coconut, margarine, and vanilla. Pour the mixture into the piecrust.

Make the meringue: In a large bowl, beat the egg whites, cream of tartar, and vanilla with a handheld mixer on medium speed until frothy, then increase the speed to medium-high and beat until they hold soft peaks. With the mixer running, gradually add the sugar, then beat until the egg whites are glossy and hold stiff peaks.

Top the pie with the meringue and sprinkle with the coconut. Bake for 10 minutes, or until the meringue is golden brown. *Makes 6 to 8 servings.*

This is one of my favorite things my wife cooks for me. I'm sure you'll enjoy it, too.

BUTTERMILK PIE

Bill Montgomery
Football, Baseball, and Men's Golf
Quarterback, 1968–1970
Golfer, 1971
First Base, 1975–1976

1 refrigerated piecrust

2 cups sugar

1 cup buttermilk

½ cup (1 stick) unsalted butter, melted

3 large eggs

3 tablespoons all-purpose flour

¼ teaspoon salt

1 teaspoon vanilla extract

Preheat the oven to 350°F.

Unroll the piecrust and place it in your favorite pie pan.

In a large bowl, combine the sugar, buttermilk, melted butter, eggs, flour, salt, and vanilla and beat with a handheld mixer on medium speed until smooth. Pour the mixture into the piecrust and bake for 30 to 40 minutes, until a knife inserted into the center comes out clean. Let cool for 5 minutes before serving. *Makes 6 to 8 servings.*

CARAMEL LAYER CHOCO-SQUARES

Courtney Deifel
Softball
Head Coach, 2015–present

½ cup (1 stick) unsalted butter or margarine, at room temperature, plus more for greasing

All-purpose flour, for dusting

1 (14-ounce) package light caramels (about 50)

⅓ cup evaporated milk

1 (13.25-ounce) box chocolate cake mix

1 (6-ounce) package semisweet chocolate pieces

1 cup chopped nuts (optional)

Preheat the oven to 350°F. Grease a 9 by 13-inch baking pan with butter, then dust it with flour, tapping out any excess.

In a heavy saucepan, combine the caramels and evaporated milk and heat over low heat, stirring continuously, until the caramels have melted and the mixture is combined. Keep warm.

In a large bowl, combine the cake mix, butter, and 1 tablespoon water. Stir with fork until the dough is crumbly but holds together. Press half the dough evenly over the bottom of the prepared baking pan, reserving the remaining dough for topping. Bake for 6 minutes, then remove the crust from the oven (keep the oven on).

Sprinkle the chocolate over the baked crust, then spread the caramel mixture over the top. Crumble the reserved dough over the caramel. Sprinkle the top with nuts, if desired. Bake for 18 minutes, then remove from the oven. It will look gooey but will set once cooled. Let cool completely, then cut into bars. *Makes about 30 bars.*

CHERRY FLUFF

Christin Wurth-Thomas
Women's Track & Field / Cross Country
800m, 1500m, 3000m, 5000m, 2000–2003

1 (14-ounce) can Carnation sweetened condensed milk

2 (21-ounce) cans cherry pie filling

1 (20-ounce) can crushed pineapple, drained

1 (12-ounce) tub Cool Whip

In a large bowl, combine the condensed milk, cherry pie filling, and pineapple. Fold in the Cool Whip until the mixture is well combined and completely pink in color. Cover and refrigerate for 2 hours before serving. *Makes 16 servings.*

CHESS SQUARES

Jim Mabry
Football
Offensive Lineman, 1985–1989

1 (13.25-ounce) box butter recipe yellow cake mix (see Note)

½ cup (1 stick) unsalted butter, melted

3 large eggs

1 (8-ounce) package cream cheese, at room temperature

1 teaspoon vanilla extract

1 (16-ounce) box powdered sugar

Preheat the oven to 325°F.

In a medium bowl, stir together the cake mix, melted butter, and 1 egg. Press the crust mixture into the bottom of a 9 by 13-inch baking pan.

In a separate large bowl, stir together the remaining 2 eggs, the cream cheese, vanilla, and powdered sugar until well combined, then pour the mixture into the baking pan over the crust. Bake until golden brown, about 1 hour. Let cool completely, then cut into squares. *Makes 18 to 24 squares.*

NOTE *Substitute lemon cake mix to make lemon chess squares.*

This is my mom's chess square recipe. They are delicious and were a common birthday request from the grandkids. Chess squares or lemon squares will be a fan favorite at Razorback tailgate parties. Go Hogs!

CHOCOLATE CARAMEL CHEESECAKE

Brandon Burlsworth
Football
Guard, 1995–1998

2 cups graham cracker crumbs

¾ cup plus ⅓ cup sugar

½ cup (1 stick) unsalted butter, melted

30 individually wrapped caramels, unwrapped

3 tablespoons whole milk

¾ cup chopped pecans (optional)

1 cup semisweet chocolate chips

3 (8-ounce) packages cream cheese, at room temperature

1 teaspoon vanilla extract

3 large eggs

½ cup mini chocolate chips, for garnish

In a medium bowl, stir together the graham cracker crumbs, 1/3 cup of the sugar, and the melted butter until well combined. Press the crust mixture over the bottom and 1 inch up the sides of a 9 by 13-inch baking pan.

In a small saucepan, combine the caramels and milk. Cook over low heat, stirring, until the caramels have melted and the mixture is smooth. Stir in the pecans (if using). Pour the caramel mixture over the crust, then refrigerate for 30 minutes.

Preheat the oven to 325°F, with racks in the center and lower third.

Place the semisweet chocolate chips in the top of a double boiler and heat, stirring occasionally, until melted and smooth. Remove from the heat and let cool to lukewarm.

In a large bowl, combine the cream cheese, remaining ¾ cup sugar, and vanilla and beat with a handheld mixer on medium speed until smooth. Beat in the eggs one at a time. Fold one-third of the cream cheese mixture into the melted chocolate, then pour the chocolate mixture into the bowl with the rest of the cream cheese mixture and mix until completely combined. Remove chilled crust from the refrigerator and pour the cream cheese mixture into the crust.

Fill a roasting pan halfway with water and place it on the lower oven rack (this will help keep the cheesecake from cracking as it bakes). Set the cheesecake on the center rack and bake for 50 minutes, or until the center is almost set. Sprinkle the mini chocolate chips over the top and then let cool in the oven with door cracked open for 15 to 20 minutes while chocolate chips melt. Refrigerate, uncovered, for at least 5 hours before serving. *Makes 12 servings.*

Brandon Burlsworth and those offensive linemen had huge appetites, and Brandon loved chips and cheesecake. He was so shy and quiet around everyone except his family and close friends. When going out to eat or at a ballgame, he would always stop and make time for those who wanted to shake his hand or ask for his autograph. He really was a gentle giant. We love you, #77.

—Recipe submitted by Marty and Vickie Burlsworth

CHOCOLATE CHEESECAKE

Bill Bakewell
Baseball
Pitcher, 1977–1979

½ cup (1 stick) unsalted butter, melted

1 cup chopped pecans

1 cup all-purpose flour

1 (8-ounce) package cream cheese

1 cup powdered sugar

1 (16-ounce) container Cool Whip

1 (3.4-ounce) package instant vanilla pudding mix

1 (3.4-ounce) package instant chocolate pudding mix

2¾ cups whole milk

Preheat the oven to 350°F.

In a medium bowl, stir together the melted butter, pecans, and flour. Press the mixture into bottom of a 9 by 13-inch glass baking dish. Bake for 20 minutes. Let cool.

In a large bowl, stir together the cream cheese and powdered sugar, then fold in half the Cool Whip. Spread the mixture over the cooled crust.

In a large bowl, whisk together both pudding mixes and milk until thick. Pour the pudding over the cream cheese mixture. Refrigerate for 1 hour to set the pudding.

Spread the remaining Cool Whip over the cheesecake and serve immediately. *Makes 12 to 15 servings.*

In Arkansas, this recipe is also affectionately known as "Possum Pie."

CHOCOLATE CHIP PUDDING COOKIES

Kelsi Musick
Women's Basketball
Head Coach, 2025–present

2¼ cups all-purpose flour

1 teaspoon baking soda

½ teaspoon salt

1 cup (2 sticks) unsalted butter, at room temperature

¾ cup packed light brown sugar

¼ cup granulated sugar

1 (3.4-ounce) instant vanilla pudding mix

2 large eggs, at room temperature

1 teaspoon vanilla extract

1 (12-ounce) bag semisweet chocolate chips

Preheat the oven to 350°F. Line a baking sheet with parchment paper.

In a medium bowl, stir together the flour, baking soda, and salt.

In a large bowl, beat together the butter, brown sugar, and granulated sugar with handheld mixer on medium-high speed until creamy, at least 3 minutes. Add the pudding mix, eggs, and vanilla and beat until fully combined and fluffy, 3 minutes more. With the mixer on low speed, slowly add half the flour mixture and mix until combined. Repeat with the rest of the flour mixture. Fold the chocolate chips into the cookie dough by hand.

Drop 1½-tablespoon portions of the dough onto the prepared baking sheet, leaving 2 inches between each cookie. Bake for 8 to 10 minutes, until the edges of the cookies are light golden brown (the centers may look a little underdone). Remove from the oven and let cool on the baking sheet for 3 minutes, then transfer to a wire rack to cool completely. *Makes 30 cookies.*

CHOCOLATE CHIP SQUARES

Jerry Carlton
Men's Basketball and Baseball
Guard, 1958–1962
Shortstop, 1958–1962

½ cup (1 stick) unsalted butter, at room temperature, plus more for greasing

1¼ cups sifted all-purpose flour, plus more for dusting

½ cup granulated sugar

½ cup packed light brown sugar

1 large egg

½ teaspoon vanilla extract

½ teaspoon baking soda

½ teaspoon salt

½ cup chopped nuts

1 (6-ounce) package chocolate chips

Preheat the oven to 375°F. Grease a 9-inch square baking pan with butter, then dust it with flour, tapping out any excess.

In a large bowl, beat the butter, granulated sugar, and brown sugar with a handheld mixer on medium speed until combined, then beat in the egg and vanilla. Gradually stir in the flour, baking soda, and salt. Stir in the nuts and chocolate chips. Scrape the batter into the prepared baking pan and spread it evenly. Bake for 25 to 30 minutes, until the edges and top are lightly golden brown. Cut into squares and serve. *Makes 16 pieces.*

CHOCOLATE SHEET CAKE

Norm DeBriyn
Baseball
Head Coach, 1970–2002

CAKE

½ cup (1 stick) margarine, plus more for greasing

2 cups all-purpose flour, plus more for dusting

2 cups granulated sugar

¼ cup unsweetened cocoa powder

½ cup Wesson oil

½ cup buttermilk

1 teaspoon baking soda

Pinch of salt

I teaspoon vanilla extract

2 large eggs, lightly beaten

ICING

1 (16-ounce) box powdered sugar

½ cup (1 stick) margarine, at room temperature

¼ cup unsweetened cocoa powder

¼ cup milk

1 teaspoon vanilla extract

½ cup chopped nuts (optional)

Make the cake: Preheat the oven to 400°F. Grease a 12 by 18 by 1-inch baking pan with margarine, then dust it with flour, tapping out any excess.

Sift the flour and granulated sugar together into a large bowl and set aside.

In a small saucepan, combine the cocoa powder, margarine, oil, and 1 cup water. Bring to a boil over medium heat, then pour the hot mixture over the dry ingredients and stir to combine. Add the buttermilk, baking soda, salt, vanilla, and eggs and stir to combine.

Pour the batter into the prepared pan and bake for 18 minutes, or until a toothpick inserted into the center comes out clean.

Make the icing: About 5 minutes before the cake is done, in a medium bowl, stir together the powdered sugar, margarine, cocoa powder, milk, vanilla, and nuts (if using) until well combined. While the cake is still hot, pour the icing over the top. *Makes 24 servings.*

CLIFF POWELL'S COCONUT CAKE

Cliff Powell

Football

Linebacker, 1967–1969

1 (13.25-ounce) box butter recipe yellow cake mix

1 (14-ounce) can sweetened condensed milk

1 (15-ounce) can Coco López cream of coconut

1 (8-ounce) container Cool Whip

2 cups sweetened shredded coconut

Prepare the cake according to the package directions for a 9 by 13-inch baking pan. Let cool, then make slits in the cake with a knife or poke holes in it with a fork or a wooden spoon handle.

In a medium bowl, stir together the condensed milk and cream of coconut. Microwave for 30 seconds to warm, then spread the mixture over the cake and let cool. Top with the Cool Whip. Sprinkle the shredded coconut over the top and refrigerate overnight before serving. *Makes 12 servings.*

Very grand happening to be a Razorback! It was by far the highlight of my football career. Dream come true.

COACH T'S FAVORITE COCONUT PIE

Ken Turner

Football

Graduate Assistant Coach, 1970

Assistant Coach, Offensive Line, Tight Ends, and Special Teams, 1973–1989

PIE

1 cup sugar

⅓ cup cornstarch

¼ teaspoon salt

3 cups whole milk

4 large egg yolks

4 tablespoons (½ stick) unsalted butter

1½ teaspoons vanilla extract

1 cup sweetened flaked coconut

1 (9-inch) prebaked piecrust

MERINGUE

3 large egg whites, at room temperature

¼ teaspoon cream of tartar

¼ cup sugar

2 to 4 tablespoons sweetened flaked coconut, for topping

Preheat the oven to 350°F.

Make the pie: In a 2-quart microwave-safe bowl, stir together the sugar, cornstarch, and salt. Add the milk and egg yolks and mix well. Microwave on high for 5 minutes, then stir and microwave for 5 to 7 minutes more, stirring every 2 minutes, until thickened. Stir in the butter, vanilla, and coconut. Pour into the piecrust.

Make the meringue: Place the egg whites in a clean medium bowl and beat with a handheld mixer on medium speed until frothy. Add the cream of tartar and beat until soft peaks form. Gradually beat in the sugar, 1 tablespoon at a time, then beat until the sugar has dissolved and stiff, glossy peaks form.

Top the pie with the meringue and sprinkle with the coconut. Bake for 5 minutes, or until browned on top. *Makes 8 servings.*

COCA-COLA CAKE

Reggie Craig
Football
Wide Receiver, 1972–1974

CAKE

1 cup (2 sticks) unsalted butter, cubed, plus more for greasing

2 cups all-purpose flour

2 cups granulated sugar

1 teaspoon baking soda

½ teaspoon salt

½ teaspoon ground cinnamon

1 (12-ounce) can cola

¼ cup unsweetened cocoa powder

2 large eggs, at room temperature

½ cup buttermilk

1 teaspoon vanilla extract

GLAZE

1 (12-ounce) can cola

½ cup (1 stick) unsalted butter, cubed

¼ cup unsweetened cocoa powder

4 cups powdered sugar, sifted

Make the cake: Preheat the oven to 350°F. Grease a 9 by 13-inch baking pan with butter.

In a large bowl, whisk together the flour, granulated sugar, baking soda, salt, and cinnamon.

In a small saucepan, combine the cola, butter, and cocoa powder. Bring just to a boil over medium-high heat, stirring occasionally. Add the cola mixture to the flour mixture, stirring just until moistened.

In a small bowl, whisk together the eggs, buttermilk, and vanilla until combined. While whisking continuously, add the egg mixture to the flour mixture. Pour the batter into the prepared pan. Bake for 25 to 30 minutes, until a toothpick inserted into the center of the cake comes out clean. Make the glaze: About 15 minutes before the cake is done, bring the cola to a boil in a small saucepan. Cook until the liquid has reduced to ½ cup, 12 to 15 minutes. Add the butter and cocoa powder and stir until the butter has melted; remove from the heat. Add the powdered sugar and stir until smooth.

Remove the cake from the oven and immediately pour the glaze over the hot cake. *Makes 12 servings.*

COCONUT MERINGUE PIE

Kevin Kopps
Baseball
Pitcher, 2017–2021

PIE

3 cups whole milk

1 cup sugar

¼ cup cornstarch

¼ teaspoon salt

4 egg yolks

3 tablespoons unsalted butter

1½ teaspoons vanilla extract

1 (3½-ounce) can Baker's Angel Flake sweetened coconut

1 (9-inch) prebaked piecrust

MERINGUE

4 egg whites, at room temperature

¼ teaspoon cream of tartar

½ cup sugar

½ teaspoon vanilla extract

¼ cup sweetened shredded coconut, toasted, for topping

Preheat the oven to 350°F.

Make the pie: In a medium saucepan, combine the milk, sugar, cornstarch, and salt. Cook over low to medium heat, stirring continuously, until the mixture bubbles and thickens, then cook for 2 minutes more. Remove from the heat.

In a separate medium bowl, beat the egg yolks lightly. While whisking continuously, gradually pour 1 cup of the hot milk mixture into the egg yolks and whisk to combine. Pour the egg mixture into the saucepan with the remaining milk mixture and bring to a gentle boil over medium heat. Cook, stirring, for 2 minutes more. Remove from the heat. Add the butter and vanilla; stir until the butter has melted. Add the coconut and mix. Pour the mixture into the piecrust.

Make the meringue: In a medium bowl, beat the egg whites and cream of tartar with a handheld mixer on high speed until foamy. Gradually add the sugar, 1 tablespoon at a time, and beat until the sugar has dissolved and the egg whites hold stiff peaks, 2 to 4 minutes. Beat in the vanilla.

Spread the meringue over the hot filling, all the way to the edge of the piecrust. Sprinkle the toasted coconut on top of the meringue. Bake for 12 to 15 minutes, until the meringue is browned. Let cool completely before slicing and serving. *Makes 8 servings.*

NOTE *For a cream pie, let the filling cool, then top with whipped cream instead of meringue.*

I'm not a big sweets person and won't typically eat any if they're presented to me. My mom started making coconut meringue pie a couple of years ago during the holidays, and it's one of the few sweets I will eat.

COLA CAKE

Ivan Jordan
Football
Defensive End, 1972–1975

CAKE

1 cup (2 sticks) unsalted butter, at room temperature, plus more for greasing

1⅓ cups granulated sugar

2 large eggs

2 cups all-purpose flour

3 tablespoons unsweetened cocoa powder

1 teaspoon baking soda

½ cup buttermilk

1 teaspoon vanilla extract

1 cup cola

1½ cups miniature marshmallows

COLA ICING

4 cups powdered sugar

½ cup (1 stick) unsalted butter, at room temperature

3 tablespoons unsweetened cocoa powder

⅓ cup cola

1 cup chopped pecans (optional)

Make the cake: Preheat the oven to 350°F. Grease a 9 by 13-inch baking pan well with butter.

In a large bowl, beat the butter and granulated sugar with handheld mixer on medium speed until fluffy. Add the eggs one at a time, beating after each.

In a separate medium bowl, sift together the flour, cocoa powder, and baking soda. Add the dry ingredients to the butter mixture, alternating with the buttermilk. Stir in the vanilla and cola, mixing well. Fold in the marshmallows. Pour the batter into the prepared baking pan. Bake for 35 to 45 minutes, until toothpick inserted into the center comes out clean. Let cool.

Meanwhile, make the cola icing: In a large bowl, beat together the powdered sugar, butter, and cocoa powder with a handheld mixer on medium speed. Add the cola and beat until smooth. Stir in the pecans (if using).

When the cake is cool, frost it with the cola icing. *Makes 12 to 15 servings.*

CREAM CHEESE BLONDIES

Clint Stoerner
Football
Quarterback, 1996–1999

½ cup (1 stick) unsalted butter or margarine, melted, plus more for greasing

3 large eggs, beaten separately

1 box yellow cake mix (approximately 19 ounces)

1 (8-ounce) package cream cheese, at room temperature

1 cup packed light brown sugar

1 cup powdered sugar, plus more for dusting

1 teaspoon vanilla extract

⅛ teaspoon salt

Powdered sugar, for dusting

Preheat the oven to 325°F. Grease a 9 by 13-inch baking dish with butter.

In a medium bowl, combine the melted butter, 1 egg, and the cake mix. Scrape the batter into the prepared baking dish.

In a large bowl, combine the cream cheese, remaining 2 eggs, the brown sugar, powdered sugar, vanilla, and salt. Beat with a handheld mixer on medium-high speed until smooth, then spread the mixture over the cake batter. Bake for 40 to 45 minutes, until golden brown. Let cool completely before slicing, as the top layer is too soft to cut well when hot. Cut into 40 squares and dust the tops with powdered sugar. *Makes 40 blondies.*

DADDY DICK BREAD PUDDING WITH WHISKEY SAUCE

Casey Dick
Football
Quarterback, 2005–2008

BREAD PUDDING

2½ cups whole milk

2 large eggs

2 tablespoons unsalted butter, melted

2 tablespoons vanilla extract

2 cups sugar

2 cups cubed sourdough bread (1-inch cubes)

⅓ cup chopped pecans

SAUCE

½ cup sugar

½ cup (1 stick) unsalted butter

½ cup heavy cream

¼ cup Jack Daniel's whiskey

Make the bread pudding: Preheat the oven to 325°F.

In a large bowl, beat together the milk, eggs, melted butter, and vanilla. While whisking, gradually add the sugar and whisk thoroughly until the sugar has dissolved.

Place the bread cubes in the bottom of a 9-inch round baking dish. Pour the milk mixture liquid over the bread, making sure all the pieces are fully saturated. Sprinkle the pecans over the bread and push them down into the bread. Bake for 50 to 60 minutes.

Meanwhile, make the sauce: In a medium saucepan, combine the sugar, butter, cream, and whiskey. Cook over low heat, stirring continuously, until the mixture comes to a low rolling boil. Remove from the heat.

Pour a small amount of the sauce over individual servings of the bread pudding. *Makes 8 to 10 servings.*

My dad, Steve Dick, also known as Daddy Dick, made the best bread pudding. One day, Daddy Dick and my mom, Mary Ellen, were cooking together in the kitchen and made this dessert as a Christmas treat. The bread pudding and whiskey sauce quickly became a favorite for the Dick family, and after that Christmas, I would request this bread pudding for every special occasion. The "Daddy Dick Bread Pudding" has become a staple for me and my family, especially since my dad's passing. Every time we make it now, we get to share in his memory.

DATE BALLS

John McDonnell
Men's Track & Field / Cross Country
Head Coach, 1972–2008

1 (8-ounce) package chopped dates

½ cup (1 stick) margarine, melted

1 cup sugar

1 large egg

2½ cups Rice Krispies cereal

½ cup chopped nuts

½ teaspoon vanilla extract

1 (14-ounce) package unsweetened coconut flakes

In a large saucepan, combine the melted margarine, sugar, and egg. Add the dates and cook over medium-high heat for 5 minutes. Remove from the heat. Stir in the Rice Krispies, nuts, and vanilla. Let cool slightly.

Spread the coconut over a shallow bowl. When the date mixture is cool enough to handle, form it into balls, then roll in the coconut to coat. The date balls can be stored in an airtight container in the refrigerator for up to 1 week or in the freezer for up to 3 months. *Makes 24 balls.*

—Recipe submitted by Heather McDonnell Hastings, John's daughter

DON'S SEAFOOD & STEAKHOUSE BREAD PUDDING

Joe Ferguson
Football
Quarterback, 1969–1972

BREAD PUDDING

9 slices white bread, torn into small pieces

1 cup sugar

1 (13-ounce) can evaporated milk

2 cups milk

I teaspoon vanilla extract

4 egg yolks

⅓ cup unsalted butter, melted

MERINGUE

4 egg whites

¼ cup sugar

RUM SAUCE

1 (8-ounce) can evaporated milk, preferably Carnation

1 cup whole milk

1 cup sugar

3 tablespoons unsalted butter

1½ tablespoons cornstarch

2 ounces rum

Joe Ferguson

Preheat the oven to 450°F.

Place the bread in a 9 by 13-inch baking pan.

In a medium bowl, combine the sugar, evaporated milk, milk, vanilla, egg yolks, and melted butter and mix well. Pour the milk mixture over the bread in baking pan. Bake for 15 minutes.

Meanwhile, make the meringue: In a large bowl, beat the egg whites and the sugar with a handheld mixer on medium-high speed until they hold stiff peaks.

Cover the bread pudding with the meringue and bake for 3 to 4 minutes, until golden.

Make the rum sauce: In the top of a double boiler, combine the evaporate milk, whole milk, sugar, and butter. Heat over medium heat until hot. Dissolve the cornstarch in a little cool water and stir it into the hot milk mixture. Cook, stirring, until thick, then remove from the heat and stir in the rum.

Pour the rum sauce over individual servings of the bread pudding. *Makes 12 servings.*

Don's Seafood & Steakhouse is one of the finest and longest-lived business in Lafayette, Louisiana. In the off season (1980s) Joe worked out with Pat Tilley (St. Louis Cardinals), Bo Harris (Cincinnati Bengals), and Larry Anderson (Pittsburg Steelers) in Shreveport. We (players and wives) went to Don's Seafood one night, and everyone was getting bread pudding . . . I was asking about chocolate, and they were horrified I wasn't getting bread pudding . . . so I got it, and later Diane Tilley gave me this recipe. It's a family favorite.

DUMP CAKE

Johnny Ray

Baseball

Second Base, 1978–1979

1 (20-ounce) can crushed pineapple, undrained

½ cup packed light brown sugar

1 (21-ounce) can cherry pie filling

1 (13.25-ounce) box butter yellow cake mix

½ cup (1 stick) margarine or unsalted butter

Preheat the oven to 350°F.

Spread the pineapple (with its juice) over the bottom of a 9 by 13-inch baking pan. Sprinkle the brown sugar over the pineapple. Layer the cherry pie filling on top. Sprinkle the dry cake mix over the cherry pie filling and lightly press down. Cut pats of butter and distibute them evenly over the top until it's covered. Bake for 1 hour, or until golden brown. *Makes 12 servings.*

COACH BROYLES, as he was fondly known, coached the Razorbacks from 1958 to 1976 and served as athletic director from 1974 to 2007. He also enjoyed a part-time college football broadcasting career for ABC television for nine years. As head coach, he won seven Southwest Conference football titles, and his undefeated 1964 team was named national champion. As athletic director, he oversaw many SWC and SEC conference championships, along with thirty-four national championships. He was involved in fundraising to improve several athletic facilities during his tenure, including new buildings for basketball, track and field, and baseball. The University of Arkansas athletic center and the field at Donald W. Reynolds Razorback Stadium are named in his honor. His many accolades include induction into the College Football Hall of Fame, the University of Arkansas Hall of Honor, and the Arkansas Sports Hall of Fame and being named National Coach of the Year. The Frank Broyles Award was established in 1996 in his honor and is given annually to the best assistant coach in college football.

Frank Broyles

FRANK'S FUDGE

Frank Broyles
Football
Head Coach, 1958–1976
Athletic Director, 1974–2007

3 tablespoons unsalted butter, plus more for greasing

3 cups sugar

6 tablespoons unsweetened cocoa powder

1 cup whole milk

3 tablespoons Karo light corn syrup

¼ teaspoon vanilla extract

1½ cups pecan pieces (see Note)

Grease a large platter with butter.

In a large saucepan, mix together the sugar and cocoa powder. Add the milk and stir well. Bring to a boil over medium heat, then stir in the corn syrup and butter. Reduce the heat to maintain a low boil and clip a candy thermometer to the side of the pot. Cook, stirring every 5 minutes, until the mixture is just past soft-ball stage (about 241°F). Remove from the heat and stir in the vanilla. Beat by hand for several minutes. Stir in the pecans, then pour the fudge onto the prepared platter. Let cool slightly, then slice the fudge into individual pieces before it gets too hard. *Makes 30 to 40 pieces.*

NOTE *It's important to use good pecans!*

This is an old family recipe, probably 150 years old. Frank said he used to make the fudge when he was young.

—Recipe submitted by Frank's daughter, Betsy Broyles Arnold

FROZEN CHEESECAKE

Amber Nicholas Shirey
Women's Basketball
Guard, 1988–1992
Graduate Assistant Coach, 1992–1993
Assistant Coach, 1993–2007; 2012–2014
Director of Operations, 2008–2012; 2014–present

1 (8-ounce) package cream cheese, at room temperature

1 cup sugar

Pinch of salt

3 large eggs, separated

1 teaspoon vanilla extract

1 cup heavy cream

1 cup graham cracker crumbs

3 tablespoons unsalted butter, melted

In a large bowl, beat together the cream cheese, sugar, and salt with a handheld mixer on medium speed until well combined. Add the egg yolks and vanilla and mix.

In a separate large bowl, whip the cream with the handheld mixer until it holds soft peaks.

Clean the mixer beaters and dry them well. In a medium bowl, whip the egg whites with a handheld mixer until they hold stiff peaks. Fold the egg whites into the whipped cream, then fold the whipped cream mixture into the cream cheese mixture.

In a small bowl, stir together ½ cup of the graham cracker crumbs and the melted butter until combined. Press the mixture evenly over the bottom of a 9-inch pie pan. Spoon the cream cheese mixture over the crumb mixture. Sprinkle the top with the remaining ½ cup graham cracker crumbs. Cover and freeze for 3 to 4 hours before serving. *Makes 6 to 8 servings.*

This was a recipe passed down to my mom by a family member. My mom used to make it a lot in the summer when I was a kid.

Amber Nicholas Shirey

GARY ADAMS'S MOTHER'S COCONUT CAKE

Gary Adams
Football
Cornerback, 1965–1968

1 (13.25-ounce) box Betty Crocker Delights French vanilla cake mix

2 (16-ounce) containers sour cream

1½ cups sugar

5 ounces sweetened flaked coconut

1 teaspoon vanilla extract

Preheat the oven to 350°F.

Prepare the cake according to the package directions for a 9 by 13-inch baking pan.

While the cake is baking, in a medium bowl, stir together the sour cream, sugar, coconut, and vanilla; set the icing aside.

Remove the cake from the oven. Poke holes in the cake with the end of a wooden spoon and let cool for 10 minutes, then pour the icing over the cake. Refrigerate overnight before serving. *Makes 12 servings.*

This is a recipe that I remember my mother cooking in the 1950s and '60s.

GERMAN CHOCOLATE BROWNIES

Haley VanFossen
Women's Soccer
Center Defender, 2017–2021

½ cup (1 stick) unsalted butter, melted, plus more for greasing

1 (13.25-ounce) box German chocolate cake mix

1 cup chopped pecans (optional)

½ cup plus ⅓ cup evaporated milk

60 individually wrapped caramels, unwrapped, or 1 (11-ounce) package caramel bits

⅓ cup semisweet chocolate chips

Powdered sugar, for dusting

Preheat the oven to 350°F. Grease a 9-inch square baking pan with butter.

In a large bowl, mix together the cake mix, pecans (if using), ⅓ cup of the evaporated milk, and the melted butter until well combined. It will be very thick. Press half the brownie mixture over the bottom of the prepared baking pan. Bake for 8 to 10 minutes, then remove the brownie base from the oven and set aside.

In the top of a double boiler, combine the caramels and remaining ½ cup evaporated milk. Heat, stirring, until melted and combined, then pour the caramel mixture over the brownie base. Sprinkle the chocolate chips evenly over the caramel. Using your hands, press the remaining brownie mixture over the chocolate chip layer. (It will not completely cover the chocolate chip layer.) Bake for 20 to 25 minutes. Remove from the oven and let cool to room temperature, then cover and refrigerate for several hours before serving. When ready to serve, slice the brownies and dust with powdered sugar. *Makes 16 brownies.*

A memory I have of this recipe was that my mom used to make a batch and bring them for my roommates and me for every home game. She would also make them for us when we were in Orange Beach for the SEC tournament!

GERMAN CHOCOLATE CAKE

Kenderick Moore
Baseball
Second Base, 1992–1996

CAKE

Nonstick cooking spray

4 ounces Baker's German sweet chocolate, coarsely chopped

1 teaspoon baking soda

1 teaspoon salt

2 cups sugar

1 cup (2 sticks) unsalted butter, at room temperature

4 large eggs, separated

1 teaspoon vanilla extract

2¼ cups all-purpose flour

1 cup buttermilk

FROSTING

3 large egg yolks

1 cup sugar

½ cup (1 stick) unsalted butter

1 cup evaporated milk

1 teaspoon vanilla extract

1⅓ cups sweetened coconut flakes

1 cup chopped pecans

Make the cake: Preheat the oven to 350°F. Coat three 8-inch round cake pans with cooking spray and line the bottoms with rounds of parchment paper cut to fit.

In a 1-quart saucepan, heat the chocolate and ½ cup water over low heat, stirring frequently, until the chocolate has completely melted; remove from the heat and let cool.

In a medium bowl, stir together the flour, baking soda, and salt.

In a separate medium bowl, beat together the sugar and butter with a handheld mixer on medium speed until light and fluffy. Beat in the egg yolks one at a time until combined. Add the melted chocolate and vanilla and beat on low speed to combine. Add half the flour mixture and beat on low speed until smooth, then beat in half the buttermilk until smooth. Repeat with the remaining flour and buttermilk.

Clean the mixer beaters and dry them well. In a small bowl, beat the egg whites on high speed until they hold stiff peaks. Gently fold the egg whites into the batter until blended. Pour the batter into the prepared cake pans, dividing it evenly. Bake for 30 to 40 minutes, until a toothpick inserted into the center comes out clean. Remove from the oven and let cool in the pans for 10 minutes. Invert the cakes onto wire racks and let cool for 1 hour more.

Meanwhile, make the frosting: In a 2-quart saucepan, stir together the egg yolks, sugar, butter, evaporated milk, and vanilla. Cook over medium heat, stirring continuously, for about 12 minutes, until thick and bubbling. Remove from the heat and stir in the coconut and pecans. Let cool for about 30 minutes, stirring occasionally, until the frosting has a spreadable consistency.

To assemble, place one cooled cake layer rounded-side down on a serving plate and spread one-third of the frosting on top. Repeat with a second layer. Top with the third cake layer, rounded-side up, and spread the remaining frosting over the top. Store the cake in an airtight container in the refrigerator for up to 3 days. *Makes 12 servings.*

GRANDMA'S RED VELVET CAKE

Chris Johnson
Women's Track & Field / Cross Country
Head Coach, 2023–present

CAKE

Butter, for greasing

2½ cups all-purpose flour, plus more for dusting

1 teaspoon baking soda

1 teaspoon salt

2 tablespoons unsweetened cocoa powder

1 cup buttermilk

2 teaspoons vanilla extract

1½ cups granulated sugar

2 cups Mazola corn oil

2 large eggs

1 teaspoon distilled white vinegar

1½ (1-ounce) bottles red food coloring

CREAM CHEESE ICING

½ cup (1 stick) unsalted butter, at room temperature

1 (8-ounce) package cream cheese, at room temperature

1 (16-ounce) box powdered sugar

1 teaspoon vanilla extract

1 cup chopped pecans, for topping

Make the cake: Preheat the oven to 350°F. Grease three 9-inch round cake pans and dust them with flour, tapping out any excess.

In a medium bowl, stir together the flour, cocoa powder, baking soda, and salt. In a measuring cup, stir together the buttermilk and vanilla.

In a large bowl, stir together the granulated sugar, corn oil, eggs, vinegar, and food coloring. Add the flour mixture to the sugar mixture in three additions, alternating with the buttermilk, and stir until just combined.

Divide the batter evenly among the prepared pans. Bake for 12 to 15 minutes, until a toothpick inserted into the center comes out clean. Let cool in the pans for 10 minutes, then turn the cakes out onto wire racks to cool completely.

Make the cream cheese icing: In a large bowl, beat the butter, cream cheese, powdered sugar, and vanilla with a handheld mixer on medium speed until well combined.

To assemble, place one cooled cake layer rounded-side down on a serving plate and spread one-third of the icing on top. Repeat with a second cake layer. Top with the third cake layer and spread the remaining icing over the top and sides. Sprinkle the pecans over the top of the iced cake and serve. *Makes 12 servings.*

GRANNY'S PECAN PIE

Ken Hatfield
Football
Defensive Back and Punter, 1961–1964
Head Coach, 1984–1989

1 cup sugar

1 cup Karo dark corn syrup

3 large eggs

2 to 4 tablespoons unsalted butter, melted

1 to 2 teaspoons vanilla extract

1 cup coarsely chopped pecans

1 (9-inch) refrigerated piecrust

Preheat the oven to 350°F.

In a small saucepan, combine the sugar and corn syrup and bring to a boil over medium heat.

In a large bowl, beat the eggs with a handheld mixer on medium speed until blended. With the mixer running, gradually add the hot sugar mixture to the eggs and beat until fully combined. Stir in the melted butter, vanilla, and pecans. Pour the filling into the pie shell. Bake for 50 to 60 minutes, until set. *Makes 8 servings.*

Dallas, Texas. January 1, 1965. Hogs are trailing 3–7, with time running out in the 4th quarter.

First & 10 for the Hogs on our own 20-yard line.

Freddie Marshall passes to Jim Lindsey, then to Bobby Burnett.

Freddie scrambles on 1st down.

Lindsey catches a short pass and rambles to the 4-yard line, where Freddie pitches to Bobby Burnett, who hurdles into the end zone. And the Tom McNelly extra point puts us ahead 10–7.

Trailing 7–10, Nebraska starts a drive, hopefully to score to tie or go ahead.

But on 4th down, near midfield, Jim Williams rushes past his blocker, runs the QB down, grabs him, and slams him to the ground—ensuring a 10–7 victory. The energy in the locker room was sky-high as we all looked in our teammates' eyes, realizing we had earned an undefeated season.

That night, we all gathered in the hotel room to pull for Texas against Alabama in the Orange Bowl. Trailing 21–17 in the closing minutes, Alabama quarterback Joe Namath tried a 1-yard sneak to win, only to be met by All-American Tommy Nobis for no gain! Preserving the Texas victory over previously undefeated Alabama, leaving the Arkansas Fighting Razorbacks (11–0) as the ONLY undefeated college team in 1964. And earning the Football Writers and Helm Athletic Foundation National Championship!

HUMMINGBIRD CAKE

Jim Mabry
Football
Offensive Lineman, 1985–1989

CAKE

1½ cups vegetable oil, plus more for greasing

3 cups all-purpose flour, plus more for dusting

2 cups granulated sugar

1 teaspoon salt

1 teaspoon baking soda

1 teaspoon ground cinnamon

3 large eggs, beaten

1½ teaspoons vanilla extract

1 (8-ounce) can crushed pineapple, undrained

2 cups chopped pecans

2 cups chopped bananas

ICING

1 (8-ounce) package cream cheese, at room temperature

½ cup (1 stick) unsalted butter, at room temperature

1 (16-ounce) package powdered sugar

1 teaspoon vanilla extract

Make the cake: Preheat the oven to 350°F. Grease three 8-inch round cake pans and dust them with flour, tapping out any excess.

In a large bowl, stir together the flour, sugar, salt, baking soda, and cinnamon. Add the eggs and oil and stir until the dry ingredients are evenly moist. Stir in the vanilla, pineapple, pecans, and bananas. Divide the batter evenly among the prepared cake pans. Bake for 25 to 30 minutes, until a toothpick inserted into the center comes out clean. Let cool in the pans for 10 minutes, then transfer the cakes to wire racks to cool completely.

Meanwhile, make the icing: In a large bowl, beat together the cream cheese, butter, powdered sugar, and vanilla with a handheld mixer on medium speed until smooth.

To assemble, place one cooled cake layer rounded-side down on a serving plate and spread one-third of the icing on top. Repeat with a second layer. Top with the third cake layer and spread the remaining icing over the top and sides. *Makes 12 servings.*

On special occasions, like Thanksgiving and birthdays, when the entire family would be together, my mom would make a hummingbird cake. It was a family-favorite dessert! My mom struggled with MS most of her life, and it took a lot of effort for her to spend the day in the kitchen baking this special cake for us. She put a lot of time and love into making it, and it made her happy to hear how much we all enjoyed it. She would stack it three layers high, and ice it herself with homemade icing. My wife and sister-in-law still make a hummingbird cake in her honor on special occasions, and everyone in the family still loves eating it!

JENNY'S FAMOUS CHOCOLATE CHIP COOKIES

Hayden Henry
Football
Linebacker, 2017–2021

¾ cup (1½ sticks) unsalted butter, at room temperature

¾ cup packed light brown sugar

¼ cup granulated sugar

1 large egg

2 teaspoons vanilla extract

2 cups all-purpose flour

2 teaspoons cornstarch

1 teaspoon baking soda

½ teaspoon salt

1 cup semisweet chocolate chips

Preheat the oven to 350°F. Line a baking sheet with parchment paper.

In the bowl of a stand mixer fitted with a paddle attachment, beat the butter and both sugars on medium-high speed until fluffy and light in color. Add the egg and vanilla and mix to combine.

In a medium bowl, stir together the flour, cornstarch, baking soda, and salt. With the mixer on low speed, gently add the flour mixture to the butter mixture. Add the chocolate chips and mix just to combine.

Scoop 1-tablespoon portions of the dough onto the prepared baking sheet, spacing them 2 inches apart. Bake for 8 to 10 minutes (if you like them a bit underdone, bake for exactly 9 minutes). Let cool on the pan for 5 minutes. *Makes about 36 cookies.*

JOHN JOHN'S YUMMY-IN-THE-TUMMY CHOCOLATE CHIP COOKIES

Jim Barnes

Football

Offensive Guard, 1966–1968

1 cup (2 sticks) unsalted butter, at room temperature

1½ cups turbinado sugar

2 large eggs

1 teaspoon vanilla extract

1½ cups whole wheat flour

1 teaspoon baking soda

½ teaspoon salt

1 cup semisweet chocolate chips

1 cup 60% dark chocolate chips

2 cups rolled oats

1 cup pecans, toasted and chopped (optional)

Preheat the oven to 375°F.

In the bowl of a stand mixer fitted with the paddle attachment, combine the butter, turbinado sugar, eggs, and vanilla and beat on medium speed to combine. Add the flour, baking soda, and salt and mix to combine. Add all the chocolate chips, the oats, and the pecans (if using) and mix well.

Spoon the dough onto baking sheets. Bake for 12 to 14 minutes, until lightly browned. Let cool on the pans for 10 minutes, then carefully transfer to wire racks to cool completely. Store in an airtight container at room temperature for up to 2 weeks. *Makes 36 cookies.*

These are a Barnes family favorite, shared at Christmas and at our annual trip to Lake Ouachita. Everyone says they're addictive! They'd be a great addition to a tailgate in the fall.

KEY LIME PIE

Barry Lunney Jr.

Football and Baseball

Quarterback, 1992–1995

Pitcher, 1993–1995, 1997

Graduate Assistant Coach, 1998–1999

Assistant Coach, 2013–2019

Interim Head Coach, 2019

CRUST

⅓ (1-pound) box graham crackers (about 12 sheets)

5 tablespoons unsalted butter, melted

⅓ cup raw sugar

FILLING

3 large egg yolks

2 teaspoons key lime zest, or 1 tablespoon regular lime zest, plus more for garnish

1 (14-ounce) can sweetened condensed milk

⅔ cup fresh key lime juice or regular lime juice

TOPPING

1 cup heavy cream

¼ cup powdered sugar

Splash of vanilla extract

Make the crust: Preheat the oven to 350°F.

Place the graham crackers in a large zip-top bag and crush them into crumbs with a rolling pin. Pour them into a large bowl and add the melted butter and raw sugar. Mix to combine. Press the crumb mixture over the bottom and up the sides of a 9-inch pie plate. Bake for about 8 minutes, until the crust is golden. Remove from the oven and set aside; keep the oven on.

Make the filling: In the bowl of a stand mixer fitted with the whisk attachment, beat the egg yolks with the lime zest on high speed until fluffy, about 7 minutes. Add the condensed milk and beat until thick, about 4 minutes more. Reduce the speed to low and gradually add the lime juice, then beat just until combined. Pour the mixture into the crust and bake for 10 to 12 minutes, until the filling is set. Let cool completely.

Make the topping: Clean and dry the stand mixer bowl and whisk attachment. In the mixer bowl, combine the cream, powdered sugar, and vanilla and whip on medium-high speed until thick. Transfer the whipped cream to a piping bag fitted with a decorating tip of your choice (a round or star shape works well). Pipe dollops of the whipped cream side by side around the edge of the filling, next to the crust. Lightly sprinkle the dollops with lime zest. Freeze for 20 to 30 minutes to set before slicing and serving. Store, tightly covered, in the refrigerator for up to 3 days or in the freezer for up to 3 months (freezing is preferred). *Makes 8 servings.*

LEMON BARS

Neil Harper
Women's Swimming & Diving
Head Coach, 2016–present

BOTTOM LAYER

1 (15.25-ounce) box lemon cake mix

½ cup (1 stick) unsalted butter, melted

1 large egg

TOP LAYER

1 (16-ounce) box powdered sugar

1 (8-ounce) package cream cheese, at room temperature

2 large eggs

Preheat the oven to 325°F.

Make the bottom layer: In a large bowl, stir together the cake mix, melted butter, and egg. Spread the mixture over the bottom of 9 by 13-inch baking dish.

Make the top layer: Set aside 2 tablespoons of the powdered sugar and place the rest in a large bowl. Add the cream cheese and eggs and beat with a handheld mixer on low speed until well combined. Pour over the bottom layer. Bake for about 50 minutes, until the edges are golden brown. Sprinkle the reserved powdered sugar on top before serving. *Makes 12 to 15 servings.*

LEMON ICEBOX PIE

Bo Busby
Football
Safety, 1973–1976

1 cup heavy cream

1 (14-ounce) can Eagle Brand sweetened condensed milk

½ cup lemon juice

1 (9-inch) prepared graham cracker or vanilla wafer piecrust

In a large bowl, whip the cream with a handheld mixer until it holds stiff peaks. In a separate medium bowl, stir together the condensed milk and lemon juice. Fold in the whipped cream. Pour into the piecrust and refrigerate until set, about 3 hours. *Makes 8 servings.*

LOUISIANA MUD CAKE

Joe Ferguson
Football
Quarterback, 1969–1972

CAKE

1 cup (2 sticks) unsalted butter or margarine, melted; plus more for greasing

1½ cups all-purpose flour, plus more for dusting

4 large eggs

2 cups Imperial granulated sugar

⅓ cup unsweetened cocoa powder

2 cups walnuts or pecans, chopped

1 cup sweetened shredded coconut

1 teaspoon vanilla extract

1 (7-ounce) jar marshmallow creme

FLOODTIDE FROSTING

½ cup (1 stick) unsalted butter or margarine, melted

6 tablespoons whole milk

1 pound (4 cups) unsifted Imperial powdered sugar

⅓ cup unsweetened cocoa powder

1 teaspoon vanilla extract

2 cups walnuts or pecans, chopped

Make the cake: Preheat the oven to 350°F with a rack in the center position. Grease a 9 by 13-inch baking pan with butter, then dust it with flour, tapping out any excess.

In the bowl of a stand mixer fitted with the paddle attachment, beat the eggs and granulated sugar on high speed for 5 minutes.

Meanwhile, in a medium bowl, stir together the melted butter, flour, cocoa powder, nuts, coconut, and vanilla. Add to the egg mixture and mix well. Transfer the batter to the prepared baking pan.

Bake on the center rack for 30 minutes, or until a toothpick inserted into the center comes out clean. Remove from the oven and spread the marshmallow creme over the top of cake. Let stand for a few minutes while you make the frosting.

Make the Floodtide frosting: In a large bowl, combine the melted butter, milk, powdered sugar, cocoa powder, vanilla, and nuts and mix well with whisk until combined.

While the cake is still warm, carefully spread the frosting over the marshmallow creme. *Makes 24 servings.*

This cake is very rich and filling, so it can be cut into small squares to feed a crowd.

MAYONNAISE CHOCOLATE CAKE

Bruce Maxwell
Football
Fullback, 1966–1969

CAKE

Butter, for greasing

2 cups all-purpose flour

1 cup sugar

¼ cup unsweetened cocoa powder

1½ teaspoons baking powder

1½ teaspoons baking soda

1 scant cup mayonnaise

2 teaspoons vanilla extract

ICING

1½ cups sugar

2 tablespoons unsweetened cocoa powder

2 teaspoons shortening

2 teaspoons unsalted butter

1 teaspoon milk

1 teaspoon Karo light corn syrup

½ teaspoon salt

Make the cake: Preheat the oven to 350°F. Grease a 9 by 13-inch baking pan with butter.

Sift the flour, sugar, cocoa powder, baking powder, and baking soda together into a large bowl. Add the mayonnaise, vanilla, and 1 cup cold water. Mix well and pour into the prepared baking pan. Bake for 30 to 40 minutes, until a toothpick inserted into the center comes out clean.

Make the icing: In a small saucepan, combine the sugar, cocoa powder, shortening, butter, milk, corn syrup, and salt. Mix well, then bring to a boil over medium-high heat and cook for 1 minute, stirring continuously to dissolve the sugar.

Poke holes in the cake and pour the hot icing over the cake. *Makes 18 to 24 servings.*

This cake and Coconut Pie (page 138) are two of my favorite things that my wife makes for me. I'm sure you will enjoy them.

MEMAW'S CHOCOLATE YUM YUM CAKE

Houston Nutt
Football and Basketball
Quarterback, 1976–1977
Guard, 1976–1977
Head Coach, 1998–2007

CAKE

1 cup (2 sticks) unsalted butter, plus more for greasing

2 cups granulated sugar

2 cups all-purpose flour

1 teaspoon baking soda

¼ cup unsweetened cocoa powder

½ cup buttermilk

2 large eggs

1 teaspoon vanilla extract

ICING

1 (16-ounce) box powdered sugar (3½ cups)

½ cup (1 stick) unsalted butter

¼ cup unsweetened cocoa powder

5 tablespoons milk

1 teaspoon vanilla extract

1 cup chopped pecans or walnuts

Make the cake: Preheat the oven to 350°F. Grease a large rimmed baking sheet with butter.

Sift the granulated sugar, flour, and baking soda together into a large bowl.

In a small saucepan, combine the butter, cocoa powder, and 1 cup water and heat over medium-high heat, whisking, until the mixture comes to a rapid boil. Pour the butter mixture over the dry ingredients and stir to combine. Add the buttermilk, eggs, and vanilla and whisk well until the batter is thoroughly combined. Pour the batter into the prepared pan and bake for 15 minutes, or until a toothpick inserted into the center comes out clean.

Meanwhile, make the icing: Pour the powdered sugar into a medium bowl and set aside.

In the saucepan you used for the batter, melt the butter over medium-high heat, then whisk in the cocoa powder and milk to combine. Bring almost to a boil, then stir in the vanilla. Remove from the heat and pour the butter mixture over the powdered sugar. Beat well with a handheld mixer on medium speed until combined. Add the pecans and beat until they're thoroughly mixed in.

Pour the icing over the warm cake and gently spread it to the edges of the cake. Slice it up and enjoy a piece of chocolaty heaven! *Makes 18 to 24 servings.*

MILLIONAIRE PIE

Devon Wallace
Softball
First Base, 2011–2015

2 cups powdered sugar

½ cup (1 stick) unsalted butter, at room temperature

1 large egg

¼ teaspoon vanilla extract

¼ teaspoon salt

2 (8-inch) piecrusts, baked

1 cup heavy cream

½ cup chopped nuts

1 (8-ounce) can crushed pineapple, drained

In a large bowl, beat together the powdered sugar and butter with a handheld mixer on low speed. Add the egg, vanilla, and salt and beat on medium speed until the mixture is light and fluffy. Spoon this mixture into the piecrusts, dividing it evenly, then refrigerate while you make the whipped cream.

Meanwhile, in a large bowl, whip the cream with a handheld mixer on medium-high speed until it holds stiff peaks. Fold in the nuts and pineapple. Divide the whipped cream evenly between the pies and refrigerate until thoroughly chilled, about 3 hours. *Makes two 8-inch pies.*

This is my favorite recipe from childhood! My Memaw would make this "Millionaire Pie" for special occasions like Thanksgiving and Christmas. I always associate this recipe with memories of her and my family during the holidays!

MOM'S APPLE PIE

Pat Bradley
Men's Basketball
Guard, 1995–1999

1 (11-ounce) box Betty Crocker pie crust mix

¼ cup all-purpose flour

¾ cup sugar

1 teaspoon ground cinnamon

8 tart apples (I prefer McIntosh), peeled and cored

1 tablespoon unsalted butter or margarine, cut into small bits

Preheat the oven to 425°F.

Prepare the dough for a double-crust pie according to the package directions. Roll out half the dough and place it in a 9-inch pie plate.

In a small bowl, combine the flour, sugar, and cinnamon. Spread about half this mixture over the unbaked bottom crust. Cut the apples into eighths (do not slice them too thin) and place the apples over the flour mixture, then sprinkle the remaining flour mixture over the top. Dot the apples with the butter.

Roll out the remaining dough and place the top crust over the pie. Crimp the edges to seal. Make about 5 slits in the top crust with a knife. To keep the edge of the crust from burning while baking, cover the edge of the piecrust with thin strips of foil. Bake for 30 minutes, then remove the foil and bake for 15 to 20 minutes more, until the filling is bubbling and the top is golden brown. Serve warm, with your favorite ice cream. *Makes 6 to 8 servings.*

This is a recipe from my mother, Maryann Bradley. She said it always brought back memories of trips with her three young sons to the apple orchard in Sterling, Massachusetts. The family would catch a hayride into the orchard, where the boys would pick apples, climb trees, and picnic.

MOM'S M&M COOKIES

Jill Gillen
Women's Volleyball
Outside Hitter, 2019–2023

2¼ cups all-purpose flour

1 teaspoon baking soda

1 teaspoon salt

1 cup (2 sticks) unsalted butter

½ cup granulated sugar

1 cup packed light brown sugar

2 large eggs

2 teaspoons vanilla extract

16 ounces M&M's

Preheat the oven to 300°F.

In a small bowl, combine the flour, baking soda, and salt. In a large bowl, beat together the butter, granulated sugar, and brown sugar with a handheld mixer on medium speed. Add the eggs and vanilla. Beat well. Gradually beat in the flour mixture. Stir in the M&M's.

Scoop tablespoon-size portions of the dough onto a baking sheet. Bake for 9 to 11 minutes, until golden brown. Let cool. *Makes 24 cookies.*

MOTHER'S SUGAR COOKIES

Kirk Botkin
Football
Tight End, 1990–1993
Assistant Coach, 2008–2009

COOKIES

1 cup granulated sugar

⅔ cup (11 tablespoons) unsalted butter

2 cups all-purpose flour, plus more for dusting

½ teaspoon baking powder

½ teaspoon baking soda

½ teaspoon salt

1 large egg

2 tablespoons milk

½ teaspoon vanilla extract

½ teaspoon lemon extract

BIRTHDAY CAKE ICING

2 pounds powdered sugar, sifted

½ cup all-purpose flour

1 cup Crisco

1½ teaspoons clear vanilla flavoring

Make the cookies: In a large bowl, beat together the granulated sugar and butter.

In a separate medium bowl, stir together the flour, baking powder, baking soda, and salt. Add the flour mixture to the butter mixture and mix to combine. Add the egg, milk, vanilla, and lemon extract and mix to combine. Cover and refrigerate the dough for at least 1 hour; overnight is best.

Preheat the oven to 350°F.

On a floured surface, roll out the chilled dough to ⅛ inch thick. Cut it into your desired shapes and place on a baking sheet. Bake for 10 to 12 minutes. Let cool while you make the icing.

Make the birthday cake icing: In a large bowl, mix together the powdered sugar and flour. Add the Crisco to the dry ingredients and mix well. Add the vanilla and ¾ cup water and stir to combine.

Ice the cookies, then let them sit at room temperature until the icing hardens. The cookies may be stacked with parchment paper between each cookie, then placed in a freezer bag or airtight container and stored in the freezer for up to 45 days. *Makes 24 cookies.*

NOTE *This is just like the decorator icing used in bakeries. This recipe makes a large amount; divide it among a few bowls and tint each with food coloring for different colors.*

My grandmother started the tradition of mixing, cutting, and decorating these cookies on holidays. When Mema passed, my mother took over the cookie baking, and my brother and I decorated. My mother said that she never made a full batch, because I ate the chilled dough so fast! This recipe is delicious and holds great memories!

NANA'S CHOCOLATE CHIP COOKIES

Nick Schmidt
Baseball
Pitcher, 2005–2007

1 cup (2 sticks) unsalted butter

1⅓ cups granulated sugar

⅔ cup packed light brown sugar

1 teaspoon baking soda

1 teaspoon salt

1½ teaspoons vanilla extract

2 large eggs

3 cups all-purpose flour

1 (12-ounce) bag milk chocolate chips

Preheat the oven to 350°F.

In a large bowl, beat together the butter, granulated sugar, and brown sugar with a handheld mixer on medium speed until smooth. Add the baking soda, salt, and vanilla and mix. Add the eggs and mix. Add the flour 1 cup at a time and mix it in by hand. Stir in the chocolate chips.

Drop spoonfuls of the dough 2 inches apart onto a baking sheet. Bake for about 10 minutes, until the tops of the cookies are barely turning brown and the bottoms are medium brown. *Makes 36 cookies.*

OATMEAL COOKIES WITH A TWIST

Rick Schaeffer
Assistant Sports Information Director, 1976–1979
Sports Information Director, 1979–2000

½ cup (1 stick) Crisco

¾ cup firmly packed light brown sugar

½ cup granulated white sugar

2 large eggs

1 teaspoon vanilla extract

1½ cups all-purpose flour

1 teaspoon baking soda

1 teaspoon ground cinnamon

1 teaspoon kosher salt

3 cups Quaker quick 1-minute oats

1 cup Nestlé milk chocolate chips

1 cup Nestlé butterscotch chips

1 cup Kellogg's Special K cereal

½ cup sweetened coconut flakes

¾ cup chopped pecans or walnuts

Preheat the oven to 375°F.

In a large bowl, beat together the Crisco, brown sugar, and granulated sugar with a handheld mixer on medium speed until creamy. Add the eggs and vanilla and beat well.

In a small bowl, stir together the flour, baking soda, cinnamon, and salt. Add the flour mixture to the sugar mixture and mix well. Add the oats and mix well. Add the chocolate chips, butterscotch chips, Special K, coconut, and pecans and mix well.

Drop rounded tablespoons of the dough 2 inches apart onto a baking sheet. Bake for 8 to 9 minutes for chewy cookies, 10 to 11 minutes for crispy cookies. Let cool on the pan for 5 minutes, then transfer to a wire rack to cool completely. Store in an airtight container at room temperature for up to 5 days. *Makes 48 cookies.*

NOTE *The dough can also be frozen for quick cookies as needed. To freeze, portion into heaping tablespoons and place on a parchment-lined baking sheet with a little room between them. Freeze until solid, then transfer to a zip-top freezer bag and freeze for up to 6 months. Bake directly from frozen, adding 1 to 2 minutes to the cooking time.*

"These cookies are everyone's favorite cookie. I call them 'bake and take' because I have to bake them and then take them out of the house!" —Adelaide Schaeffer

OREO DESSERT

Tim Horton
Football
Wide Receiver and Punt Returner, 1986–1989
Assistant Coach, 2007–2012

1 (18.12-ounce) package Oreo cookies, crushed

4 tablespoons (½ stick) unsalted butter, melted

½ gallon vanilla ice cream, softened

1 (8-ounce) carton frozen whipped topping, thawed

Hot fudge sauce (optional)

½ cup chopped pecans (optional)

Set aside 1½ cups of the crushed Oreos. In a medium bowl, stir together the remaining crushed Oreos and the melted butter, then press the mixture over the bottom of a 9 by 13-inch baking dish. Spread the ice cream over the Oreo mixture. Spread the whipped topping over ice cream. Sprinkle the reserved 1½ cups crushed Oreos over the whipped topping. If desired, drizzle hot fudge sauce over the Oreos and sprinkle with pecans. Cover and freeze for several hours, until set. Let stand at room temperature for 15 minutes to soften before serving. *Makes 15 to 18 servings.*

This is a fast, easy, and delicious recipe! I try to keep the ingredients on hand so I'm ready to serve this at a moment's notice.

"This is one of Coach Horton's favorite recipes, and it is a favorite of the many players we have fed throughout the years! The recipe was given to me by Jannese Knaus, a dear coach's wife and friend in Texas." —Lauren Horton

OREO FRUIT COCKTAIL

Jarrell Williams
Football
Defensive Back and Offensive Back, 1958–1960

1 (13.3-ounce) package Oreo cookies

1 (15-ounce) can fruit cocktail

Crumble the Oreos into the bottom of a serving bowl. Pour the fruit cocktail, including the juice, over the Oreos, and enjoy! *Makes 4 servings.*

I go out to eat because I don't cook. If I get hungry at home, I put together this recipe!

OREO PEANUT BUTTER PIE

Martine Bercher Jr.
Football
Safety and Defensive Back, 1964–1966

½ (8-ounce) package cream cheese

¾ cup sugar

2 tablespoons cornstarch

¾ cup crunchy peanut butter

⅓ cup whole milk

1 (8-ounce) tub Cool Whip

6½ ounces Oreos, broken into small pieces

2 ounces chopped roasted peanuts

1 Oreo piecrust (see Note)

In the bowl of a stand mixer fitted with the paddle attachment, combine the cream cheese, sugar, and cornstarch. Beat on high speed for 3 minutes. Add the peanut butter and milk. Beat on medium speed for 5 minutes. Fold in the whipped topping, then 4½ ounces of the Oreo pieces. Scrape the mixture into the Oreo crust. Top with the remaining 2 ounces Oreo pieces and the peanuts. Cover and refrigerate overnight to set (or freeze to set the pie more quickly) before serving. The pie can be made ahead and stored in the freezer for up to 3 months. Transfer to the refrigerator to thaw for several hours before serving. *Makes 8 servings.*

NOTE *If you can't find a prepared Oreo piecrust, make your own by putting 16 Oreos in a food processor and pulsing until they are broken down into crumbs. Transfer to a medium bowl, add 4 tablespoons (½ stick) melted unsalted butter, and mix well. Press the mixture into a 9-inch pie plate and bake at 350°F for 5 minutes, then let cool completely before filling.*

This was one of our best-selling pies at our restaurant in Fort Smith.

—Recipe submitted by Carole Bercher

PAUL'S PUMPKIN BARS

Hunter Yurachek
Director of Athletics, 2017–present

BARS

4 large eggs

1 cup vegetable oil

1⅔ cups granulated sugar

1 (16-ounce) can pure pumpkin puree

2 cups all-purpose flour

2 teaspoons baking powder

2 teaspoons ground cinnamon

1 teaspoon salt

1 teaspoon baking soda

ICING

½ (8-ounce) package cream cheese, at room temperature

½ cup (1 stick) butter, at room temperature

1 teaspoon vanilla extract

2 cups powdered sugar

Make the bars: Preheat the oven to 350°F.

In a large bowl, beat together the eggs, oil, sugar, and pumpkin with a handheld mixer on medium speed.

In a medium bowl, stir together the flour, baking powder, cinnamon, salt, and baking soda. Add the flour mixture to the pumpkin mixture and stir to combine. Pour the batter into a 10 by 15-inch jelly roll pan. Bake for 25 minutes, or until a toothpick inserted into the center comes out clean. Remove from the oven and let cool.

Meanwhile, make the icing: In the bowl of a stand mixer fitted with the paddle attachment, beat together the cream cheese, butter, vanilla, and powdered sugar on medium-high speed until well combined.

Spread the icing over the cooled pumpkin bars, then cut into 24 pieces. *Makes 24 bars.*

Nothing is better than pumpkin bars and a glass of milk or coffee on a cool fall evening. A batch never lasts long, and I've never met anyone who doesn't like them.

PEANUT BUTTER SHEET CAKE

Ronn Reynolds
Baseball
Catcher, 1979–1980

CAKE

2 cups all-purpose flour

2 cups granulated sugar

1 teaspoon baking soda

½ teaspoon salt

¾ cup (1½ sticks) unsalted butter

½ cup vegetable oil

½ cup peanut butter

2 large eggs

½ cup buttermilk

1 teaspoon vanilla extract

FROSTING

½ cup (1 stick) unsalted butter

½ cup peanut butter

⅓ cup whole milk

1 teaspoon vanilla extract

3½ cups powdered sugar

Make the cake: Preheat the oven to 350°F.

In a large bowl, stir together the flour, granulated sugar, baking soda, and salt. Set aside.

In a medium saucepan, combine the butter, oil, peanut butter, and 1 cup water. Bring to a boil over medium-high heat, stirring to combine. Pour the mixture over the dry ingredients and mix well to combine. Add the eggs, buttermilk, and vanilla and mix, then pour into a high-sided rimmed baking sheet. Bake for 12 to 15 minutes, until a toothpick inserted into the center comes out clean. Let cool slightly before frosting.

Make the frosting: In a medium saucepan, combine the butter, peanut butter, milk, vanilla, and powdered sugar. Bring to a boil over medium-high heat, stirring to combine. Remove from the heat.

While the cake is still warm, spread the frosting over the top. *Makes 18 servings.*

PINEAPPLE CAKE

Pat Morrison
Football
Tight End, 1967–1970

CAKE

2 cups all-purpose flour

2 cups sugar

2 teaspoons baking soda

½ teaspoon salt

1 (20-ounce) can crushed pineapple, undrained

¼ cup vegetable oil

2 large eggs, beaten

1 teaspoon vanilla extract

TOPPING

1 cup PET evaporated milk

1½ cups sugar

¾ cup (1½ sticks) margarine

½ teaspoon vanilla extract

1 cup sweetened shredded coconut

1 cup chopped pecans

Make the cake: Preheat the oven to 350°F.

In a large bowl, stir together the flour, sugar, baking soda, salt, pineapple, oil, eggs, and vanilla until well combined. Pour the batter into a 9 by 13-inch baking pan. Bake for 40 minutes, or until the cake is golden brown and a toothpick inserted into the center comes out clean.

Meanwhile, make the topping: In a medium saucepan, combine the evaporated milk, sugar, margarine, and vanilla. Bring to a boil over medium-high heat, then reduce the heat to maintain a simmer and cook for 10 minutes. Remove from the heat and stir in the coconut and pecans.

Poke holes in the top of the cake with a fork and pour the hot topping over the entire cake. Let stand for about 20 minutes to let the cake cool slightly and allow the topping to soak in before slicing and serving. *Makes 12 to 15 servings.*

This recipe was my mom's and was always my favorite.

POUND CAKE

Mark Miller
Football
Quarterback, 1973–1975

1 cup Crisco, plus more for greasing

3 cups all-purpose flour, unsifted,
plus more for dusting

3 cups sugar

6 extra-large eggs

½ teaspoon salt

2 teaspoons vanilla extract

1 cup buttermilk

½ teaspoon baking soda

Preheat the oven to 350°F. Grease a 9-inch round tube cake pan with Crisco, then dust it with flour, tapping out any excess.

In a large bowl, beat together the Crisco and sugar with a handheld mixer on medium speed. Add the eggs one at a time, beating after each addition. Add the salt and vanilla and mix.

In a measuring cup, stir together ½ cup of the buttermilk and the baking soda; set aside.

Alternate adding the flour and the remaining ½ cup buttermilk to the Crisco-sugar mixture, then add the buttermilk–baking soda mixture and mix. Pour the batter into the prepared pan, shaking gently to even the batter and make the top smooth. Bake for 1 hour

15 minutes, or until the cake is golden brown on top and a toothpick inserted into the center comes out clean. Let cool in the pan for 10 minutes, then place a plate over the pan and invert the plate and pan together to turn the cake out onto the plate. Let cool completely, then slice and serve. *Makes 12 servings.*

RED VELVET CAKE

Ron Calcagni
Football
Quarterback, 1975–1978

CAKE

½ cup (1 stick) unsalted butter, plus more for greasing

2 cups all-purpose flour, plus more for dusting

1½ cups sugar

2 large eggs

2 tablespoons unsweetened cocoa powder

1 ounces red food coloring

1 cup buttermilk

1 teaspoon vanilla extract

1 teaspoon salt

1 tablespoon distilled white vinegar

1½ teaspoons baking soda

FROSTING

1 cup milk

5 teaspoons all-purpose flour

1 cup sugar

1 cup (2 sticks) unsalted butter

1 teaspoon vanilla extract

Make the cake: Preheat the oven to 350°F. Grease two 9-inch round cake pans with butter, then dust them with flour, tapping out any excess.

In a large bowl, beat together the butter, sugar, and eggs with a handheld mixer on medium speed.

In separate small bowl, stir together the cocoa powder and food coloring to make a paste. Add the paste to the butter mixture and mix to incorporate.

In a measuring cup, stir together the buttermilk, vanilla, and salt, then add to the butter mixture, alternating with the flour. In a small bowl, stir together the vinegar and baking soda, then fold into the batter. Divide the batter evenly between the prepared pans and bake for 30 minutes, or until a toothpick inserted into the center comes out clean. Let cool while you make the frosting.

Make the frosting: In a small saucepan, combine the milk and flour and heat over low heat until the mixture thickens and starts to boil. Remove from the heat and let cool to room temperature.

In a medium bowl, beat together the sugar and butter with a handheld mixer on medium-high speed until fluffy. Add the vanilla and mix to combine. With mixer on medium speed, add the cooled flour mixture a little at a time until all is incorporated, then beat on high speed until all is white and fluffy.

To assemble, place one cooled cake layer rounded-side down on a serving plate and spread frosting over the top. Top with the second cake layer and spread the remaining frosting over the top and sides of the cake. Slice and serve. *Makes 12 servings.*

Enjoyed making lifetime friends . . . Once a Razorback, always a Razorback!

ROCKY ROAD CANDY

Dean Weber
Head Athletic Trainer, 1978–2008

1 (10-ounce) package miniature marshmallows

1 to 2 cups chopped pecans

2 tablespoons salted butter or margarine

1 (12-ounce) package chocolate chips

1 (14-ounce) can Eagle Brand sweetened condensed milk

Line a 9 by 13-inch pan with wax paper.

In a large bowl, combine the marshmallows and pecans. Set aside.

In top of a double boiler, melt the butter and chocolate chips. Slowly pour in the condensed milk. Fold the chocolate mixture into the marshmallows and pecans. Spread the mixture evenly over the prepared pan. Refrigerate for 2 hours, or until firm.

Remove the candy from the pan, peel off and discard the wax paper, and cut the candy into squares. Store in an airtight container at room temperature for up to 1 week. *Makes 24 to 30 pieces.*

ROSSI'S COOL WHIP PIE

Rossi Morreale
Football
Wide Receiver, 1997–1999

1 (8-ounce) tub Cool Whip

1 (7.6-ounce) bag Reese's peanut butter cups or other candy of your choice, lightly chopped

1 Oreo piecrust or graham cracker piecrust

In a medium bowl, stir together the Cool Whip and peanut butter cups. Fill the piecrust with the Cool Whip mixture, cover loosely, and freeze until set, about 3 hours. Enjoy! *Makes 8 servings.*

SCOTCH-A-ROOS

Chris Bucknam
Men's Track & Field / Cross Country
Head Coach, 2008–present

1 cup Karo light corn syrup

1 cup sugar

1 cup creamy peanut butter

6 cups Rice Krispies cereal

1 cup butterscotch morsels

1 cup chocolate morsels

In a 3-quart saucepan, stir together the corn syrup and sugar and bring to a slow boil over low heat. As soon as it boils, remove from the heat and stir in the peanut butter. Mix in the Rice Krispies (2 cups at a time is easiest). Spread the mixture in a 9 by 13-inch baking pan.

In the top of a double boiler, melt the butterscotch and chocolate morsels. (It's easiest to start to melt the butterscotch first, then add the chocolate.) Stir until well combined and smooth, then spread the chocolate mixture over the Rice Krispies mixture. Let the topping harden, then cut into squares. For best results, do not refrigerate. *Makes 18 to 24 squares.*

Scotch-a-Roos were a family tradition on holidays at my house. Although my track guys shouldn't indulge in eating them, they're the perfect treat for coaches and others to enjoy.

SOPAPILLA CHEESECAKE

Parker Goins
Women's Soccer
Forward and Midfield, 2017–2021

2 (8-ounce) packages cream cheese, at room temperature

1½ cups granulated sugar

1 tablespoon vanilla extract

Milk, if needed

2 (8-ounce) cans crescent rolls (nonperforated work best)

½ cup cinnamon sugar

½ cup (1 stick) unsalted butter, melted

Preheat the oven to 350°F.

In a large bowl, beat together the cream cheese, vanilla, and granulated sugar with a handheld mixer on low speed until smooth. If the mixture is not blending smoothly, add 1 teaspoon milk.

Open one can of crescent rolls and lay the dough over the bottom of a 9 by 13-inch glass baking dish. Spread the cream cheese mixture evenly over the crescent rolls. Open the second can of crescent rolls and place them on top of the cream cheese mixture to cover. Brush the melted butter over the crescent rolls and sprinkle evenly with the cinnamon sugar. Bake according to the crescent roll package directions until browned on top, 30 to 35 minutes. Let cool for 30 minutes before serving. *Makes 12 servings.*

SOUR CREAM COOKIES

Christin Wurth-Thomas

Women's Track & Field / Cross Country

800m, 1500m, 3000m, 5000m, 2000–2003

COOKIES

4 cups all-purpose flour, plus more for dusting

2 teaspoons baking powder

1 teaspoon baking soda

1 cup shortening

1¾ cups granulated sugar

2 large eggs

2 teaspoons vanilla extract

1 cup sour cream

ICING

¾ (16-ounce) bag powdered sugar

4 to 5 tablespoons unsalted butter, at room temperature

1 teaspoon vanilla extract

Dash of milk

Make the cookies: In a medium bowl, stir together the flour, baking powder, and baking soda. Set aside.

In a large bowl, stir together the shortening, granulated sugar, eggs, and vanilla until well combined, then mix in the sour cream. Add the flour mixture and stir to combine. Refrigerate overnight (6 to 8 hours).

Preheat the oven to 350°F. Line cookie baking sheet with parchment paper.

Using a tablespoon or cookie scoop, portion the chilled dough and use floured hands to roll each portion into a ball, placing them on the prepared baking sheet as you go. Bake for 8 to 10 minutes, until golden brown. Let cool.

Meanwhile, make the icing: In a medium bowl, stir together the powdered sugar, butter, vanilla, and milk until smooth and well combined.

Spread the icing over the cooled cookies. *Makes 36 cookies.*

STRAWBERRIES AND CHOCOLATE

Jarrell Williams

Football

Defensive Back and Offensive Back, 1958–1960

Hulled fresh strawberries

Hershey's chocolate syrup

Slice the strawberries in half and put them in a bowl. Pour chocolate syrup over the strawberries and enjoy. *Makes 1 serving.*

I don't cook, so if I get hungry at home, this is one of the two desserts I make (see page 162 for the other one).

STRAWBERRY BANANA PUDDING

Joe Adams

Football

Receiver, 2008–2011

2 (3.4-ounce) boxes instant vanilla pudding mix

2 cups whole milk

3 ripe bananas, diced

2 (10-ounce) bags vanilla wafers

12 ounces strawberries, sliced

In a medium bowl, whisk together the pudding mix and milk until smooth.

Layer half the vanilla wafers over the bottom of a 9 by 13-inch glass baking dish, then top with a layer of half the bananas and strawberries. Pour half the pudding over the top and repeat the layers until all the ingredients are gone. Serve immediately or cover and refrigerate until ready to serve. *Makes 12 servings.*

STRAWBERRY CAKE

David Bazzel
Football
Linebacker, 1981–1985

CAKE

1 (15.25-ounce) box white cake mix

1 (6-ounce) box strawberry Jell-O mix

3 tablespoons self-rising flour

1 cup Wesson oil

4 large eggs

1 (10-ounce) package frozen strawberries, thawed (liquid reserved)

ICING

½ (8-ounce) package cream cheese, at room temperature

1 (16-ounce) box powdered sugar

Make the cake: Preheat the oven to 350°F.

In a large bowl, stir together the cake mix, Jell-O mix, flour, oil, and ½ cup water. Beat in the eggs one at a time until well combined. Stir in 1 cup of the strawberries, reserving the rest (and any liquid in the package) for the icing. Pour the batter into three 8-inch round cake pans or a 9 by 13-inch sheet cake pan. Bake for 1 hour, or until a toothpick inserted into the center comes out clean. Let cool.

Make the icing: In a large bowl, beat the cream cheese, powdered sugar, remaining strawberries, and 2 to 3 tablespoons of the strawberry liquid with a handheld mixer on low speed until combined.

For a layer cake, place one cooled cake layer rounded-side down on a serving plate and spread one-third of the icing on top. Repeat with a second layer. Top with the third cake layer and spread the remaining icing over the top and sides of the cake. Refrigerate for 1 hour before slicing and serving (this helps the cake hold its shape). For a sheet cake, spread the icing over the top of the cooled cake. *Makes 12 servings.*

STRAWBERRY PAVLOVA

Jason Watson
Women's Volleyball
Head Coach, 2016–present

4 large egg whites, at room temperature

¼ teaspoon cream of tartar

Pinch of salt

1 cup sugar

1 tablespoon cornstarch

1 tablespoon distilled white vinegar

1 teaspoon vanilla extract

2 cups heavy cream

2 tablespoons orange liqueur

4 cups strawberries, hulled and halved

Preheat the oven to 250°F. Line a baking sheet with parchment paper.

In a large bowl, combine the egg whites, cream of tartar, and salt and beat with a handheld mixer on medium speed until soft peaks form. Beat in the sugar 1 tablespoon at a time until stiff peaks form. Add the cornstarch, vinegar, and vanilla and beat until blended.

Spread the meringue in a 10-inch round on the prepared baking sheet, with a raised edge and slight indention in the center. Bake for about 1 hour 15 minutes, until the meringue is a cream color and firm to the touch. If the meringue appears to be browning, reduce the oven temperature to 225°F. Remove the meringue from the oven and let cool.

When ready to serve, place the cream in a large bowl and whip with a handheld mixer on medium-high speed until stiff peaks form. Gently stir in the liqueur until incorporated.

Peel the parchment off the bottom of the meringue and place the meringue on a serving plate. Spread the whipped cream over the meringue, leaving the edge of the meringue visible. Top with the strawberries. Cut into wedges and serve. *Makes 8 servings.*

"Every year on Jason's birthday, our daughter Kara makes him a pavlova, just like clockwork. It's a tradition that started because this light, fresh dessert is perfect for summer birthdays in Australia, even if we are bundled up in coats here in the States. She's got the recipe down, and honestly, I couldn't imagine anyone else making it for him." —Larissa Watson

SUGAR COOKIES

Mark Miller
Football
Quarterback, 1973–1975

1 cup (2 sticks) unsalted butter, at room temperature

1¼ cups sugar

2 large eggs

1 teaspoon vanilla extract

2½ cups all-purpose flour, plus more for dusting

1½ teaspoons baking powder

Pinch of salt

Icing (optional)

Preheat the oven to 400°F. Line a baking sheet with parchment paper.

In a large bowl, beat together the butter and sugar with a handheld mixer on medium speed. Add the eggs and vanilla and mix to combine.

In a small bowl, stir together the flour, baking powder, and salt, then add to the butter mixture and mix to combine. Refrigerate the dough for 1 hour.

Lightly dust a work surface with flour. Roll out the chilled dough to ¼-inch thickness. Cut out shapes with any cookie cutter and place them 1 inch apart on the prepared baking sheet. Bake for 5 to 6 minutes, until just barely brown. Enjoy plain or iced. *Makes 24 to 30 cookies.*

SWEET POTATO PIE

Bill McClard
Football
Kicker, 1968–1971

3 or 4 large sweet potatoes (about 2¼ pounds)

½ cup (1 stick) unsalted butter, at room temperature

2 cups sugar

4 large eggs

1 (13-ounce) can PET evaporated milk

1 teaspoon ground cinnamon

½ teaspoon ground nutmeg

½ teaspoon salt

¼ teaspoon ground cloves

2 (9-inch) refrigerated Pillsbury Pet-Ritz deep-dish piecrusts

Marshmallows, for garnish (optional)

Preheat the oven to 375°F. Place a baking sheet in the oven to preheat as well.

Place the sweet potatoes in a large pot with water to cover. Bring to a boil over high heat, then cook until the sweet potatoes are easily pierced with a fork, 20 to 30 minutes. Drain and let cool slightly, then peel the sweet potatoes and place the flesh in a large bowl. Beat with a handheld mixer on medium speed until smooth. Stir in the butter and sugar. Beat in the eggs one at a time. Mix in the evaporated milk, cinnamon, nutmeg, salt, and cloves.

Pour the mixture into the piecrusts and set them on the preheated baking sheet. Bake near the center of the oven for 70 minutes, or until a knife inserted into the center comes out clean. Let cool on a wire rack. Garnish with marshmallows before serving, if desired. *Makes two 9-inch pies.*

We love this pie much better than pumpkin pie.

TIRAMISU

Barry Switzer
Football
Center and Linebacker, 1955–1959
Assistant Coach, 1961

4 (8-ounce) containers mascarpone cheese

2 cups heavy cream

2 cups sugar

Dash of vanilla extract

Dash of rum extract

1½ cups brewed espresso or instant espresso

4 to 6 (7-ounce) packages good-quality Italian or French ladyfinger cookies

Unsweetened Marsala wine

Unsweetened cocoa powder

FOR SERVING

Powdered sugar

Whipped cream

Cherries (maraschino, Amarena, or fresh)

In the bowl of a stand mixer fitted with the paddle attachment, combine the mascarpone, cream, sugar, vanilla, and rum extract. Beat on medium speed until the mixture is creamy. Set aside.

Line the bottom of a 10 by 12-inch cake pan with rows of ladyfingers. Spoon some espresso onto each ladyfinger (cover the cookies, but do not drench them). Pour half the mascarpone filling over the ladyfingers and spread it evenly. Top with another layer of ladyfingers and spoon espresso over each ladyfinger. Drizzle the Marsala over this layer. Top with the rest of the mascarpone filling and spread it evenly. Sprinkle evenly with cocoa powder. Cover and refrigerate for 24 hours.

To serve, cut into small squares and use a small square spatula to scoop each portion onto a plate. Sprinkle with powdered sugar and garnish with whipped cream and a cherry. *Makes 12 to 15 servings.*

INDEX

Page numbers in *italics* indicate photographs.

C

D

E

ABOUT THE AUTHORS

BECKY BULL, a University of Arkansas alumna who grew up right across the Arkansas border in Joplin, Missouri, has lived and owned businesses in Arkansas for over forty years. She is married to former Razorback quarterback and pitcher Scott Bull. After living in the San Francisco Bay Area during Scott's time with the 49ers, they came back to make Arkansas their permanent home. They have two children and three granddaughters who also live in Northwest Arkansas.

KAREN VAN HORN, a University of Arkansas alumna who grew up in Little Rock, spent thirty years working in architecture, engineering, and construction. She worked for three universities, including the University of Arkansas. She is married to former Razorback second baseman and current Razorback head baseball coach Dave Van Horn. After marrying in Fayetteville, they spent fifteen years working in four states, then returned in 2002 to make Fayetteville their permanent home. They have two children and three grandchildren who also live in Northwest Arkansas.

BECK CHERICO KASTOR L

DEBRIYN STEWART MUSSEL

CALIPARI DAILEY MOORE

GRABLE-BARNES SADLER

RICHARDSON ENGLAND FORS

SHADDY BUSBY TRAINOR

WELLS MCREYNOLDS CALC

BROWN WALLACE WEBER

COX SCHAEFFER HOUSE